KV-012-600

Mormon Identities in Transition

Edited by Douglas J. Davies

UNIVERSITY OF WOLVERHAMPTON
LIBRARY

Acc No. 2132670

CLASS

CONTROL
0304336866

289.
3

DATE
27. JUL. 1998

SITE
WL

MOR

CASSELL

Cassell
Wellington House, 125 Strand, London, WC2R 0BB
127 West 24th Street, New York, NY 10011

© The editor and contributors 1996

First published 1996

All rights reserved. No part of this publication may be reproduced or transmitted in
any form or by any means, electronic or mechanical, including photocopying,
recording or any information storage or retrieval system, without permission in
writing from the publishers.

British Library Cataloguing in Publication Data
A catalogue record for this book is available from the British Library

ISBN 0-304-33686-6

Library of Congress Cataloging-in-Publication Data
Mormon identities in transition / edited by Douglas J. Davies.
    p. cm.
    Proceedings of the Conference on Mormon Studies held in Apr. 1995
at the University of Nottingham.
    Includes bibliographical references and index.
    ISBN 0–304–33686–6
    1. Sociology, Christian (Mormon)–Congresses.   2. Mormons–
Congresses.   3. Group identity–Congresses.   4. Church of Jesus
Christ of Latter-Day Saints–Membership–Congresses.   5. Reorganized
Church of Jesus Christ of Latter Day Saints–Membership–Congresses.
  6. Mormon Church–Membership–Congresses.   7. Identification
(Religion)–Congresses.   I. Davies, Douglas James.   II. Conference
on Mormon Studies (1995: University of Nottingham)
BX8637. M655   1996
289. 3–dc20   96–1635
                                                               CIP

Typeset by Falcon Oast Graphic Art
Printed and bound in Great Britain by Biddles Ltd, Guildford and King's Lynn

Contents

Part VII   The Future of Mormon Studies

List of contributors

Lynn Matthews Anderson A graduate of Brigham Young University and author of the *Easy to Read Book of Mormon* as well as numerous articles on Mormon feminism.

Andrew Bolton Lecturer in Religious Education at Westminster College, Oxford. With his wife he is joint pastor of the Leicester congregation of the Reorganized Church of Jesus Christ of Latter Day Saints.

Bruce Chadwick Professor of Sociology and Director of the Center for Studies of the Family at Brigham Young University. He has published several books and articles on family topics.

Christie Davies Professor of Sociology at the University of Reading, England. His first degree and doctorate were taken at Cambridge University and he has been visiting lecturer in India, Poland and the USA. His papers on the sociology of religion have been translated into German, Italian and Polish.

Douglas J. Davies Trained in both anthropology and theology at Durham and Oxford Universities, he engaged in his first research on British Mormonism in 1969 and now leads Mormon Studies at Nottingham University where he is Professor of Religious Studies. Other research and publications include studies of death and contemporary funerary rites.

James T. Duke Professor of Sociology at Brigham Young University. His recent research has focused on culture wars in the US Congress, conversion rates and changes in religiosity through the life-cycle and social factors fostering LDS church growth.

Jessie L. Embry Assistant Director of the Charles Redd Center for Western Studies and instructor in history at Brigham Young University. Has published *Black Saints in a White Church* (1994) and is still researching the experiences of ethnic American Mormons.

H. Dean Garrett Associate Professor and Assistant Chair in the Department of Church History at Brigham Young University. He has published widely in journals of religion and social science.

Melvyn Hammarberg An anthropologist and psychologist in the Department of Anthropology at the University of Pennsylvania, his interest in the LDS goes back to 1971 and to a paper given at the Society for the Scientific Study of Religion on the rise of the Church as a revitalization movement and the role of the family. He is currently Director of the graduate program in American Civilization.

Thomas B. Holman Associate Professor of Family Sciences and Director of the Family Studies Interdepartmental program at Brigham Young University.

Massimo Introvigne Director of CESNUR, the Centre for Studies on New Religions, in Turin, Italy. Lecturer in new religious movements at Queen of the Apostles University in Rome. Author or editor of some twenty books in Italian, French and German.

Daniel K. Judd Assistant Professor of Ancient Scripture at Brigham Young University with a doctorate in counselling psychology.

Roger R. Keller Holds an MDiv from Princeton Theological Seminary and a PhD from Duke University. Currently an Associate Professor of Church History and Doctrine at Brigham Young University where he specializes in world religions.

David Knowlton An anthropology graduate of the Universities of Utah and Texas at Austin, Dr Knowlton has extensive experience of fieldwork in Bolivia and Chile. He currently teaches at Colorado College.

Seth D. Kunin A graduate of Columbia and Cambridge Universities, Dr Kunin currently lectures in the social anthropology of religion at Nottingham University. His expertise in Structuralism complements an additional interest in Judaism.

Roger D. Launius A specialist in military history and Chief Historian, National Aeronautics and Space Administration (NASA), Washington, DC. Roger Launius engages in extensive research on the Reorganized Church of Jesus Christ of Latter Day Saints, from whose perspective he writes.

E. Dale LeBaron Associate Professor of Church History at Brigham Young University. In 1978, when the revelation on the priesthood was received, he was presiding over the only organized LDS mission in Africa, the Johannesburg Mission in South Africa. He has collected more than 500 oral histories from black Mormon converts in 13 African nations.

Armand L. Mauss Professor of Sociology and Religious Studies at Washington State University and past editor of the *Journal for the Scientific Study of Religion*. His most recent book is *The Angel and the Beehive: The Mormon Struggle with Assimilation* (1994).

L. C. Midgley A graduate of Brigham Young and Brown Universities, Dr Midgley is now Professor of Political Science at Brigham Young University, specializing in the history of political philosophy and political theory.

David L. Paulsen Professor of Philosophy at Brigham Young University. Also holding the Richard L. Evans Chair for Religious Understanding.

Gordon K. Thomas A doctoral graduate in English of Tulane University and now Professor Emeritus of English at Brigham Young University.

Malcolm R. Thorp Professor of History at Brigham Young University with a particular interest in British history, as attested in his important joint work with Richard L. Jensen, *Mormons in Early Victorian Britain* (1989).

Grant Underwood Professor of Religion at Brigham Young University-Hawaii, Grant Underwood published his prize-winning *Millenarian World of Early Mormonism* in 1993.

David J. Whittaker Dr David Whittaker is the Curator of Western and Mormon Manuscripts at the Harold B. Lee Library of Brigham Young University and President of the Mormon History Association (1995–96).

Acknowledgements

This book followed very naturally from a most successful academic conference devoted to Mormon Studies held at Derby Hall in the University of Nottingham in April 1995. I must thank all delegates for their support, especially those whose papers comprise the following chapters, and who have allowed me a free hand in editing for publication texts originally prepared for verbal delivery.

I much appreciated the group of American scholars whose encouragement of Mormon Studies within the Theology Department of the University of Nottingham led them to active participation in what was, probably, the first ever academic conference held in England, and probably in Europe, devoted to Latter-day Saint life and culture.

Mrs Mavis Withnall, the Warden's Secretary of Derby Hall, served as Conference Secretary and did much to foster its success through her personal contacts before and during the event. Miss Esther Elliott, one of my postgraduate students, assisted in the organization and also helped produce the bibliography for this book.

We are grateful to the editor of *Faith and Philosophy* for permission to include an abridged version of David Paulsen's 'Must God be incorporeal?,' which was originally published in that journal (6 January 1989: 76–87). I must, personally, also thank Dr Paulsen, as the individual responsible for the Richard L. Evans Chair in Religious Understanding at Brigham Young University in Utah, for hosting my own visit under the auspices of that Chair in May and June 1995. He, along with several other contributors, especially Drs Malcolm Thorp, David Whittaker and James Duke, facilitated my continuing LDS researches, and preparation for this book, in Utah, and extended friendship and hospitality during my stay.

The production of this volume, so soon after the conference, has been facilitated by Janet Joyce of Cassell, an enthusiastic publisher with whom it has been a pleasure to collaborate.

It may be that some of the delegates noticed that the conference began on April 6, the same day as the Church of Jesus Christ of Latter-day Saints was founded in 1830. In retrospect, this book marks the one event in the light of the 165th anniversary of the other.

Professor Douglas J. Davies
Department of Theology,
University of Nottingham

December 1995

Introduction: Scholars, Saints and Mormonism

Douglas J. Davies

This introduction explores the relationship between knowledge and spirituality as a background to the rest of this book, whose chapters originated in an academic Conference on Mormon Studies which I convened at the University of Nottingham in April 1995.

While many of the contributors are Latter-day Saints, they are also scholars who reflect a broad spectrum of opinion from rather conservative to quite liberal standpoints. Others, like the editor, are not Mormon and also represent a variety of intellectual and religious perspectives. This breadth of interest has resulted in an interdisciplinary collection of papers which, together, present a picture of contemporary Mormon life that is hardly to be found in any other single book. Even Cornwall, Heaton and Young's excellent volume on *Contemporary Mormonism* (1994), given its avowed social scientific focus, does not quite embrace the breadth of material presented in the following chapters.

I entitle this introduction 'Scholars, Saints and Mormonism' not only to reflect this breadth of authorship and interest but also to emphasize the more subtle theoretical importance of the relationship between academic analysis and religious commitment in the study of religion, which is particularly important as far as Mormon Studies are concerned.

Wilfred Cantwell Smith's distinction between what he called *faith* and *cumulative tradition* was an important contribution to the history of religions in helping to indicate both the depth of meaning offered by a religion to individuals in their personal *faith*, and the dimensions of the *cumulative tradition* subsisting in the historical and cultural framework of their religious life within which faith might be fostered and flourish (1963: 17). Smith's distinction ought to be more widely known for its usefulness in drawing attention to the method and motives involved in religious studies. I dwell on it here to draw attention to the part played by educational institutions in influencing the way religious positions are framed and presented both to students and to other scholars, not least because of the important position of Mormon educational bodies in relation to Mormon Studies as a whole.

Smith's category of *faith* is closely related to confessional theology, that formal analysis of belief grounded in the assumption of the truth of particular religious beliefs and used as the basis for discussing the consequences and implications of religious creeds for a wide variety of issues. Many European universities, for example, even possess Protestant and Catholic Faculties of Theology where the appropriate assumptions of faith are normative and explicit. When such centres turn their attention to the *cumulative tradition* of their own religion they do so with the eye or heart of *faith* but when they focus on other religions they, often, do so by stressing the *cumulative tradition* at the expense of the *faith* of the other groups. This, as Cantwell Smith showed, can lead to a distorted vision of the other tradition in that when I consider my own religion I do so by focusing on my inner core of faith, but when I consider someone else's religion I look only on its outward forms and traditions, ignoring its inner core. This means that like is not compared with like. In the following chapters we find expressions of *faith* as well as analyses of aspects of the Mormon *cumulative tradition*.

The place of universities in the study of religion is, obviously, of some importance to Mormon Studies as in the study of any other religion but it is particularly important for this book because many of the authors are academics at the Mormon Church's Brigham Young University at Provo in Utah.

While much could be said about the question of religious orthodoxy and academic responsibility, it is important to raise this issue for general consideration by briefly setting it within a broader framework since this is a field often left quite untouched. English universities, for example, do not, by and large, operate on the principle of denominational faculties. Departments of Theology and also of Religious Studies explicitly stress the study of the *cumulative traditions* of religions and do not see themselves as grounded in any confessional theology. Partly because of this, the major churches within England have established their own confessional theological colleges for the training of priests and ministers even though these students may also take courses at neighboring universities. This very co-existence of university departments of theology and theological colleges in England reflects Smith's dichotomy between *cumulative tradition* and *faith*. This is not to say that individual teachers within the state university system do not have their own religious commitments and motivation which are very likely to influence their teaching and research, and it is not to say that there is not an implicit form of confessionalism which can exert a significant influence. This is, perhaps, especially important in situations like Oxford, Cambridge and Durham where some academics hold official religious appointments as chaplains or canon-professors at cathedrals and where there exists what ought perhaps to be called an implicit dominance of a confessional theology, albeit in the slightly diffuse form of Anglican academic theology which has largely absorbed the scholarly traditions of historical-critical methods which, to a degree are still problematic in some Mormon contexts.

Against that background Brigham Young University (BYU) presents an interesting and important profile as far as this book is concerned and also in relation to Mormon studies. This merits more than a passing comment because of the strong participation of BYU staff in the Conference organized at the non-confessional University of Nottingham. Their involvement was much appreciated and helped contribute to the success of the event; indeed just about a half of all the following chapters were written by BYU Faculty members as can be seen from the list of contributors. But these contributions themselves reflect a diversity of approach. Some are expressly confessional in form, not because they deal with theological issues but in the way they discuss their chosen topic, as in Dale LeBaron's important description of the way in which black Africans came to receive the Mormon Priesthoods and Roger Keller's sketch of Mormonism in India. So too in Gordon Thomas's historically creative and quietly reflective 'English Romantics and the Restoration.'

Other chapters are more descriptive and follow the normal practice of particular academic disciplines as in James Duke's sociological study of tension between cultural continuity and secularization in Mormonism, or Daniel Judd's more psychological analysis of mental health amongst Latter-day Saints.

In the task of editing their contributions the authors have, when necessary, graciously allowed me a relatively free hand in turning papers written for verbal delivery into scripts suitable for reading. In doing so I have retained all language which reflects religious adherence, and have often left the oratorical style to speak for itself.

Where I have considered it appropriate the abbreviation LDS replaces Latter-day Saint(s) and RLDS Reorganized Latter Day Saints, BYU replaces Brigham Young University, and titles such as those of President or Elder have occasionally been omitted. American spelling and punctuation has been retained. Appropriate abbreviations have often been used for titles of LDS writings such as the Doctrine and Covenants (D&C), Pearl of Great Price (PGP) and Book of Mormon (BM). While some notes have been retained at the end of each chapter, most information has been placed within the text and a single bibliography covers all chapters.

Scholars, Saints and knowledge

After these preliminary points I can now raise the question of the relation between the nature of knowledge and spirituality as far as Mormonism is concerned, since this is of prime concern for Mormon Studies.

Mormonism possesses a deep commitment to knowledge grounded in its own metaphysical system which sees persons as eternally progressing and developing intelligences. The early establishment of schools led, through an initial Academy of 1875, to the Brigham Young University of 1903. This institution grew into today's flagship of Mormon education.

From an anthropological perspective there is a sense in which Brigham Young University stands as a complementary symbol to Mormon Temples.

This may, initially, seem a strange thing to say, given that most Western cultures foster schools and colleges while the Temple stands as a unique feature of Mormonism. Temples are prime institutions which both define Mormonism and set it apart from all other Christian traditions as places where lessons are learned about the pre-existence of humanity, its fall, salvation and process of exaltation. They are also places where important rituals are performed for the ultimate salvation both of the living and the dead.

As sociological types the Mormon Temple and the Mormon University are, in a very particular way, symbols of each other in the sense that a symbol participates in that which it represents. Broadly speaking we might suggest that the Temple is a symbol of a University in that it is a place of committed learning. But, conversely, it might also be suggested that a Mormon University is a symbol of the Temple because it runs contrary to most modern and secular ideals of University life. Though Mormons do not make this point in any explicit way, I think it could be argued that the University is symbolic of the Temple in that the gaining of knowledge is believed to involve an interaction with divine processes.

I have argued elsewhere that the ideal Mormon *Homo religiosus* involves the dimensions of peace, knowledge and achievement (Davies, 1987: 135). All of these furnish part of what Mormons call their testimony, that inward certainty of the Church as the prime source of truth. While it is easy to argue that the Mormon *Homo religiosus* is peculiarly related to the Temple and its ritual, it is also important to see the University as a parallel arena of this ideal type of Mormon being. At his inauguration as the eighth President of Brigham Young University, Dallin H. Oaks said, 'Our reason for *being* is to be a university. But our reason for *being a university* is to encourage and prepare young men and women to rise to their full spiritual potential as sons and daughters of God' (1971: 18).

For this reason the University is a place that requires boundaries just as much as does the Temple; the honour code to which students are asked to subscribe is, thus, as important as the rules of ritual purity underlying the capacity of a church member to obtain a temple recommendation, enabling access to the sacred rites. Similarly, in a symbolic sense, the academic staff will be expected to foster the religious goals of the University and not to undermine them, whether in their teaching or in their moral lives. Here the goals of scholarship become inextricably linked with those of spirituality, and it is in this sense that I speak in this chapter of 'Scholars, Saints and Mormonism.' For it is a Mormon ideal that scholars be saints, not simply in the titular sense of being Latter-day Saints, but in their double commitment to knowledge and faith.

Given the explosion of interest in hermeneutics in recent decades this is so obvious that it need not even be mentioned but, because many aspects of the general academic life of the Western world have moved from liberal intellectualism into either post-modern idiosyncrasy or obscurantism, this distinctive feature of Mormon scholarship needs emphasis. This is not to say that Mormons lack their liberals, reformists and even revolutionaries, some of whom are represented in the following chapters, but it is to affirm the lively ideal that knowledge of God and a sense of the divine presence is closely related to the academic quest. This is precisely why the quest for truth, both by scholars and by central church authorities, can stir deep emotion in Mormon communities.

As we have already indicated, one of the goals of LDS life is to gain and foster what Mormons call a 'testimony,' a word describing an experience which convinces individuals that they really do belong to a unique church, with a uniquely restored message and a uniquely authoritative prophetic leader. Knowledge is one of the media through which a testimony should be gained and within which a testimony should be allowed to express itself.

But here one important problem arises. It concerns the critical method of analytical scholarship as the distinguishing feature of Western liberal intellectualism during most of the twentieth century. This perspective followed naturally from the nineteenth century's fostering of methods of historical, textual and literary criticism and has, in the late twentieth century, become the very arena of the epistemological debate of post-modernism. These critical methods bore upon the Bible and church history within the academic circles of many Protestant churches and influenced the way in which faith came to be understood. Many rejected the reductionist consequences and affirmed more fundamentalist attitudes to the Bible and to faith as described in Massimo Introvigne's chapter which compares Catholic and Mormon attitudes to sacred scriptures.

Unlike Catholicism's concern over church authority or Protestantism's interest in biblical authority, Mormonism, despite its very real engagement with these topics, has been preoccupied with history. Many have argued that, for Mormons, history functions in the way in which theology works in other religions. This is understandable given the Mormon belief that God restored truth to the earth through particular divine manifestations which were given to Joseph Smith in the 1820s and 1830s. These foundational events are viewed as the *sine qua non* of Mormon religion. While heresy in other churches takes the form of denial of particular doctrines, especially Christological doctrines, the functional equivalent of heresy in Mormonism lies in the denial of these foundational events and of the status of Joseph Smith as a prophetic founder of a distinctive church with new revelation. In fact heresy may be seen as the logical opposite of possessing a testimony. And this is why the canons of the historical critical method are so problematic to Mormonism.

In the light of these various issues Mormon Studies will, increasingly, be an area of deep academic interest for non-Mormon scholars of religion as well as for Mormons themselves. Papers such as that of Seth Kunin, himself a non-Mormon anthropologist, bring the distinctive method of Structuralism to bear upon Mormon sacred texts in a unique way. Some Mormons might find this an intrusion into a privileged area while other Saints may find it illuminating and respond with increased scholarly activity in this field of analysis. By such dialogue between religious and scholarly perspectives knowledge will increase. Certainly, the inter-disciplinary nature of this book interacts with the varied, though implicit, religious positions of each contributor to emphasize the complexity under-lying any exercise in the study of a religious group, a complexity grounded in the identity of each contributor.

Indeed, if one theme emerges more than any other throughout the following chapters it is that of identity. Because of this we begin with Armand Mauss's important reflections on identity and boundary main-tenance in Mormonism as it faces an expansionist future. That chapter reflects the important contribution Mauss has made to a critical self-awareness of Mormon social development over time. Christie Davies's subtle analysis of the Word of Wisdom shows the importance of compara-tive study in establishing the identity markers of religious sub-cultures over time. Dale LeBaron's chapter, by contrast, furnishes an important document in Mormon self-awareness as he tells the story of how the priest-hood came to be open to African Mormons.

The issue of identity is raised in quite a different way by Roger Launius and Andrew Bolton, one an American and the other a British member of the Reorganized Church of Jesus Christ of Latter Day Saints. Their contri-butions not only mark the distinction between their Church and that of the 'Utah' Mormons but also show how a sense of group identity can change over time and in relation to wider political pressures. Bolton's chapter is, also, a highly creative contribution to the interpretation of LDS scriptures in their social contexts. In a very similar way, though on the entirely dif-ferent issue of gender and church identity, Lynn Matthews Anderson pre-sents an impassioned and moving discussion of women and the priesthood.

On a canvas drawn much wider than that of Latter-day Saint concerns, the topic of hermeneutics is explored by Massimo Introvigne, whose com-parative study of Catholic and Protestant approaches to scripture will be highly informative to theological readers from many traditions. Theologians will also be interested in David Paulsen's spirited debate on the embodiment of God.

The detailed and valuable work of David Knowlton takes us from theology into the world of social anthropology to show how Mormonism's expansion into South America possesses important consequences for church organization. This reinforces the issues raised by Jessie Embry for ethnic Americans and Roger Keller for India.

These, and the other chapters by Thorp and Underwood on history and society, by Hammarberg, Judd and Holman on more psychological issues, and by Chadwick and Garrett in their observation of Mormon behavior combine to furnish a stimulating volume for scholars from many fields. The resources available for studying Mormonism, so fully documented by David Whittaker, end the book with an appropriate challenge for future research.

Part I
Dimensions of Identity

1 Identity and boundary maintenance International prospects for Mormonism at the dawn of the twenty-first century

Armand L. Mauss

> But ye are a chosen generation, a royal priesthood, an holy nation, a peculiar people; that ye should shew forth the praises of him who hath called you out of darkness into his marvellous light; which in time past were not a people, but are now the people of God . . . (1 Peter 2:9–10)

Mormons have always thought of themselves as the 'peculiar people' to which Peter's epistle refers. Of course, other religious movements and denominations have also appropriated that term and concept; yet for Mormons, at least those in North America, such a distinctive identity has become somewhat problematic in recent years. I have explored the implications of this issue at some length in my recent book (Mauss, 1994), so I shall not belabor it here. Let me simply summarize my general thesis in this way: After a stormy relationship with American society owing to nineteenth-century Mormon 'peculiarities,' the Mormon leadership and people devoted the first half of the twentieth century to living down their disrepute and passing as mainstream Americans. By about mid-century, however, many Mormons, including some key leaders, began to feel that assimilation had perhaps gone too far. The predicament of disrepute had become a predicament of respectability. The 'peculiar people' were not so peculiar anymore, at least not in very conspicuous ways. The boundaries between Mormons and non-Mormons had eroded, maintained neither by the geographic separation nor by the same degree of social distance on either side of that boundary that had prevailed throughout the nineteenth century.

During the past few decades, the Mormon leadership and people, at least in North America, have been engaged in a retrenchment process apparently intended to reverse some, though certainly not all, of the elements in the assimilation or 'Americanization' that had occurred during the first half of the century. This retrenchment has been expressed at both the official and the folk levels. At the official level, it has taken the form of renewed emphasis upon certain authentic traditional Mormon doctrines and ideals, including modern revelation and temple worship, as well as a conservative turn in social and political policies occurring well ahead of the comparable turn in America at large during the 1980s. At the folk level, the retrenchment motif has taken the form of a considerably less authentically Mormon borrowing from Protestant fundamentalists in religious style and even in content. It is as though the Mormons had spent the first half of the century in partial emulation of the Episcopalians and Congregationalists, only to turn during the second half of the century in the direction of the Southern Baptists and Assemblies of God.

I conclude my book by suggesting that this process of alternating periods of assimilation and retrenchment constitutes a kind of 'natural history' for new religious movements, at least for those that survive across time as truly distinctive denominations. For too much 'peculiarity' cannot be sustained indefinitely, and new religions that fail to make assimilative concessions will eventually be repressed into oblivion, even in relatively free societies. On the other hand, too much assimilation is just another form of oblivion, in which the social boundary between the new religion and its host society gradually disappears, and along with it any unique sense of identity on the parts of the religious adherents. If I am right about this theoretical proposition, then Mormons and Mormonism will experience everywhere in the world a replication, in some form, of the same process that has occurred during the past hundred years in North America (Mauss, 1994: ch. 12). This paper is concerned with the implications of that prospect.

Boundaries and identity

Yet what has all this to do with the issue of identity, which is the main theme of this paper, and, indeed, of other contributions in this collection? As I understand modern social psychology, the concepts of 'identity' and 'boundaries' are inextricably linked, implicitly if not explicitly (e.g. Stryker, 1992). Our identities are the products of symbolic and other forms of interaction between ourselves and others. Through that process, we learn not only our roles and identities as individuals *vis-à-vis* others in each of our reference groups; we also learn our identities as reference group members *vis-à-vis* other groups, the 'us versus them' identity, as it were. It is this latter form of identity in which the boundaries between 'us and them' are especially important. Such boundaries can take many forms, of course, including national, spatial, social, ethnic, symbolic, linguistic, and others, separately or in combination. The boundaries can be maintained primarily either by the reference group itself, as in monastic orders; or by the external society, as in the case of pariah peoples; or by a combination of internal and external efforts, as in the case of diaspora Jews throughout most of their history. Similarly, an erosion of boundaries can be predicted to the extent that relaxation occurs on either side in the boundary-maintenance process. It is important to add that the significance of identity lies not merely in an internal, psychological state; for identity is always expressed in behavior: We act on who or what we think we are – another way of understanding the maxim (Proverbs 23:7) that 'as (one) thinketh in his heart, so is he' (Stryker, 1992).

Cast in these terms, my argument is that during the first half of the present century the boundary was gradually relaxed on both sides between the Mormons and the surrounding American society, spatially, socially, and symbolically; but that since mid-century the Mormons have been attempting to redefine and strengthen this boundary, and with it the partially eroded Mormon identity as a special or 'peculiar' people. Some of these efforts might be regarded as ill-advised or even bizarre, especially at the level of folk religion, or at least as not coming out of an authentic Mormon heritage. *Yet it must be conceded, I think, that the future success, or even survival, of the Mormon religion in North America depends precisely upon this retrenchment process,* with the accompanying redefinition of boundaries and rehabilitation of the Mormon identity. The alternative is an increasingly blurred identity, both at the individual and at the institutional levels, as Mormonism, in Troeltschian terms, is inexorably (if slowly) assimilated into the great ecumenical blandness of today's mainline denominations (Finke and Stark, 1992; Perrin, 1989; Troeltsch, 1931; Witten, 1993).

This perspective accords quite well, furthermore, with the 'rational choice' theoretical framework so pervasive among contemporary sociologists of religion in the United States, among whom Rodney Stark and his associates are probably the best known exponents (e.g. Stark and Bainbridge, 1985; Iannaccone *et al.*, 1995; Warner, 1993). This theoretical orientation is not without its critics, of course, especially in Britain and elsewhere in Europe (e.g. Barker *et al.*, 1993; Bruce, 1993; Dobbelaere, 1987; Robertson, 1992). Yet it offers a heuristic convergence with my argument about the Mormon case in particular. From this viewpoint, a clear and secure identity, as part of a distinctive religious community, is one of the 'products' offered on the religious market. Not everyone, of course, will be inclined to look to the religion 'industry' for this product, finding their identity instead in their professions, in various other voluntary associations, in their ethnic groups, or in their extended families. Yet in the religion segment of the 'identity market,' consumers are likely to be attracted and retained most often by a religion offering an identity that is clear, distinctive, and reassuring about meaning, particularly the meaning of action, both existentially and teleologically. Religions compete in other markets besides the identity market, of course, and their adherents or consumers might be seeking any number of other kinds of products; but surely a secure identity is one of the most important products of a religious enterprise, especially in an age in which other traditional identities have become so problematic (e.g. Fulton and Gee, 1994; Ramet, 1993).

As with other products in any market, religious products, including a secure identity, will be gained only at some cost. If a 'purchase' is to occur, especially on a recurring basis, the cost must be regarded by the consumer as commensurate with the value of the proffered identity. Part of the cost of a religious product is determined by the degree of cultural tension between a religious community and its host society. To the extent that the community exhibits culturally deviant traits, that tension will be great, and the demands placed upon adherents or consumers will be stigmatizing and therefore costly (Young, 1994). At the same time, however, the accompanying identity is likely to be all the more distinctive and secure; for the boundary between 'them and us' will be maintained on both sides. Obviously it is possible for a religious community to misestimate, either quantitatively or qualitatively or both, what it can demand as the cost for an identity or for the other products that it offers in a given market. Not only the sheer number, but also the types of consumers a religion attracts will therefore fluctuate according to its success in estimating how much and what kinds of costs the market will bear. That is, no religion will be equally successful in all market niches, even in the same society.

Religious identities as exports

It is in this connection that the world-wide export of Mormonism (or of any other religion) becomes an especially intriguing issue. For, understood in terms of markets, products, and costs, the Mormon enterprise faces the necessity of 'marketing identities' and other goods that can be sold in a variety of cultural settings without seriously undermining the integrity of what remains essentially an American product, indeed even a western American product. Since the nature, as well as the degree, of cultural tension between Mormonism and the host society will vary from one culture to another, a 'Mormon identity' will clearly mean different things, and require different costs, in different cultures. For the institutional church, with its headquarters in Salt Lake City, the crucial question will always be: How much tailoring and customizing of the religion can be permitted in order for the Mormon identity to 'work' in each setting?

In some settings, it might be enough simply to change the packaging, or to remove the most conspicuous marks signifying *Made in the USA*. In other settings, a Mormon identity will never 'sell' without significant modifications, perhaps even structural ones. How many, and what kinds of modifications can be made before the product is no longer recognizably Mormon, however palatable it might have become in a given locale? One of the deterrents to the marketing of American automobiles in Japan, and perhaps in the UK as well, has always been the unwillingness of some American manufacturers to put the steering wheel on the right side. No car will ever acquire a Japanese identity as long as its steering wheel is on the left! One wonders at the obstinacy of the American manufacturers, for a change in the position of the steering wheel would not seem an unreasonable concession to local preferences.

By analogy, we might ask which modifications in Mormon products can be made that would be the equivalent of changes in the position of the steering wheel, and which ones would have to be resisted as threatening the integrity of the entire mechanism. As an historical parallel, the Roman Catholic Church has always grappled with the problem of how to make the religion truly catholic, which is to say less Roman, without sacrificing its Christian essence. Some might say that the Catholic Church has made too many accommodations with local syncretisms. The ethnic variations in Islam raise exactly the same issue.

One can easily judge from official Mormon publications (e.g. Cowan, 1993; Johnson, 1993: 35) that the church leadership understands this predicament *in principle;* but as yet it has not articulated any general criteria by which to resolve the predicament operationally from one cultural setting to another. Different Mormons, and even different leaders, seem to have different conceptions of these crucial criteria; but we have not yet been formally instructed as to which traditional Mormon doctrines and practices constitute the irreducible core, the *sine qua non,* of Mormonism, as opposed to those which might be modified, or even dispensed with, in creating local adaptations of the religion and thus local variations in the nature of the Mormon identity. Furthermore, it is not yet clear whether the LDS leadership conceives of the Mormon culture and identity as ideally new, neutral, and *separate* from all worldly cultures or as infinitely adaptable and capable of *integration* with various local cultures. The Spring 1996 issue of *Dialogue* contains a number of perceptive papers devoted to the theme of adapting Mormonism to various cultural settings in the twenty-first century.

Mormonism as a new world religion?

It is well known that Mormonism has grown rapidly, especially during 'retrenchment' since mid-century, and perhaps partly *because* of that retrenchment, which has increased somewhat the cost of being Mormon, at least in the US, but has also correspondingly sharpened and strengthened the Mormon identity there. What is less often recognized is that the Mormon membership, and particularly its rapid growth, are almost entirely *Western Hemisphere phenomena.* About 85 per cent of the world's nine million Mormons live in the Western Hemisphere; the remaining 15 per cent are scattered throughout Europe, Asia, Africa, and the entire rest of the world (Bennion and Young, 1996; Knowlton, 1996). Furthermore, outside the US, at least 90 per cent of all Mormons have joined the Church since about 1960, which means that their children, the first second generation of appreciable size outside North America, have only just begun to reach maturity. The retention rates for this second generation range from modest to abysmal, depending on the part of the world in question (Bennion and Young, 1996; Numano, 1996; Shepherd and Shepherd, 1996; van Beek, 1996). In light of these considerations, it is obviously quite premature to speak of Mormonism as a 'world religion' in a practical sense.

The rapid spread of Mormonism in the Western Hemisphere can be attributed mainly to the relative openness of the 'religious markets' in the countries of that hemisphere, an historic reality in the US, and increasingly true also in Latin America with the decline of Roman Catholic hegemony there (e.g. Mariz, 1994; Torres, 1992). As Stark and his colleagues have emphasized, a politically unregulated religious market is not only necessary for any meaningful competition to occur, but it is also crucial to the vitality and prosperity of the market as a whole (Iannaccone, 1991 and 1992; Stark and Iannaccone, 1992). Yet, as certain European observers have noted (e.g. Barker *et al.*, 1993; Dobbelaere and Voye, 1990; Hervieu-Leger, 1990), many national and cultural settings cannot be adequately understood in terms simply of the amounts and kinds of formal legal regulation of the religious market, as Americans are inclined to think of it. In many European societies, at least on the continent, the access of new religions to the market is determined at least as much by social structure and by fundamental cultural 'habits of the heart' as by formal law. That is, in those societies, religion has a complex *organic* relationship to the entire cultural heritage, not simply the kind of statutory or legal relationship implied by the American notion of separation of church and state. Even in the United States, as Phillip Hammond (1992) has demonstrated, a truly open religious market was not achieved simply by the legal disestablishment of churches during the early Republic period but only after a second 'disestablishment,' with the loss of the Protestant cultural hegemony, or even a third one, the increasing decline of *any* theistic hegemony.

In any case, there is clearly a sense in which conversion to Mormonism, or to any other culturally foreign religion, in many societies inevitably brings some displacement of one's identity as a true member of that society in favor of the newly acquired Mormon identity. In Poland, for example, there is a sense in which a Mormon convert somehow becomes less truly 'Polish' in the eyes of other Poles. The same sort of thing seems to occur also in Germany, Italy, or, for that matter, even in Japan; for despite the perfunctory and minimal levels of religious practice in those societies, their traditional religions permeate and inform their fundamental cultures, and derivatively the very identities of the people as individuals (Dobbelaere, 1987; Dobbelaere and Voye, 1990). In these terms, the religious situation in Britain, and in other English-speaking countries, might be somewhere in between the American and the European cases. We must thus begin with an understanding of this kind of fundamental difference in the organic centrality of religion from one society to another, if we are to understand the differential growth rates of Mormonism and the differential costs of adopting a Mormon identity. For if a Mormon identity is to develop and endure, especially at the individual level, it must take the form of a tapestry that interweaves authentically Mormon strands with those from each local cultural heritage.

Future prospects for international Mormon identities: some illustrations

Let us begin by reminding ourselves that the construction of local identities is more than a local enterprise; it is a bilateral process between exporters and importers. On the one side, when the 'original' Salt Lake City product itself is exported to each locale, it does not arrive as a culturally neutral orthodoxy, all ready to be interwoven harmoniously with the local colors. Its very orthodoxy, or at least what most American Mormons take for granted as orthodoxy, is already permeated with American ideas and maxims. These include, at the very least, a glorification of the American constitution and form of government as divinely inspired (LDS D&C 101: 77–80); the retroactive 'Mormonization' of the American founding fathers (and other culture heroes) through vicarious temple rituals (Alexander, 1986b: 299–300); an adaptation of nineteenth-century British Israelism that portrays American Mormons as literal Israelites almost by definition (Allen, 1930; McConkie, 1966: 389–90; Millett and McConkie, 1993); the enshrinement of a family model closely resembling Victorian patriarchy (Foster, 1979); and the presumption of American holiday observances in meeting schedules and lesson manuals (Numano, 1996). Such Americanisms might be readily replaced in many cultures by local counterparts, but how much such replacement could be tolerated by the Salt Lake City headquarters is another question.

Yet it is the other side of that bilateral process that interests us the most here – namely the efforts to construct Mormon identities in each locale. In Latin America, for example, many Mormon communities have adopted and adapted the Lamanite identity from the Book of Mormon, especially in urban areas, to displace their historically stigmatized identities as urban Indians or as *mestizos* (Knowlton, 1996); some Guatemalan Mormons have even found parallels between the Book of Mormon and their own ancient Popul Vuh (Murphy, 1996); in New Zealand, the numerous Mormon Maoris have embraced an identity as remnants of Israel, bestowed on them by Mormon missionaries, and used it as a weapon to help legitimize key elements of their culture against periodic government campaigns for total assimilation (Barber and Gilgen, 1996). Even the Mormon version of patriarchy (which sometimes seems so oppressive to Mormon women in the US) is regarded by many Mormons in Mexico, especially the women, as preferable to the local *machismo* tradition.

Such then, are a few of the features of the Salt Lake City import that Mormons in various other locales have found assimilable, not only in their belief systems but, more to the point here, in their very identities, their very understandings of who they are and therefore how they should live. Perhaps the especially rapid Mormon growth in Latin America is attributable in part to the availability of such elements in the Utah religion that can be appropriated in each local Mormon identity at relatively low cultural cost, or perhaps at a profit. Yet even in Latin America, the widespread perception of Mormonism as a political and economic toehold of US colonialism has made Church membership there costly, even fatal at times (Young, 1994).

In France, where we might expect people with a strong anti-clerical tradition to be put off by the hierarchical governing structure of Mormonism, French Mormons instead are attracted by the lay ministry, in which leadership at the local level comes from their friends and neighbors and it is at the local level, after all, that most people experience their religion on a regular basis. In that sense, the French see themselves as identifying with a religion of the people, rather than one of the elite (Jarvis, 1991). A third of the Mormons converted in France, furthermore, have been born elsewhere, including the former African colonies, so that the new Mormon religion becomes the basis, again, for *a new identity that cuts across former boundaries of birth and culture* to unite all into the new Mormon community.

Disproportionate conversion of converts born elsewhere is very common also in other countries with large immigrant populations. For these displaced persons, the new Mormon identity is much more attractive and much less costly than among their native-born and unstigmatized neighbors. (In this regard, see also van Beek, 1996, on Holland.)

In Japan, where immigration is a minor factor, both native and imported religions from previous centuries have been amalgamated in such a way as to build into each individual Japanese identity a strong sense of connection to ancestors, to the contemporary extended family, and to future generations. This sense is obviously convergent with orthodox Mormon teachings about the role of family in the eternal cosmic scheme; but Japanese Mormons get the additional assurance, from the temple rituals, that their ancestors can be brought into the Mormon fold with them, sealed to them with a special divine authority lacking in earlier religions, and resurrected with them (Numano, 1996). Such supplements to the traditional Japanese family identity might come at too high a cost, however, for many Japanese, who have to give up a lot of their Japanese identity more generally in order to be Japanese Mormons. Indeed, the whole idea of an identity deriving from membership in 'the only true church' is an alien idea in Japan, as in most of Asia, where different religions are understood as standing in complementary or even symbiotic relationships to each other, rather than being mutually exclusive.

To move to a less exotic location, Nottingham's own Professor Davies, in his work on Mormons in Wales, has discussed many of the elements that went into the construction of a Welsh Mormon identity, though with reference mainly to the nineteenth century (D. J. Davies, 1987). The Welsh converts found some of their new identity in connecting not only with ancestors, as the Japanese do, but also with God's people generally throughout the ages by means of genealogy and temple work. Even at times when persecution by the government itself raised the cost of their new Mormon identity, the early Welsh saints understood their plight as simply reliving the episodes in the Bible and in the Book of Mormon, in which God's people suffered at the hands of wicked rulers. Thus they could link up with a long collective memory not only of earlier generations of Mormons but of earlier generations of God's people in all times and places. At a somewhat less fundamental level, the merger of the Welsh and the Mormon choral traditions, with the hymns of Evan Stephens and the acclaimed Welsh Mormon choirs even in Utah, helped in the synthesis of a new Welsh Mormon identity (D. J. Davies, 1987).

Indeed, even the subtle and not-so-subtle racism in traditional Mormon doctrine has at times resonated with local traditions and helped to create bridges by which Mormon and other local identities could be joined. We tend to forget, for example, that early Mormons, at least, were taught to see themselves as literal and not merely spiritual descendants of Israel, comprising particularly a remnant of Ephraim destined to comprise the vanguard of the gathering process in the last days (McConkie, 1966: 389–90; Millet and McConkie, 1993). This idea has obvious convergence with British Israelism, and certain counterparts on the continent, a popular doctrine in the nineteenth and early twentieth centuries, even among intellectuals (Allen, 1930). I have not documented an explicit recognition of this ideological convergence among early British converts to Mormonism, but it might well have provided one of the links between the British and the Mormon identities. As long as Mormon conversions were taking place so disproportionately among English-speaking and European peoples, such a connection to biblical Israel was probably useful; but surely the same idea will prove increasingly dysfunctional in the efforts to export Mormonism to more exotic cultures in the twenty-first century, especially outside the Western Hemisphere. Accordingly, I expect a noticeable erosion to occur during the next century in that traditional Mormon doctrine linking converts literally to the biblical tribe of Ephraim, or even to Abraham's lineage more generally.

These few examples are only suggestive, but I think not idiosyncratic, indications of the possibilities for building Mormon identities by merging or reconstructing elements from the Mormon heritage with the various other cultural heritages around the world. Let us be clear, however, that I am talking about identity construction (or reconstruction) not merely as a process of superficial, external behavior change, but rather as a profound psychological change in self-definition that is only reflected in behavioral change. Two anecdotes acquired in my travels will illustrate the distinction I am trying to make between internal identity change and mere behavioral change.

First, a colleague and former student of mine studied several wards and branches of the church in France (Jarvis, 1991). In one branch, the president, who had been a member of the church for less than a year, announced to his flock one Sunday that he and his family would be gone for the next month on vacation to a well-known nudist colony, in accordance with long-standing family custom. A minority of the branch, but a large minority, reacted with shock and horror, especially the missionaries serving in that branch from Utah. The ensuing controversy was at length resolved when the president came to understand that even though there might not be any gospel principle at stake here, his family's custom was nevertheless a source of offence and contention among the members of his branch from cultures other than France. The family accordingly changed its vacation plans to an innocuous camping trip in the mountains, not, I must emphasize, because they, or most of the French members of the branch, saw anything 'unMormon' or 'unChristian' about nudism under these circumstances, but only in deference to the feelings of the other, non-French members. In this instance, the family had not internalized psychologically, as part of their new Mormon identity, the feeling that we are Mormons, and Mormons 'don't do nudism.' They simply altered their external behavior out of consideration for the feelings of others. There were no implications for identity.

The second anecdote comes from a colleague who has conducted church-sponsored surveys in the Philippines. After overseeing the training of a number of local Philippine interviewers, all of whom were recent LDS converts, he arranged for the interviewing team to begin its first day of interviewing with a meeting at the local LDS church building, where final instructions were to be given and the designated samples of interviewees would be distributed. This turned out to be an inauspicious beginning for the project, however, for when the research director called for the interviewing team to assemble at 'the church,' he neglected to specify that he meant the small LDS branch meeting house. Accordingly, a large proportion of the interviewers gathered instead at the local Catholic church, which was what the term 'church' had always meant in their lives theretofore. This is perhaps not a terribly crucial example, but it does illustrate how new converts can sometimes fail to internalize, as part of their new identity, the very concept that they have totally changed churches – that they are now part of the one, exclusively true, divinely sanctioned religion, an important element in orthodox Mormonism. In this case, neither the behavior nor the identity seems to have changed with 'conversion.'

Mormon institutions in identity-building

Of course, some institutionalized Mormon practices have greater potential than others to promote that melding of the local and ecclesiastical elements that will comprise the Mormon identity in each culture. One of these institutions is the missionary system, with reference here to what the missionary experience does for the missionary himself or herself. It is by no means to be taken for granted that the missionary experience has the same meaning and impact for every missionary (Shepherd and Shepherd, 1996). For some, both in the U.S. and elsewhere, the mission call is accepted for a variety of expedient reasons. However, for those who accept the call with a degree of genuine religious commitment, it provides an ideal opportunity to learn how to solidify the Mormon identity in their own cultural terms – or, in other words, to learn how to 'own' their Mormonism authentically but locally.

Finally, I would like to point to one other rather unique Mormon institution with special prospects and problems for identity construction. I refer to the temple. In a symbolic sense, the Mormon temple is analogous to a cathedral in the Roman and the Anglican Catholic traditions. Of course, its functions are in no way analogous to those of cathedrals, but symbolically it bespeaks a certain Mormon strength and a permanent Mormon presence. It offers a solid, material focus for the collective, community identity of all the Mormons in its locale, and especially for the individual Mormon identities of all who use it. One's Mormon identity is reinforced to some extent even by visiting the grounds. As one who grew up in a period when there were only four temples outside of Utah, and none in my home state of California, I can well remember how especially Mormon I felt as I urged all my non-Mormon friends to visit the Oakland Temple before its final dedication.

How much greater is the reinforcement of the Mormon identity as one proceeds first through the interviewing process to gain access to the temple, and then through the temple rituals themselves. There is nothing like them anywhere else in Mormonism, to say nothing of anywhere else in the world! Whatever may be the disparate sources of the various ideas and elements of the temple ritual, it is unique enough as an eclectic product to stand outside of any of the world's existing cultures, at least potentially. The fundamental doctrines and major covenants of the temple ritual, which are its main purposes, could be taught and recited in language and media which are quite neutral in cultural context and impact. Yet they have not been so taught, or at least not yet. In its many devolutions, the temple ritual has increasingly dispensed with elements originating in the American Mormon experience (Alexander, 1986b: 291–303; Buerger, 1987). Yet much in the film that now provides the dramatic framework for the ritual is still quite culture-bound, still dependent upon literal biblical understandings of creation, deity, and the other world.

If the processes of devolution and evolution in the temple ritual should continue, we might well eventually see adaptations of that ritual to various cultural settings, not only with local actors in the ritual drama, but with some uses made of local traditions and myths in the drama itself. The fundamental covenants and doctrines would, of course, be the same in all the temples, but the composition of the context or medium for these covenants and doctrines might vary somewhat from one culture to another. To the extent that such might occur, the temple ritual would be more fully 'owned' by local Mormons and more readily appropriated as a natural part of their own Mormon identity. In any case, as Mormon temples increasingly dot the world's map, there being some 50 now in operation, they will make an increasing contribution to the construction and maintenance of local Mormon identities. Yet, whatever the Church leadership does about temples, it will ultimately be up to the Mormons in each part of the world to find the faith, the ingenuity, and the motivation to construct their own enduring Mormon identities from harmonious combinations of local culture and authentically Mormon ideas and practices. The future of Mormonism in the world certainly depends upon their success in so doing.

2 Modernity, history and Latter-day Saint faith

L. C. Midgley

It has been argued that communities 'are constituted by their past – and for this reason we can speak of a real community as a "community of memory," one that does not forget its past.' Hence a genuine 'community is involved in retelling its story, its constitutive narrative, and in so doing, it offers examples of the men and women who have embodied and exemplified the meaning of the community' (Bellah, 1985: 185).

> The stories that make up a tradition contain conceptions of character, of what a good person is like, and of the virtues that define such character. But the stories are not all exemplary, not all about successes and achievements. A genuine community of memory will also tell painful stories of shared suffering that sometimes creates deeper identities than success . . . . The communities of memory that tie us to the past also turn us toward the future as communities of hope. (ibid.)

Martin Marty, the most distinguished American church historian, holds that both individuals and religious communities ground their identity on stories. And we are formed into communities to the degree that we share a common story with a recognizable plot. He insists that:

> . . . life is not lived one-on-one, or by one's self: we are social beings, born in and destined for some sort of social, communal, and corporate existence. And here story, and history, come in even more suggestive ways. We have no access to a past beyond our own memory unless someone has taken pains to tell or write stories about it, to make it thus accessible. (1989: 7)

Without texts we have no past other than our own or shared communal memories. But we do not really live by what is produced by antiquarians or professional historians, for 'religious communities are not made up of antique-collectors. For instance, the Christian Church is not a memorial society,' because 'the church is not a "keeper of the city of the dead." While tradition keeps it healthy, when it loves tradition it is not a community of traditionalists.' Instead, 'it lives by stories. These can engender doctrines' (ibid.: 9). The tradition provides the network of stories which constitutes a link with the past that forms the identity of a community. Marty also denies that philosophy or anything like it could 'have come to the detail of the narratives which engendered Jewish, Christian, and later believing communities dependent upon them' (ibid.).

Community grounding stories, according to Marty, are not exactly what is often meant by 'history' in academic circles. Why? A rich network of stories provides the grounding for communities of believing Jews, Muslims, Christians and Latter-day Saints. On this issue one would do well to consider the fine book by Yosef Yerushalmi, which contains remarkable illustrations of the power of biblical history in constituting Jewish identity and community (1982). This book also constitutes a cautionary tale for those interested in the preservation of communities of faith and memory.

Christians 'see God's activity in the events, words, circumstances, and effects of Jesus Christ and tell the story of his death and resurrection as constitutive of the faith that forms their community,' while others either 'extend the sense of story through the ages,' or repudiate intervening Christian history and live off the original story of Christianity (Marty, 1985: 10).

But Latter-day Saint faith is perhaps more history-grounded than that of Muslims and other Christians. Marty refers to the Saints as a people who act 'upon the basis of their history, their story' (ibid.: 12). He correctly notes that they:

> have not made much of doctrine, of theology: they especially live as chosen and covenanted people in part of a developing history. Much is at stake when the story is threatened, as it potentially could have been when forged documents concerning Mormon origins agitated the community and led to tragedy a few years ago. (ibid.)

He has in mind the forgeries of Mark Hofmann. Why would forgeries of historical documents or the recent attacks on the Book of Mormon generate concern among the Saints? The answer is that for the Saints to begin to see the Book of Mormon as frontier fiction, as the product of a trance by a magic or occult saturated, dissociative 'genius,' fundamentally transforms the story of the Restored Gospel. Much is therefore at stake when such matters are debated.

Marty correctly senses that the faith of Latter-day Saints has always 'been characterized by its thoroughly historical mode and mold' (1992: 170). He sees the faith of the Saints as:

> 'historically classical' in its tradition. When Latter-day Saints argue, they argue about morals based on history, or about historical events and their meaning – about how the contemporary community acquires its identity and its sense of 'what to do and how to do it' from the assessment of the character, quality, content, and impetus of that story. (ibid.)

It is therefore crucial for the faith of the Saints that the story of the generative or founding events remain in place in the hearts and minds of the Saints. Those who become Saints do so because they find meaning in the accounts of those events, their own story and the story of the restoration then become linked. And those who leave do so because the story no longer has power to regulate and give meaning to their lives.

The Saints thus have their own distinctive ties to the past. A story fills their memory and forms the identity that melds then into a community of faith and memory. That which disputes, dilutes, or transforms the distinctive Mormon past will also alter and erode the community. And that which refines, tells more fully and accurately the story, will preserve and build the Kingdom.

Marty describes a crisis of faith taking place within the Mormon community analogous to similar and related crises experienced by other Christians confronted with Enlightenment skepticism about the miraculous, attacks on natural theology, historical-critical studies of the Bible, and so forth. The Mormon development, he believes, is a 'crisis comparable to but more profound than that which Roman Catholicism recognized around the time of the Second Vatican Council (1962–65)' (1992: 169).

Marty refers to the 'acids of modernity' which flow from the ideologies of the 'God-killers' which have corroded the faith of many Muslims, Jews and Christians (1959: 298–301). The resulting crises of faith have come in waves and degrees, and with different effects in each case. For the Saints, the crisis is not one that centers on abstruse philosophical issues or on systematic or dogmatic theology, but on history – on how the story is told and understood. The primary source of the crisis is the emergence of an 'historical consciousness' that leaves a faith grounded in historical events problematic because history no longer seems to contain any certainties.

Marty is correct about the importance of history for Latter-day Saints, for it is in accounts of the past that we find the ground and content of faith. Are the Saints really undergoing a 'crisis of historiography' that challenges their faith? One can find support for this view. But it is not the whole story, for the understanding of the generative events for the most part seems not to have eroded or transformed but deepened and refined among the Saints since World War II. And since the Mormon faith has always been characterized by 'its thoroughly historical mode and mold,' the current crisis, to the degree that it is accurate to speak of such a thing, was unavoidable. Why? Because a new historical consciousness has yielded 'what some might regard as a dramatic and traumatic shift among Mormon intellectual' (1992: 170). But for most Saints there is no crisis or they have passed through it with a more refined and stronger faith.

The primary challenge generated by modernity to the faith of the Saints has not been skepticism concerning natural theology, since that sort of thing has played virtually no role in forming a Mormon identity. And skepticism concerning miracles has only minimal impact on Latter-day Saints, since the miraculous has been pictured by the Saints in ways that have diverted or blunted most criticisms of miracles. The primary challenge is from attacks on the network of stories that form the identity of the Saints. Part of what seems necessary to maintain LDS identity includes maintaining the viability of the stories that ground their faith, since challenges to these clearly threaten to modify, weaken or destroy group identity.

Marty argues that the challenge to communities of faith by Enlightenment rationalism, if not met in some effective way, tends to dilute, modify, or destroy faith. If religious communities, that is, in the larger sense Muslims, Jews and Christians, each in their own way, depend for their identity upon a story they more or less share within their own communities and that forms both the content and grounding of their particular faith, the life and health of those communities depends at least to some extent upon whether they manage to find ways of meeting challenges to their stories. Hence, we can speak of communities of faith and memory, and we can begin to sort out what generated, perpetuates, and threatens such communities.

Of course, what Marty (1959: 296) labels as the 'acids of modernity' may not threaten individual or group identity when believers exist in a condition that he describes as 'primitive naivete,' borrowing that label from Paul Ricoeur (Marty, 1992: 171). This label merely describes the understanding of the world that is held by those who have not confronted the possibility that the world can be understood differently by those outside the community of faith. When a range of alternative explanations and competing stories is encountered, an individual must find some way of avoiding the challenge or reach an accommodation with the new competing view, or abandon faith.

The Saints cannot avoid the impact of the culture that surrounds them and hence have often found themselves in an environment in which they confronted competing and contradictory understandings of reality. And some of them, of course, have experienced a crisis of faith that they had to resolve in some way. This is especially the case when they have experienced the allure of a different and perhaps alien world made available through secular education. And Latter-day Saints have coped with such crises in a number of ways, with some ceasing to believe. The current debate over the historical authenticity of the Book of Mormon going on at least in part on the fringes of the Mormon intellectual community is an indication that some of the Saints have experienced the impact of explanations having their assumptions in secular modernity (Midgley, 1992).

There are a few accounts of the Book of Mormon and the related story told by Joseph Smith that are clearly recognized as 'naturalistic explanations of Joseph Smith's theophanies' done in entirely 'secular terms.' And even the most ardent apologist for what is vaguely labeled a 'new Mormon History' grants that such naturalistic explanations end up denying 'the possibility of genuine individual creativity or [divine?] inspiration' (Alexander, 1986a: 30). And it is exactly that kind of revisionist history that some of those he defends think of as approaching objectivity precisely because they boast that they are not subservient to or involved in the faith. And it is precisely those accounts, if they were to become popular, that would transform or destroy the Latter-day Saint community of faith and memory.

By complaining about revisionist accounts of the Book of Mormon and Joseph Smith's prophetic charisms, which I believe interdict the story that forms the community of faith and memory (Midgley, 1994), I do not question the need for accurate, profound, and fruitful accounts of the Mormon past by Latter-day Saints (or sympathetic, better-informed accounts of others), nor do I deny that important advancements have taken place in writing about the Mormon past in the last 30 years. Furthermore, I deplore pictures of the Saints as faultless heroes. Attempts to conceal the frailties or shortcomings among the Saints are silly. Recognizing that historical accounts, as well as the understanding of certain texts on which they rest and by which they are transmitted, have a crucial role in the perpetuation of communities of faith and memory, my concern is with the way artifacts such as the Book of Mormon and the related prophetic truth claims of Joseph Smith are understood. To this point at least, for the most part the acids of modernity have not corroded the faith of the Saints, as they have the faith of many other Christians.

3 The Book of Mormon wars
A non-Mormon perspective

Massimo Introvigne

In 1976 Harold Lindsell, a founding faculty member of the Evangelical Fuller Theological Seminary in Pasadena, California, published his now famous book *The Battle for the Bible*. It chronicled the battle for the doctrine of inerrancy of the Bible within the Southern Baptist Convention, the Lutheran Church – Missouri Synod, and the Fuller Theological Seminary itself, where moderately liberal Bible scholars were teaching by the 1970s.

While Lindsell's book is still a favorite among American fundamentalists, Lindsell himself made clear that it would be inaccurate to reduce the large variety of Protestant positions on the Bible to two camps only, of liberal and fundamentalist, since, in fact, dozens of different positions between the two extremes seem to exist. Scholarly studies on Protestant fundamentalism, not to mention the study of fundamentalism as a broader category not necessarily confined to the Protestant world (see Marty and Appleby, 1991–94), have boomed in the last two decades. Since the publication of the movement's manifesto, *The Fundamentals*, between 1910 and 1915 ('Two Laymen,' 1910–15) fundamentalism was often represented as a reaction against science. Recent scholarship, on the other hand, has suggested an alternative explanation, seeing fundamentalism as an attempt to secure for biblical truth the same certainty that science enjoyed according to the Newtonian and positivist paradigm.

Evangelicalism and fundamentalism had, according to George M. Marsden (1991: 129), 'a love affair with Enlightenment science' and hailed 'objective scientific thought . . . as the best friend of the Christian faith and of Christian culture generally.' As there was only one 'true' science, needless to say, not including evolutionary theories, the fundamentalists reasoned that there could be only one objective 'truth' about the Bible: that it was the inerrant, infallible Word of God. Marsden (1980) has proved that hostility to science was originally foreign to fundamentalism and emerged as a later development, when science started to be secularized and to change its own paradigm. Fundamentalism, as a consequence, has been particularly hostile to late modernist and post-modernist assumptions that there is no 'one science' only, but that science could be a collection of conflicting points of view, often selected for practical purposes without necessarily implying that one is more 'true' than the other. Paradoxically, fundamentalism maintained the objectivity of 'scientifical truth' when this claim was no longer made by mainline science itself (Marsden, 1991: 122–52).

Nineteenth-century Mormons were certainly not biblical fundamentalists. Philip L. Barlow (1991) has demonstrated that, although they sincerely professed a strong general belief in the Bible, 'early Mormon leaders limited the authority of the Bible by (1) promulgating an extra-biblical canon, (2) placing primacy on living prophets over received Scriptures, (3) representing Scriptures as but one source of truth among others, (4) stressing the corruptions in the received text of the Bible, and (5) dismissing portions of it as uninspired' (Mauss and Barlow, 1991: 406). Only in the twentieth century did the Mormon changing use of the King James Version of the Bible exhibit some features of a Mormon 'assimilation' to the Protestant (conservative) establishment (Mauss and Barlow, 1991: 410–11). Michael Quinn (1983) has emphasized the importance of the 'fundamentalist' attitudes, and the association with the conservative Protestant lobby during his diplomatic career, of J. Reuben Clark (1871–1961), who served as a member of the First Presidency from 1933 to 1961. Clark was instrumental in importing the fundamentalist attitudes on the Bible into Mormonism. Recent Mormon editions of the King James Version have been 'Mormonized' through specific notes, but the notes, at the same time, have guided the readers toward what has been called a 'fundamentalist' interpretation (Ashment, 1990: 237–64). While 'fundamentalism' is normally used in Mormon circles to designate the splinter groups who still practise polygamy or maintain nineteenth-century theories no longer regarded as orthodox by the Mormon Church, Armand Mauss (1994) has noted in the new Mormon attitudes towards the Bible one of the features showing that contemporary Mormonism is in a phase of 'retrenchment,' where at both the popular and hierarchical levels traits emerge that could be called 'fundamentalist' in the usual non-Mormon sense of the term.

In contemporary Mormonism the main battle is not about the Bible. Although it would be wrong to conclude that Mormon scholars are uninformed or uninterested in non-Mormon biblical exegesis, what in other denominations is a battle for the Bible is in contemporary Mormonism a battle for the Book of Mormon. This battle is fought not around interpretation, but around the very nature of the Book of Mormon. Is it what it claims to be? Or is it merely a product of Joseph Smith's creative genius or religious imagination? Those claiming that it is neither of the two, but a fraud, exclude themselves from the debate and join the ranks of mere anti-Mormonism. While the debate is not identical with the Protestant battle for the Bible, ultimately the question is whether the Book of Mormon, not unlike the Bible in the Protestant controversy, is 'true.'

Historians are more crucial to the Mormon debate than to the Protestant, for the obvious reason that the Book of Mormon was first published in 1830 and the circumstances of its translation are more open to historical research. While the Church-approved *Encyclopedia of Mormonism* claims that 'for most Latter-day Saints the primary purpose of scripture studies is not to prove to themselves the truth of scriptural records, which they already accept, but to gain wisdom and understanding about the teachings of these sacred writings' (Ricks, 1992: 205), in fact the 'truth' of the Book of Mormon may be defined in conflicting ways, and the battle for the Book of Mormon has largely become the battle for Mormon history. Accordingly, essays on Mormon historiography, such as those collected in *Faithful History* (G. D. Smith, 1992), in fact concern the battle for the Book of Mormon not less than specific studies of Mormon Scripture itself.

Faithful History, including some conservative views together with a majority of liberal perspectives, was published by Signature Books, while most of the liberal authors had been published in the independent Mormon journals *Dialogue* and/or *Sunstone.* These journals also publish articles by conservative authors, and it would be inaccurate to claim that they have a single, if hidden, liberal agenda especially since Mormon liberals exhibit a whole spectrum of different nuances. Signature also published *The Word of God* (Vogel, 1990), and *New Approaches to the Book of Mormon* (Metcalfe, 1993), arguably the two most controversial books representing the liberal side in the battle for the Book of Mormon. Signature was strongly criticized, to put it mildly, by conservative Mormons; one of whom, Stephen E. Robinson, went so far as to propose a parallel between the Salt Lake City press and Korihor, 'the infamous "alternate voice" in the Book of Mormon,' claiming that 'in its continuing assault upon traditional Mormonism, Signature Books promotes . . . precisely this same naturalistic assumptions of the Korihor agenda in dealing with current Latter-day Saint beliefs.' In short, 'Korihor's back, and this time he's got a printing press' (Robinson, 1991: 312).

Robinson's criticism was published in 1991 in the *Review of Books on the Book of Mormon,* a publication started in 1989 by FARMS, the Foundation for Ancient Research and Mormon Studies, based in Provo, Utah; the *Review* epitomizes the conservative or, as it would prefer to say, orthodox, Mormon side in the battle for the Book of Mormon. The battle was not merely metaphorical, since Signature asked its attorney to write to FARMS threatening what FARMS called 'the appeal to Caesar' (Peterson, 1992). Undeterred, in 1994 the *Review of Books on the Book of Mormon* devoted a whole issue to a strongly worded attack to *New Approaches to the Book of Mormon* edited by Brent Lee Metcalfe for Signature (Metcalfe, 1993). Controversies on the Book of Mormon surely had a role in the 1993–94 excommunications of liberal Mormon intellectuals together with one conservative and millennialist scholar, Avraham Gileadi. Metcalfe and another of the authors of *New Approaches,* David P. Wright, were among those excommunicated.

It would be tempting, and the non-Mormon press has occasionally succumbed to the temptation, to label as 'fundamentalists' the authors writing for FARMS publications, including the *Journal of the Book of Mormon Studies,* and as 'modernists' those published by Signature Books and by the independent Mormon journals. This would simply be to regard the battle for

the Book of Mormon as an LDS version of the Protestant funda-
mentalist/modernist controversy and battle for the Bible. The comparison
would, however, be only partially accurate. Of course, Mormon conservatives share with Protestant fundamentalists a commitment to sacred scriptures, to the support of denominational hierarchies and, to some extent, to
tradition. It is also probable that they would agree more readily with
Protestant fundamentalists than with liberal Protestants on issues like
abortion or homosexuality. On these and similar attitudes and preferences,
conservative Mormons would, however, agree also with many Protestants
who would never call themselves fundamentalists. More deeply, the basic
epistemology of Mormon conservatives is entirely different from the
fundamentalist paradigm. We have mentioned earlier that, contrary to
popular prejudice, Protestant fundamentalists, according to the most
recent scholarly interpretations, are in fact deeply committed to
Enlightenment concepts of 'objective knowledge' and 'truth.' Post-modern,
anti-Enlightenment epistemology is rather used by their liberal counterparts. Not so in the Mormon controversy. Liberals, to start with, are
staunch defenders of the Enlightenment. Edward Ashment credits 'the
Enlightenment' with having 'introduced a new morality of knowledge
which is similar to that of today's scholarly world.' He approvingly quotes
Van Harvey to the effect that 'the Enlightenment was what one scholar has
called a "declaration of independence against every authority that rests on
the dictatorial command: Obey, don't think" ' (Ashment, 1992: 287–8; see
Harvey, 1966: 39). Of course, very few historians would agree with such a
caricature of pre-Enlightenment scholarship and with the idea that the
world had to await the Enlightenment to see 'standards of truth and
honesty' prevail (Ashment, 1992: 294). This is, however, not the point.
More crucial in understanding the peculiarities of the Mormon controversy
is that, unlike many Protestant modernists, Mormon liberals are persuaded
that, thanks to Enlightenment rationalism, an objective concept of 'science'
and 'truth' may allow them to reach factual, empirical, 'scientifical' conclusions on the Book of Mormon and its origins. Not surprisingly the transition from a religious to this truly secularized perspective of history and
knowledge has been described by David P. Wright (1992: 28) as a 'conversion experience.' He has offered a typical conversion narrative of how he
'grew up a traditional Mormon,' in college 'found that many of the traditional historical assumptions that [he] held did not make sense' and finally
'by the end of [his] graduate education' came 'to own the critical framework.'

On the other hand, the late modernist and post-modernist position that
knowledge is by no means objective, and that 'true,' universally valid,
historical conclusions could never be reached, is held by Mormon conservatives. One of the most articulate expositions of this point of view has been
advanced in the last twelve years or so by David Bohn, a professor of political science at Brigham Young University. In a 1994 *Sunstone* article Bohn
(1994: 45–63) summed up his position quoting Jacques Derrida and other
post-modernist luminaries to argue that historical conclusions are not

'true' photographs of reality but are politically negotiated narratives. When liberal historians such as Michael Quinn use 'professionism as a defense,' Bohn retorts that they do not seem 'to understand that these methodological claims of professional historiography are precisely what are in question.' It would do no good, Bohn insists, to retreat to a moderate position where objectivists may argue that 'they are only trying to approximate neutrality and objectivity.' No, 'they miss the point altogether,' because 'neutrality and objectivity cannot even be approximated.' Bohn denies that we could work 'within some absolute universe;' we could only work 'within agreed-upon universes whose boundaries and standards of measure are a product of history, defined by conventions which for one reason or another we decide to use.'

Bohn goes on to attack the Enlightenment paradigm, using the phenomenology of Edmund Husserl and the hermeneutics of Hans-Georg Gadamer. Similar arguments have been used against the same targets by Louis Midgley (1992), another professor of political science at Brigham Young University, and are largely presupposed in many of the essays by FARMS scholars criticizing Metcalfe's *New Approaches*, although Bohn is probably more favorable to the post-modernist paradigm than most of FARMS associates. Conservative Mormons often quote Peter Novick's indictment of objectivism and positivism in American historiography (see Midgley, 1990). Novick (1988) is representative of a whole school of theoretical historiography claiming that 'objective truth' for the historian is an objectivistic prejudice, a 'noble dream' never to be achieved. Interestingly, Novick addressed Mormon intellectuals at the 1988 Sunstone Symposium.

At this stage, an outside observer expecting conservative Mormons to adopt a fundamentalist view of truth, and liberal Mormons to adopt a post-modernist one, may easily claim that something should be wrong. The attitudes are in fact almost reversed. Historical truth is regarded as a mere social product by Mormon conservatives, while a rather naive sociology of knowledge claiming that historical-critical methodologies may indeed achieve 'truth' lies behind the liberals' attitude. The 'love affair with Enlightenment science' of American fundamentalists described by Madsen does not find a counterpart among Mormon conservatives; conversely, Enlightenment's claim for certainty and objectivity is still defended in the liberal camp. It is not surprising that liberals accuse 'Mormon apologists' almost of cheating.

Edward Ashment (1992: 288–90), the Enlightenment enthusiast contributing to Signature Books publications, whom FARMS prefers to define as 'a California insurance salesman who once studied Egyptology' (Peterson, 1994: x), is suspicious of Mormon conservatives who 'adopt a deconstructionist strategy when it serves their purpose' and accuses them of being 'relativistic.' While accusing others of 'relativistic' attitudes is a strange claim from scholars claiming to be part of the modern secular historiographic tradition, it is true that Mormon conservatives, having embraced post-modernist attitudes on the social construction of 'truth,' should find a way to save the idea that the religious tenets of Mormonism are, nevertheless, 'true.' At least some of them are well aware of the methodological and philosophical problems involved. First, they claim that once contemporary sociology of knowledge has proved that all scholarly enterprises are politically conditioned they, as Bohn writes, 'much prefer research in which no effort is made to hide the guiding prejudice of the writer over that which feigns neutrality.' They could also resort to 'the Mormon view of God, time, and agency, . . . incompatible with traditional eschatologies and their metaphysical assumptions,' and remind us that, after all, 'Mormonism does not hold that God is the final cause of every historical fact,' thus allowing for a certain contradiction both in history and in human ability to grasp historical facts. Ultimately, however, Mormon conservatives are persuaded that 'the truth of the Restoration . . . stands beyond the power of secular discourse to authorize or annul' (Bohn, 1994: 45–63).

A non-Mormon perspective

The position of Mormon conservatives may easily be dismissed as a mere claim to faith, and probably would be regarded just as such, by many scholars socialized in the secular tradition. It is, however, not unique. While conservative Mormons use Gadamer and Husserl, other religious scholars, including Joseph Cardinal Ratzinger, one of the most prominent scholars in the Catholic Church before becoming one of the main officers in that denomination, have used the ideas of Karl Popper and his school in order to claim that science, both natural and social, does not produce 'truth' but only provisional theories capable of being 'falsified' by subsequent and better, though still provisional, new theories. Although the late Sir Karl Popper may have thought otherwise, Ratzinger and other religious scholars have argued that the argument is only valid with respect to secular science, while religion is situated in an entirely different domain where the Popperian paradigm is not applicable.

Ultimately, such use of Popper or, in a different context, of Gadamer is premised on general metaphysical and theological options which are, in turn, difficult to evaluate in terms of being 'true' or 'false.' At any rate, although probably secular scholars do not care to read it, there is a rich religious literature confronting the question of truth arguing that 'true' or 'false' are still meaningful labels in the field of theology and religion even in a post-modernist world where they have lost their meaning, and rightly so, this literature claims, in both natural and social sciences. In the Evangelical field Harold A. Netland (1991) has made his point with similar arguments in favor of 'Christian exclusivism' against relativist theologians such as Paul Knitter or Wilfred Cantwell Smith. In the Roman Catholic world the absolute value of religious truth in a post-modern world has been forcefully argued by Pope John Paul II (1993) in the most philosophically-oriented of his encyclicals, *Veritatis Splendor* ('The Splendor of Truth Shines') of 1993. Again, both Evangelical texts such as Netland's and *Veritatis Splendor* are not 'fundamentalist' in any sense of the word. Fundamentalists, in fact, do not even bother to ask themselves the question of truth, and would not accept the idea that modern social sciences, including the sociology of science, have deconstructed the notion of 'truth' with respect to our knowledge of both nature and history. As we mentioned earlier, fundamentalists in general are rather entrenched in the defense of a general objectivistic paradigm of knowledge, and would claim that 'legitimate' or 'good' science is still capable of letting us know the 'objective truth.' Even their assault on evolutionism is not conducted in the name of a criticism of science but rather of an alternative, 'creationist' science (see Numbers, 1992; Toumey, 1994).

On the question of truth and the respective claims of science (natural and historical) and religion, Mormon conservatives are more similar to Catholic and moderate Evangelical conservatives than to fundamentalists. They have, however, three problems that Mormon intellectuals, liberal and conservative alike, would probably be compelled to explore more deeply in years to come. The first problem is peculiar to Mormonism. The Evangelical, and conservative Catholic, claim for religious truth in the age of post-modernity ultimately appeals to a theological premise connected with the sovereignty of an omnipotent God. 'Truth' in religion is a participation of the absolute truth of God. It has been argued that the Mormon concept of a limited God does not allow for such claims. If God is limited, theological 'truth' should be not less provisional than historical or scientific 'truth' as restricted by post-modern criticism. This argument has been advanced by anti-Mormons such as Latayne C. Scott (1992: 25–8) in a rather trivial way, mentioning the Mormon 'open canon,' the appeal to the 'burning in the bosom' and even the exaggerations of Elder Paul H. Dunn as evidence that Mormons do not really believe in 'truth.' Not all anti-Mormons, however, present their case in such a simplistic way. Francis J. Beckwith (1992), a lecturer in philosophy at the University of Nevada, Las Vegas, has argued more astutely against any possible claim for an absolute truth in Mormonism, starting from the Mormon concept of a limited God (see also Beckwith and Parrish, 1991). Ultimately, I am personally not impressed by Beckwith's arguments, but perhaps they deserve a closer scrutiny.

There is a second problem common to Mormon and other Christian conservatives. Is the epistemological argument premised on Gadamer, Popper, or post-modernism really in touch with what the average everyday Church member really feels and thinks? Common folks in the pews not only ignore the very names of the likes of Gadamer or Popper, but are probably persuaded that both science, including social science and history, and religion produce 'truth,' without being aware of the semantic differences between the respective concepts of 'truth' in religion and science.

Post-modernist defences of Christianity, or Mormonism, risk remaining of limited sociological relevance in that the average Church member is not even aware that there are problems with the 'truth' which history or science may offer. Post-modernist approaches to the 'truth' of religion, the

Bible, or the Book of Mormon are not, however, anachronistic. Sociological inquiries tell us that even among professionals, such as computer operators and medical doctors, belief in witchcraft and magic is growing, as Luhrmann (1989) shows for the UK. Popular faith in science is decreasing and approaching, in countries like Italy, what is probably an all-time low (see Berzano and Introvigne, 1994). Post-modernity, as a reaction to the Enlightenment paradigm, is becoming more socially relevant. In this context Gadamer may not become a household name, but the possibility that science, including history, may produce 'truth' safer than religion will be increasingly questioned. And, if the socialization of the post-modern paradigm advances, conservatives will enjoy a tactical advantage over liberals in future stages of the battle for the Book of Mormon.

The third problem concerns the need to clarify the relationship between exegesis and hermeneutics. This problem is central in the position paper prepared in 1993 by the Pontifical Biblical Commission (1993) for the Roman Catholic Church, *The Interpretation of the Bible in the Church.* The paper is not, strictly speaking, a document of the Catholic magisterium, but it was published with an endorsement by the Pope who recommended it as an 'excellent work,' and with a 'Preface' by Joseph Cardinal Ratzinger, the highest authority in the Roman Catholic Church in matters of faith and doctrine. The document is premised on the distinction between exegesis and hermeneutics. Exegesis tries to collect as much information as possible about the text, while hermeneutics offers 'more' on the relationship between the text and its readers.

The first part of the document examines six styles or traditions of exegesis. All are, partially, acceptable, but none of them is 'neutral.' Their philosophical presuppositions should be identified, and some of them should be exposed as not compatible with the Christian faith. The historical-critical method is seen as 'indispensable' but, at the same time, in need of being handled carefully, since it is often a disguised secularist and rationalist agenda, and also needing to be integrated with other methods based on literary analysis, sociology, psychology, anthropology, and gender studies. Each of these latter methods, in turn, should be carefully disassociated, when necessary, from the ideological premises inherently hostile to religion often embraced by its proponents.

The second part of the Vatican document deals with hermeneutics. It is remarkable that a semi-official document by the largest Christian denomination takes seriously modern philosophical hermeneutics and discusses Gadamer's position at length. Gadamer's idea, much quoted, as we have seen, in the Mormon debate, that 'anticipations and preconceptions affecting our understanding stem from the tradition which carries us' is quoted approvingly. The document then examines Gadamer's idea of hermeneutics as a dialectical process, based on *Horizontverschmelzung*, the fusion of the differing horizons of text and reader, and *Zugehörigkeit*, or 'belonging,' as a fundamental affinity between the interpreter and his or her object. Since both literary and historical criticisms are necessary but not sufficient, in the scholarly context of post-modernity the Commission (1993: 73–7) notes 'the absolute necessity of a hermeneutical theory which allows for the incorporation of the methods of literary and historical criticism within a broader model of interpretation.' 'All exegesis . . . is thus summoned to make itself fully complete through a "hermeneutics" understood in this modern [i.e. Gadamer's] sense.' Entering directly into controversies not unfamiliar to the Mormon community, the Vatican Commission states that 'contemporary hermeneutics is a healthy reaction to historical positivism and to the temptation to apply to the study of the Bible the purely objective criteria used in the natural sciences.' On the other hand, the Commission thinks that hermeneutics still needs exegesis. Hermeneutics entirely detached from historical and literary studies may generate 'purely subjective readings.' This criticism is not far from the warnings of Umberto Eco, a deeply secular author and one not quoted in the Vatican document, that interpretation has its limits, and post-modernists at times seem to claim that simply any interpretation would do (Eco, 1990).

Of course, it would be inappropriate for a non-member to offer suggestions to the Mormon community on how to deal with the present Book of Mormon controversies on exegesis and hermeneutics. It is perhaps less inappropriate for the non-Mormon scholar, however, to offer comparisons with what is being culturally negotiated in other Christian communities. The Roman Catholic experience may offer a useful comparative perspective on at least three points.

First, it could contribute to show that it is naive to claim that the historical-critical method is the only method acceptable to approach the text of a sacred scripture. 'Exegesis' in the contemporary, scholarly sense of the word is larger than the historical-critical method, and also includes other methods. It is also useful to remember that the historical-critical method is often packaged with all the elements of a secularizing tradition inherently hostile to religion and the supernatural. It would seem that at the exegetical level a better understanding of the Book of Mormon could take advantage of studies based on approaches other than the historical-critical method, where the problems of historical criticism may be temporarily set aside.

Second, the historical-critical method remains useful when approached in full recognition of what it is and what its agendas may be. No appeal to hermeneutics could make historical and critical studies on Joseph Smith and how the Book of Mormon was translated and published in the nineteenth century irrelevant; these studies, of course, would include attempts to determine what 'translation,' in this context, may mean. Hermeneutics without exegesis risks offering what Eco calls 'the infinite interpretation,' a sequel of subjective claims no less destructive to a Christian community than the naive surrender to historical-critical exclusivism and to its claim to generate 'true' and 'objective' reconstructions.

Third, although 'pure' hermeneutics without exegesis would run the risk of an extreme subjectivism, not even advocated by Gadamer, hermeneutics remains crucial. It is, after all, in the hermeneutic circle of *Horizont-verschmelzung* and *Zugehörigkeit* that each of us will encounter a sacred text, hear the text's and God's voice, and decide what attitude he or she wants to take towards the narrative. Exegesis is needed by hermeneutics in order that this crucial decision is not uninformed, purely subjective, or merely emotional. On the other hand, exegesis should be modest enough not to pretend to break the hermeneutic circle and leave us with only one alternative. Sciences, including social and religious sciences, could only debunk the totalitarian claims and, at the same time, confirm the relative value of each exegetical tradition and approach, leading us to the center of the hermeneutic circle. When we are there, we are alone with ourselves and God, and no science could decide for us.

4 Coffee, tea and the ultra-Protestant and Jewish nature of the boundaries of Mormonism

Christie Davies

The Mormon refusal to drink coffee or tea is an oddity, a sociological puzzle that needs to be explained. No other Christian denomination, except for the Seventh-day Adventists,[1] bans these beverages, and indeed, because they cause a mild elevation of mood without ever producing inebriation or unseemly behavior, they are often served at church-based social occasions. Whilst attempts have been made to justify this peculiar Mormon practice on health grounds, the case is not a strong one, and certainly cannot justify the current Mormon insistence that active members should rigidly follow this particular rule. Such an insistence seems to treat tea and coffee as if they were polluting substances and as such is contrary to the ancient injunction so central to Christianity that:

> Not that which goeth into the mouth defileth a man; but that which cometh out of the mouth, this defileth a man. (Matthew 15:11)

Origins and development of the ban

The ban on tea and coffee is to be found in a divine revelation received by Joseph Smith, the founding prophet of Mormonism, in 1833 and is recorded in the following section of the Doctrine and Covenants (89:5, 7–9), widely known as the Word of Wisdom,

> 5. That inasmuch as any man drinketh wine or strong drink among you, behold it is not good neither meet in the sight of your Father . . .
> 7. And again strong drinks are not for the belly, but for the washing of your bodies.
> 8. And again, tobacco is not for the body, neither for the belly, and is not good for man, but is an herb for bruises and all sick cattle to be used with judgement and skill.
> 9 And again hot drinks are not for the body or belly.[2]

What is perhaps particularly significant for our present purposes is the way in which this doctrine has become more strongly emphasized over time. John L. Brooke, a historian of Mormonism, has noted that:

> The Word of Wisdom doctrine forbidding tobacco, alcohol, coffee and tea had only been sporadically enforced in the last quarter of the nineteenth century, but starting in 1901, the church mounted a campaign of enforcement, culminating in 1921, when adherence to its code was required for attendance in the temple. (1994: 291–2; cf. N. Anderson, 1942: 439, Lyon, 1992; P. H. Peterson, 1992)

The significance of this has been further emphasized by Thomas F. O'Dea, one of the leading sociologists of religion to have made a study of the Mormons, who stated that:

> Admission to the temple and hence permission to take part in the ceremonies performed there – temple marriages, sealings, baptism for the dead – are denied to Mormons who do not abide by the proscription of smoking and the command to abstain from coffee, tea and liquor. Moreover, this commandment has become for Mormons a most salient mark of their membership in the Church ... Abstention from the practices forbidden in the Word of Wisdom appears to have replaced plural marriage as the badge of Zion, the sign of the gathered, in these days of accommodation to and integration into the larger gentile community. Frequently defended and rationalized in terms of bodily health and hygiene, the Word of Wisdom is the symbol of Mormon concern with the things of this world. (1957: 146)

Coffee, tea and health

The defence and rationalization of the Mormon prohibition of smoking in terms of bodily health and hygiene is understandable given the growing medical evidence linking smoking to heart disease, lung cancer, chronic bronchitis, emphysema, peripheral neuritis, and other ailments that kill and cripple; there is similar evidence available to indicate the threat to health caused by the old American custom of chewing tobacco and spitting on the floor. Moderate alcohol consumption, though, may actually be beneficial to the health of the individual (D. Anderson, 1992); but alcohol is also a drug which, when used unwisely, can lead to antisocial behavior, and undermine the character of those dependent on it. From this point of view it is easy to see why the Mormons would have tightened up their prohibition on the consumption of alcohol in the early twentieth century, at a time when they were seeking respectability in the eyes of the main Protestant denominations for whom temperance was an important moral issue (Brooke, 1994: 292; Lyon, 1992: 1585; P. H. Peterson, 1992: 416). Likewise in the latter part of the twentieth century, when health has become almost an ideological obsession in America, with tobacco being singled out as an especial threat to health, it is clear why the Mormons, like the Seventh-day Adventists, should stress the health benefits and increased longevity derived from their distinctive diet and way of life that excludes alcohol, tobacco, tea and coffee and discourages the consumption of meat (Bull and Lockhart, 1990: 10–11; Rogers, 1989: 11–15; Lyon, 1992: 1585).

The problem items in the list are tea and coffee, since it is unlikely that moderate consumption of them has any major detrimental effect on health (Paul, 1993). The drinking of coffee and tea may well produce minor negative effects overall in relation to particular illnesses and causes of death but equally these may well be offset by benefits in other aspects of health. A detached, secular, rational utilitarian free to pick and choose those items of the Word of Wisdom, or of the dietary creeds of other religious groups which seem prudent, and to discard the others would almost certainly not bother to observe the ban on tea and coffee, any more than he or she would choose to follow the kosher dietary rules observed by Orthodox Jews. The kosher rules can be justified as health measures (Maimonides, 1963), but non-Jews, with the partial exception of some nineteenth-century Seventh-day Adventists, have never been sufficiently convinced of this to adopt them. Indeed Mormons might even have been better advised to interpret the ambiguous phrase 'hot drinks' in the original text as referring to excessive temperature[3] rather than being a prescient warning about the caffeine present in cold cola drinks as well as in hot coffee and tea. It is possible that tomorrow's pharmacologists may discover that even the moderate consumption of caffeine and allied substances is massively harmful, but equally it may turn out to be greatly beneficial. To tie a revealed doctrine too closely to the uncertainties of future scientific discovery is to give a valuable hostage to a very uncertain fortune. Insofar as Mormons do obtain health benefits from their abstention from coffee and tea, these may well derive from the sheer arbitrariness and irrationality of a rule that sets them apart from people of other religions. To be a secure member of a peculiar people (cf. W. E. Smith, 1992: 1072–4) with its own moral code and an enhanced sense of solidarity and collective identity can in and of itself provide psychological benefits for the individual that result in improved health. Also in such a social environment, characterized by a relative absence of egoism and anomie, not only suicide but other less direct forms of self-destruction may be inhibited by the strength of the individual's ties to the group and by the group's ability to regulate the lives of its members (Durkheim, 1970). The ban on tea and coffee, precisely because it has little physiological basis and is thus not shared by knowledgeable outsiders, outsiders well aware of the health hazards posed by tobacco and alcohol, strengthens collective Mormon identity and thus quite possibly improves the health of individual Mormons.

Coffee, tea and the collective identity and boundaries of Mormons, Jews and Seventh-day Adventists

For the Mormons, as for the Seventh-day Adventists, abstention from coffee and tea serves as an important boundary marker between the members of the group and outsiders which operates at two levels. In the first place the rule makes it relatively difficult for members to share social events even with those who belong to relatively restrictive Protestant denominations that disapprove of the use of alcohol and tobacco. It means that commensality is made difficult and that Mormons and Seventh-day Adventists are relatively more likely to form patterns of sociability restricted to members of their own group and following their own rules. They are not going to be tempted to join the coffee mornings or tea parties of their Baptist, Methodist or Presbyterian neighbors, let alone indulge in shared smoking and drinking with Episcopalians or Roman Catholics. The boundary is complete. Second, the duty to abstain from substances indulged in and regarded as harmless by the vast majority of the population is a daily reminder that they are a peculiar people, a group set apart, who live in the world but are not of the world.

There is an obvious parallel here with the much more elaborate, detailed and sophisticated food rules and prohibitions observed by the Jews, which serve to set them apart from the Gentiles, a term that is also significant in the Mormon vocabulary. The Jewish dietary rules were edited and codified during their period of exile in Babylon, based on a set of traditions derived from their earlier time of exile in Egypt (J. R. Porter, 1976). Their explicit purpose was to preserve the distinctive religious and national identity of the Jewish people, when forced to live in exile among strangers; they provide a set of internal, social boundaries that are a substitute for the isolation and geographical boundaries that are the more usual basis of national identity (C. Davies, 1982, 1983; Douglas, 1966, 1975). Their success is shown by the survival of a diaspora of Jewish communities throughout the world for nearly two thousand years, which in our time have provided the basis for the recreation of a Jewish state in Israel. Other peoples scattered in this way have tended to lose their identity and to be merged out of existence into their neighbors, but the Jews have survived repeated exile and persecution as a distinct and coherent people, i.e. their laws and religion have worked exactly as they were intended to do.

In the case of the Seventh-day Adventists the connection between their dietary code and that of the Jews is a fairly direct one, for their Prophetess Mrs Ellen G. White was directly inspired by her reading of the Old Testament. She was opposed to the eating of meat and in principle favored vegetarianism, but she also permitted the eating of clean meat as defined by the Jewish dietary rules and fiercely denounced the consumption of pork (Lindén, 1978: 320–1; White, 1864). Indeed, at one stage she came close to teaching that the dietary laws laid down for the Jews in Leviticus still applied to Christians in the nineteenth century (Lindén, 1978: 331).

Given that the Seventh-day Adventists keep the Sabbath on Saturday in the Jewish fashion from sunset to sunset, they have clearly moved away from mainstream Christianity back towards Judaism, for the Sabbath and the dietary rules were, and are, the very core of a separate Jewish identity. Indeed, one of the key ways in which Christianity broke away from its Jewish origins to become a distinctive religion was by repudiating the dietary laws, along with circumcision, in order that it might carry its distinctive religious message to the Gentiles and become a universal church rather than simply the religion of a particular people, though the Jewish people had, of course, been a chosen people charged with a special mission to others (1 Corinthians 10:25). Had the Seventh-day Adventists readopted the dietary laws of the Jews, they would have reversed this process to a very substantial extent and become a Judaized Christian sect. By favoring vegetarianism, they have, to a large extent, avoided the problem since the Jewish dietary rules are largely concerned with meat: animals must be killed in a particular way, such that the blood, the life of the animal, is removed; meat and dairy products may not be consumed together; and only clean animals, birds and fish, belonging to precisely defined categories, may be consumed. Vegetarianism requires no such rules and can be justified to members and to potential converts on ethical or health grounds that are at least reasonably compatible with the Christian tradition (Soulay, 1973).

The links between the Mormon dietary rules and the mores of the Jews of the Old Testament are less direct but just as interesting. The Seventh-day Adventists, as indicated by the title of their sect, came to define themselves as set apart from other denominations in the nineteenth century, by shifting the keeping of the Sabbath from the first day of the week to the seventh, in keeping with the custom of the Jews (Lindén, 1978: 115; Burgon, 1992: 1423). The Mormons of the nineteenth century adopted a far more morally radical Old Testament tradition: polygamy, or more specifically polygyny, the taking of a plurality of wives in the tradition of the Patriachs of the Old Testament (Brooke, 1994: 14; Bachman and Esplin, 1992: 1092). It was a direct reversal and repudiation of what is perhaps one of the most central and peculiar, perhaps even unique, moral principles of Christianity, for the original Christian tradition alone, in contrast to that of all other major religions, insisted on lifelong monogamy with no bigamy, no divorce, and no recognized status for concubines (C. Davies, 1993a, 1993b). For Christians, a man could not take a second wife during the lifetime of the first, nor could any children he might have by some other woman enjoy any kind of recognized status. Other religions either accepted polygyny as a matter of course, as Islam or Judaism did, or else provided for ways round the peculiar dilemmas that could arise in societies based on patrilineal inheritance when the first wife failed to produce a suitable or surviving heir. In time Christianity became more flexible in matters of annulment and divorce but the prejudice against bigamy remained and indeed was exported to the rest of the world and often imposed on people of other faiths. Jews in Christian, but not in Muslim, countries adopted monogamy over time, probably more from a wish to avoid giving the Christians one more excuse for persecuting them than from any spontaneous evolution of their own religious morality.

Likewise, in the 1890s the Mormons were forced to repudiate their revived tradition of Old Testament polygamy which had flourished in the Zion they had created in Utah, out of reach of the United States federal government (Bachman and Esplin, 1992: 1094). In the 1870s and 1880s the United States Congress passed a series of Acts that savagely suppressed polygamy and directly attacked the Church of the Latter-day Saints as an institution and the civil rights of its members (D. J. Davies, 1987: 44–5; Davis, 1992: 52–3). The United States Supreme Court refused in 1879 in *Reynolds v United States* to accept the Mormon view that the anti-polygamy laws violated their constitutionally guaranteed right of the free exercise of their religion (Riggs, 1992: 1229). Indeed it later became clear that not merely polygamous marriages but polygamous cohabitation and the advocacy of polygamy as a religious doctrine could and would lead to imprisonment, deprivation of property, or the loss of civil rights and that there were no constitutional limits to the persecution of polygamous Mormonism by an American government in the grip of a characteristically American moral frenzy.

Thus by the beginning of the twentieth century, the Mormons had lost both the local theocratic power they had enjoyed for a time in Utah and their most distinctive and distinguishing institution, namely polygamy. They had been forcibly integrated into the ordinary political and social institutions of American society. It is no coincidence that it was at this point that the Mormon authorities began to lay great emphasis on the observation of the rules of the Word of Wisdom by individual members of the Church, for they were now exiles in a strange land (O'Dea, 1957: 146). They needed an alternative way of creating a strong boundary between Mormons and Gentiles but one which would not inflame the latter to further acts of persecution. Refraining from coffee and tea as well as alcohol and tobacco now came to perform this function; like the Jewish kosher rules, this held one's members apart from the Gentile world, but could also be represented as a virtuous extension of one of Protestant America's other moral crusades, Prohibition. Indeed, Mormon proselytizing could now even take the form of saying in effect to possible converts from a conservative Protestant background, 'look, we are even more restrictive, socially responsible and healthy than you yourselves, an even finer example of your own virtues.' In this way a wall could be built that was permeable in one direction because its particular and restricting social functions for those securely held within the wall could be justified in other and universal terms to those on the outside wondering whether to enter.

Mormons, Jews and ultra-Protestants

One of the most distinctive features of the Protestant Reformation of the sixteenth century was its rejection of the elaborate celibate hierarchies that formed the organizational core of the Roman Catholic Church with its priests and members of religious orders who had taken vows of lifelong chastity. In doing so they destroyed a distinctive and venerable system of authority based not just on tradition and continuity but on the sacred quality of a rigidly bonded hierarchy set apart by its abstention from sexuality and from family life (see C. Davies, 1982, 1983, 1993). In its place Protestants, and particularly the more radical reforming Protestants who were inclined to reject all vestiges of the old hierarchy, 'root and branch,' have tended to place a special emphasis on the authority of the Bible, on the special importance and sacredness of marriage, which regulated sexuality in a world in which there was no particular merit attached to celibacy and total sexual abstinence, and on the keeping of the Sabbath.

Those Protestants who emphasized the centrality of the scriptures in this way, at the time of the Reformation and particularly those of the early nineteenth-century religious movement in America known as the Second Great Awakening, during which time Mormonism first emerged, have often been termed 'Restorationists' since they were perceived as seeking to recover the original vitality of the New Testament Church – John Dillenberger and Roger B. Keller have argued that the

> Latter-day Saints were more comprehensively restorationist than any other group, particularly since revelation is seen as being as requisite today as in the past; and that, as in the New Testament Church, the scriptural canon is not closed. (1992: 1221)

This is no doubt a fair comment, for clearly the primitive church has been a major source of inspiration to Protestant reformers generally and to the Church of Latter-day Saints in particular, but the Old Testament and its covenants have equally been a source of inspiration to many Protestants, particularly where they have felt themselves to be members of a group set apart by national identity, or by a time of exile spent among or in retreat from hostile strangers. The Protestant stress on marriage, with an acceptance of divorce, as opposed to the Roman Catholic exaltation of celibacy, and on the regular and rigid observation of the Sabbath, represent a return not so much to the teachings of the New Testament as to the Jewish traditions of the Old Testament (e.g. Ramsay, 1873).

From this point of view, the Mormons, like their fellow tea and coffee abstainers the Seventh-day Adventists, are ultra-Protestants who have gone even further in an Old Testament Jewish direction than the other Protestant reformers and restorationists. The Seventh-day Adventists' stress on keeping the Sabbath on Saturdays, and obsessive interest in Leviticus (Lindén, 1978), and the nineteenth-century Mormon belief in the practice of plural marriage, are all of Jewish origin and inspiration. There is nothing in the New Testament to justify any of these and the inspired revelations of Joseph Smith and Mrs Ellen G. White on these points are clearly rooted in their knowledge of and reverence for the Old Testament. Consider further the importance for many Latter-day Saints when they learn from their Patriarchal Blessings 'that they are literally of the lineage of Israel [Doctrines and Covenants 86:8–9], primarily the tribes of Ephraim and Manasseh' (S. K. Brown, 1992: 706; Stewart, 1992: 708). It becomes clear that there exists a very strong subjective identification between the Latter-day Saints and ancient Israel, far more so than is the case for other

Christian denominations, who in the main do not seek to identify a
genealogical blood line, nor even a line by adoption to one of the tribes of
Israel. It is one more indication of the Jewish quality of the Latter-day
Saints, which in turn may be related to the ultra-Protestantism they share
with the Seventh-day Adventists.

The complexity of the argument advanced here can perhaps best be illustrated and simplified by reducing the key variables to a single dimension
in which the end sections are Roman Catholicism and Judaism respectively. Roman Catholicism represents the furthest point from Judaism to
which Christianity has moved. The various Protestant denominations, and
particularly the Mormons, represent a reaccommodation with Old Testament tradition through the distinctive Protestant preference for seeking
continuity through scripture and marriage (in the Mormon case, including
celestial marriage, genealogy and baptism of one's dead ancestors), rather
than through a celibate hierarchy expressing the Apostolic succession of
bishops and denying the importance of a specifically genetic lineage.

Table 4.1 Attitudes to sex and marriage

Roman Catholic	Reformed Protestant	Mormon	Jewish
The celibate priest is the moral ideal. Church's key boundary an internal one between a celibate hierarchy and a laity for whom marriage is a lesser form of service to God. Within the hierarchy, celibacy, if strictly enforced, destroys lineage.	Married clergy not decisively set apart from the laity. Marriage the central sacred sexual institution in absence of sacred celibacy.	Church leaders in 19th century often polygamous.	Rabbis and religious scholars expected to marry. Marriage and family are central institutions within which many religious cere-monies are carried out at home, notably those involving meals.
		Polygamy abandoned owing to Christian hostility.	Polygamy abandoned owing to Christian hostility.
Polygamy forbidden.	Polygamy forbidden.	Great stress on lineage and celestial marriage.	Strong stress on lineage.
Divorce forbidden.	Divorce permitted.	Divorce permitted.	Divorce permitted.

Table 4.2 Attitudes to food and drink

Roman Catholic	Reformed Protestant	Mormon	Jewish
Food rules apply only to particular days, fast periods or religious orders. Alcohol is universally accepted. Roman Catholic temperance movements only significant in countries where strong Protestant influence in this direction.	No significant rules about food. Strong temperance movements, often seeking to enforce total abstinence and prohibition of alcohol. Opposition to tobacco not unusual.	Weak rules about diet, meat and grain; not stringently observed. Very strong ban on coffee, tea, alcohol and tobacco.	Very strong and detailed dietary rules distinguishing between kosher and traife, i.e. permitted and unclean foods. Alcohol, coffee and tea drunk in moderation with meals in family setting, so long as there is no mixing of meat and milk.

It is clear from the tables that Mormonism is best regarded not as a new religion but as merely a forward position on a Protestant line of advance away from Roman Catholicism and back towards the traditions of the Old Testament. Whether we should then in general speak of the 'Jewishness' or of the 'ultra-Protestantism' of Mormonism is a debatable question, but at least the Church of Jesus Christ of the Latter-day Saints lies *on* and *not detached from* a very familiar religious continuum. To look at the Latter-day Saints in this way may well at least prove more productive than indulging in further semantic disputes about whether they constitute a church, a sect, a denomination or an established sect, for this particular classification has not proved particularly helpful in the past in assisting us to understand the nature and history of Mormonism.

Concluding thoughts on coffee, tea, Protestants, Jews, and Mormons

Mormon scholars have mistakenly tended to see both the dietary rules of Leviticus and their own ban on coffee and tea as health measures, when in point of fact they function rather as social codes that set apart the members of each group from the Gentiles outside, even though explanations in terms of health can be and are provided to justify the presence of particular items. For the Jews, the dietary rules ensure that members are retained within a secure boundary, and since no attempts are made at proselytizing and recruitment to Judaism there is no reason for revising them or for seeking to justify them to outsiders. The Mormons are by contrast a strongly proselytizing and expanding church who have to consider at all times what is their best set of marketing techniques. If they were to move too close to the patterns of belief and behavior of their nearest religious neighbors, the conservative American Protestant denominations, they would gain greater respectability and social acceptance, but would lose their distinctive appeal and image in a competitive religious market-place. By contrast, if the Mormons were to introduce or reintroduce a pattern of moral behavior such as polygamy, that totally outraged middle America, this could again lead to the kind of conflict and confrontation that would threaten to destroy their, by now, stable, accepted and tolerated Church. Even those 'liberals' who speak approvingly of 'alternative' family forms, involving disappearing, unstable, replaceable, promiscuous fathers of either sex, seem to be hostile to the orderly respectable rule-governed plural marriages still to be found on the heterodox unofficial Fundamentalist fringes of official Mormonism and would presumably be willing to send in gun-toting federal agents to suppress such families.

For the Mormons, abstaining from coffee, tea and cola drinks is an ideal middle way of resolving such a problem in moral marketing. It is a sufficiently unusual and peculiar pattern of everyday behavior to set individual Mormons, and even more importantly their children, decisively apart from their peers, and to contain them securely within the group. At the same time, the banning of these substances can be represented as an extension of acceptable tendencies already present in conservative Protestantism, such as the temperance movement which disapproves of alcohol, and the current health crusade against tobacco, whose emphasis on the cleanliness of the unpolluted body is a secular version of earlier campaigns for the moral purity of the soul. For the Mormons, of course, there is no such clear contrast between the soul and the material temple that contains it (Mason, 1992: 580), and they are thus particularly well placed to exploit the contemporary obsession with healthism, though they may in the long run pay the price of an inner secularization of their religion, as seems to have happened with some of the Seventh-day Adventists (Bull, 1990: 245–61). The Mormon abstention from coffee and tea represents in a very clear way the paradoxical position of the Mormons as a group that maintains a Jewish, and very non-Christian, mode of defining its boundaries and identity through dietary taboos and an obsession with genealogy and descent and yet which also displays an ultra-Protestant, and very non-Jewish, concern with attaining an ascetic total abstention from even the mildest of legal drugs of sociability and euphoria.

Notes

1. See Bull and Lockhart (1990) and Lindén (1978) on the Seventh-day Adventists. For the marked contrast with the practices of conservative Protestants in this respect see Towns (1994).
2. See Ludlow (1992: Section 89, 5: 7–9; J. Smith (1845).

3. This view has been taken by the Reorganized Church of Jesus Christ of Latter Day Saints: see Fox (1995: 1197). It is notable that this point is presented as part of a description of the movement of the Reorganized Church away from being an exclusivist sect to being a denomination, and thus seeking to minimize the distance between itself and other Protestant denominations.

5 Latter-day Saint exceptionalism and membership growth

James T. Duke

Has the Church of Jesus Christ of Latter-day Saints been able to promote an exceptional rate of growth (Stark, 1984) in its 165-year history? What are the social conditions that facilitate such growth? I address these questions with an analysis of data from the General Social Surveys comparing LDS people to other Americans.

Through research on the growth and success of the LDS Church, Rodney Stark (1987) developed a model of the conditions necessary for the success of new religious movements. This model embodied eight conditions, two of which are addressed in this paper. If a new religious movement is to succeed, it must (1) maintain cultural continuity with other social institutions in the host society, yet (2) maintain a medium level of tension with that society.

Social scientists have not yet developed robust empirical measures of either cultural continuity or tension. Lacking such a metric, they have engaged in fruitless debates concerning the extent to which tension fosters growth or decline.

I use a single measure of both continuity and tension that has plausibility but does not put to rest the controversy. I assert that the vital feature of cultural continuity is similarity between members of a religious group and those of the host society, especially on the dimensions considered to be essential features of the way of life of both groups. People who are alike are more likely to feel a sense of solidarity, unity, and fellowship. If members of two groups are indistinguishable from each other, it is not likely they will feel tension or conflict when they interact. However, there are many subgroups within any society and the members of any religion are diverse. Therefore, members of any church may fit better with some people than with others.

Conversely, the essential test of tension is anxiety and conflict, either at the personal or social level. Such tension can arise from many sources, but is likely to be present when there are substantial differences between the two groups, especially when these differences are judged to be unusual, peculiar, or bizarre. The greater the difference, the greater the tension and the greater the probability that members of the religious group will be stigmatized and rejected by members of the larger society. Many of the tensions experienced by Latter-day Saints involve either (a) making sacrifices, such as paying tithing, serving two years in the mission field, fasting, and having more children, or (b) exerting self-discipline not expected of others, such as practicing chastity and forgoing alcohol, tobacco, tea and coffee.

Methodology

I used data from the combined General Social Surveys (GSS) (Davies and Smith, 1994). In all of the GSS surveys completed from 1972 to 1994, there were 430 LDS respondents, or 1.3 per cent of all respondents. I compare this group of LDS people with the 32,389 other Americans in the combined GSS samples. The findings apply specifically to people in the United States, but by testing Stark's theory, we hope to generalize to other societies.

LDS Church figures show that Mormons represent about 1.7 per cent of the American population, so Latter-day Saints are under-represented in the GSS surveys. GSS studies before 1979 did not sample Mormons adequately, especially those living in Utah. The GSS samples probably represent adequately the LDS population outside of Utah, while its representation of LDS people inside Utah is suspect.

The specific questions used here were selected to explore the accuracy of commonly-held beliefs held by many Americans that Latter-day Saints are religious, pro-family, hard-working and middle class, chaste and wholesome, healthy, patriotic, and politically conservative (see Duke, 1996). Because of the extreme differences in the size of the numbers of the two groups being compared, I do not report statistical significance, although with such large sample sizes a difference of only 2 or 3 per cent would be statistically significant.

Findings

Table 5.1 compares responses by LDS people with those of other Americans. The data are presented as percentage differences. I arbitrarily define a substantial difference as 20 per cent, a difference likely to produce a tangible level of tension. A moderate difference is defined as from 6 to 19 per cent, and continuity with American society is defined as a difference of 5 per cent or less.

Table 5.1 Comparisons between Latter-day Saints and other Americans

Dimension	Latter-day Saints		US average	
	Males	Females	Males	Females
N =	(181)	(249)	(14,070)	(3531)
Religious questions	%	%	%	%
Strong affiliation with church	59.0	64.4	31.9	44.7
Belief in life after death	94.5	94.0	75.2	80.8
Average yearly contributions	$1846	$1562	$421	$403
Family questions				
Current marital status	%	%	%	%
Married	77.9	69.1	64.4	54.7
Divorced or separated	5.0	9.6	10.5	15.5
Widowed	1.7	12.8	4.1	15.3
Never married	15.5	10.4	21.0	14.5
Ever been divorced	18.2	19.3	18.0	17.4
Ideal number of children				
0–1	0.8	1.2	3.7	3.3
2	25.2	30.7	51.5	51.4
3	20.3	16.3	24.0	22.2
4+	44.0	42.7	14.9	17.3
As many as you want	9.8	9.0	6.0	5.8
Indicators of well-being				
General happiness: very happy	40.0	39.8	31.5	33.0
Marital happiness: very happy	63.7	69.5	66.1	62.4
Very satisfied with job or housework	46.0	45.9	47.5	47.4
Condition of health: excellent	49.6	32.5	34.2	29.6
Ever drink alcohol	33.3	22.8	77.7	65.7
Currently smoke	15.2	12.1	40.5	30.9
Conditions on sexuality				
Premarital sex is always wrong	54.4	58.9	23.7	33.4
Teen sex age 14–16 is always wrong	84.6	87.9	63.0	73.4
Extramarital sex is always wrong	91.5	90.6	70.0	77.3
Homosexual sex is always wrong	94.4	86.4	73.7	72.8
Number of sex partners last year				
None	21.2	29.3	15.2	26.9
One	5.0	65.9	67.3	64.2
More than one	3.8	4.9	17.4	8.9

Socio-economic status				
Average years of school completed	13.4	13.0	12.4	12.1
Subjective class identification	%	%	%	%
Lower class	2.3	4.7	4.5	5.7
Working class	43.7	44.9	47.4	44.9
Middle class	50.6	47.5	45.0	46.3
Upper class	3.4	3.0	3.1	3.1
Current family income				
Below average	28.1	29.8	26.0	30.4
Average	44.4	51.2	49.7	53.6
Above average	27.5	18.9	24.3	16.0
Family income when 16				
Below average	20.9	34.2	32.1	31.7
Average	53.1	49.6	50.9	53.1
Above average	26.0	16.3	17.0	15.2
Could find an equally good job				
Very easily	23.3	26.7	25.0	25.6
If rich, would continue working	86.4	61.0	73.5	67.5
Political questions				
Political party: moderate or strong republican	62.4	58.2	35.0	33.2
Political ideology: slightly or extremely conservative	56.3	48.8	36.4	31.3
Served in armed services	33.3	0.7	41.4	1.4
Media questions				
Watched X-rated movie last year	11.0	10.2	28.8	16.6
Read a newspaper every day	52.2	43.3	58.4	52.6
Hours per day watching TV	2.37	2.48	2.78	3.15

Source: Combined General Social Surveys 1972–1994, National Opinion Research Council

Substantial differences

These data show that there are five substantial differences between Latter-Day Saints and other Americans. LDS people:
1. are more likely to be highly religious – to believe oneself to be a strong member of one's church, to believe in life after death, and to make greater financial contributions to the church (Hoge and Yang, 1994);
2. are less likely to use tobacco or alcohol;
3. have a higher ideal family size and a larger number of children actually born (Heaton, 1989);

4. are more politically conservative and more likely to identify with the Republican Party;
5. are less likely to approve of premarital sex, extramarital sex, and homosexual sex, and less likely to have multiple sex partners. However, the difference between LDS and non-LDS people is greater for premarital sex than the other types of sexual behavior, and greater for LDS men than women.

Moderate differences

There are also a substantial number of ways in which LDS people are moderately different (from 6 to 19 per cent) from others. LDS people:

1. are more likely to be married;
2. are more likely to be remarried following divorce;
3. have a higher level of general happiness, and LDS women are more likely to be very happy in their marriages;
4. are more likely to have completed a high level of education, although this does not result in a higher average income or occupational status;
5. are less likely to have served in the armed services;
6. are less likely to have seen an X-rated movie, and less likely to read a newspaper or watch television every day.

In addition, LDS men:
7. are more likely to consider their health to be excellent;
8. are more likely to say they would work if they were suddenly to became rich, while LDS women are somewhat less likely than other American women to work if rich.

Similarities with other Americans

The data in Table 5.1 also show some areas in which Latter-day Saints are similar to other Americans – that is, in which they maintain cultural continuity:

1. LDS people are equally likely to have been divorced;
2. LDS men are equally likely to say they are very happy in their marriages, and both LDS men and women are about as happy with their jobs and housework as are other Americans;
3. LDS women are as likely to say their health is excellent, even though those who practice the LDS lifestyle have a much lower mortality rate (Enstrom, 1989);
4. LDS people are as likely to identify with the middle class and to assess both their current family income and their income at age 16 as average. However, Mormon men are more likely to say the income of their families at age 16 was above average;

5. LDS people are as insecure about finding a new job as other Americans.

In addition to these questions, there are many other ways in which LDS people are similar to others. These include vast areas of work experience, economic and financial activities, travel and leisure pursuits, cultural beliefs and values, and food and other consumer preference.

Discussion and conclusion

The conventional beliefs held by Americans concerning Latter-day Saints were supported, with one exception. Members of the LDS Church tend to be religious, family-oriented, middle class, chaste, politically conservative, and healthy. However, they are *less* likely than other Americans to exhibit patriotism by serving in the armed services. These findings support previous research on Latter-day Saints (Duke, 1996) and reflect positively on the church and its members. The church teaches that there are beneficial consequences to living gospel teachings, and church members see evidence of such consequences.

In some areas of social life particularly significant to them, Latter-day Saints are substantially different from other Americans. There are also areas of moderate differences and many areas of continuity. We lack a method of combining these differences into a broad scale to indicate tension. Does a combination of substantial, moderate, and low differences add up to a medium level of tension? My answer is affirmative yet tentative. All things taken together, most LDS people in the United States probably experience a medium level of tension with the host society. Further, it is plausible but as yet not demonstrated that such tension is a contributing condition to the growth of the LDS Church.

It is not an easy task to maintain continuity with the host society while sustaining a medium level of tension with that society. Latter-day Saints maintain continuity by being like others on a great many dimensions, yet they experience tension by being different on some significant social dimensions. The schism between wanting to be accepted and wanting to be different requires constant personal and organizational adjustment and adaptation. Church leaders advocate maintaining church standards while being different and 'peculiar.'

The conditions of continuity and tension in Stark's model are difficult to measure, so we still are far from being able to test his model with powerful measurement techniques. Until the time when such measurement is possible, studies such as this will serve as plausible substitutes.

6 Neither Mormon nor Protestant? The Reorganized Church and the challenge of identity

Roger D. Launius

Several years ago Clare D. Vlahos (1980) analyzed what could only be considered a narrow path, walked by the Reorganized Church of Jesus Christ of Latter Day Saints (RLDS) since its formation, between the seemingly radical Mormonism that emerged in Nauvoo and was carried to its logical conclusion in the Great Basin, and the overtly accommodationist mainstream Protestantism that is so prevalent in the United States. The latter represented a watered-down form of Christianity that the Restoration had emerged to counteract in 1830, while the former seemed to the early RLDS an excessive religious vision that went far beyond and ultimately did violence to the appropriate prophetic legacy of Joseph Smith Jr.

In essence the traditional RLDS identity was built on the tensions between the desire to remain faithful to the stories, symbols, and events of early Mormonism and the yearning for respectability among and hence openness to Protestants (Blair, 1973; Vlahos, 1981). Because of this the RLDS have largely been the people in the middle, steering between the Scylla of excessively authoritarian, speculative Nauvoo Mormonism and the Charybdis of rigidly creedal, congregational Protestant sectarianism. These tensions were held in creative balance until the last generation, when a theological reformation fundamentally reshaped the RLDS into a new church. For good or ill, it seems, the present-day Reorganization is only tangentially an inheritor of the legacy of the prophetic leadership of Joseph Smith.

Perhaps the fundamental ingredient in the identity of the early RLDS was that it coalesced out of a group of independently-minded people who had at one time or another stood up in the various factions of Mormondom and said in essence, 'up with this I will not put.' Because of this attribute, the RLDS was primarily an inheritor of a legacy of dissent that had been present as a minority movement within the early Mormon church. That legacy had manifested itself repeatedly almost from the very beginnings of the church as members debated the direction of church policy, organizational structure, and doctrinal conceptions (Launius, 1991). Because of the uniqueness of its founding, the peculiarities of its early leadership, the fortunes of its environment, and the doctrinal biases of those making up the RLDS as it emerged in the 1850s, the group embraced and gloried in a moderate expression of Mormonism in the American Midwest. Fundamental to its *Weltanschauung* was a commitment to greater membership involvement in the church's decision-making process (Draper, 1968). When the Reorganization began to coalesce in the early 1850s and as members coming out of this experience affiliated with it, the result was an emphasis on individual and congregational rights and prerogatives, an emphasis that remained strong for more than 100 years (Alder and Edwards, 1978; Launius, 1988).

As a dissenting movement, the fundamental ingredient in the Reorganization's historic sense of identity, it had to forge a place for itself in relation but also in opposition to the Utah-based faction of Mormonism. This was remarkably easy to do in the nineteenth century when the group first coalesced. Plural marriage provided the most easily recognizable means of establishing an identity as a Mormon group outside of the Utah faction. Simply put, the Rocky Mountain Mormons embraced the doctrine as a positive good and publicly practiced it until forced to stop by the power of the United States government while the Midwestern Mormons rejected it as an evil prostitution of the legacy of the Restoration. Plural marriage, with its demonstrable effects everywhere present in Utah, was an issue that resonated in the larger American population, not as an abstruse theological construct but as a concrete social issue. By standing in opposition to plural marriage but still claiming the legacy of early Mormonism, the RLDS made a legitimate place for itself in the nether world between Mormonism and Protestantism (Launius, 1987a and b).

The easiest period in which the RLDS could forge a reasonable identity as a separate religious institution was between 1852, when Utah Mormons publicly announced that they were practitioners of polygamy, and 1890, when the LDS church announced that it would no longer sanction its practice (Howard, 1983; Blair, 1985). Because of its inflammatory nature, plural marriage provided the needed context that set the RLDS brand of Mormonism apart from the Rocky Mountain variety. When that decisive difference between the two churches was removed in 1890 it inadvertently set up the more difficult task of maintaining boundaries between the RLDS and the Mormons that were less easily grasped by both the larger community and the membership of the Reorganization.

The nineteenth century, therefore, represented the 'golden age' of an RLDS identity as the people in middle. Vlahos observed of this era that 'The early Reorganization waited, caught somewhere in between, neither gentile nor Mormon' (1985: 184; cf. Conrad and Shupe, 1985). Vlahos makes an important but perhaps not altogether convincing case. His conclusion that the RLDS waited and was caught as a people in between the groups implies that this happened by accident and that it was a negative position for the church. Instead, the RLDS membership aggressively defined an identity in this middle place. They saw it as a strength, a way to legitimacy that might not have been possible on one or other ends of the scale. Indeed, in the twentieth century as the church sought to move toward the 'gentile' side of the scale and to distance itself from traditional Mormon identity it has found it increasingly impossible to ensure legitimacy as a separate institution.

Perhaps the central theme of American religion in the twentieth century has been its encounter with modernity, that set of priorities, assumptions, and values present in larger society as a response to emerging concepts in science, technology, economics, politics, philosophy, and the overall *Weltanschauung*. The response to modernity, according to Martin E. Marty, fundamentally changed the landscape of American religion in this century (1986).

The RLDS felt this challenge keenly, as it tried to redefine itself upon the landscape of American religion in the wake of Utah Mormonism's renunciation of polygamy. This process took off during the years following World War II and fundamentally reshaped the nature of the institution in the 1960s and 1970s. Several factors were at play in this process. One of the important ones was the rise in the standard of living of most of the RLDS's membership.[1] While this development, perhaps, did not cause, it certainly abetted a greater openness to Protestantism and accommodation to modern society than was ever present in the church before. The church as a body began to be more open to the influences of the society around it and in the process it moved into the mainstream secular world of the United States (Launius and Spillman, 1991).

Concomitant with the economic development of the RLDS church lay a theological reformation which began in the 1950s and was truly felt in the 1960s when Reorganization liberals engaged in a reorientation of the traditional RLDS consensus. The theological reformation had been initiated long before it began to be apparent in the Reorganization, and certainly had as one of its ingredients the need to refine its place in the middle as both ends of the scale shifted in response to their own considerations of modernity. This set the stage for a debate over authority, structure, and theology, with revisionists prevailing in most cases. The seeds of theological debate were harvested during the presidency of W. Wallace Smith, 1958–78, the time during which these questions began to emerge in a serious way in the Reorganization. But although W. Wallace Smith did not begin the theological reformation, clearly his policies allowed it to prevail. In its totality, the process enabled the shift of the church's theological milieu farther from the Mormon side of the spectrum and more into synchronization with mainstream Protestantism in the United States (Launius, 1995a and b; Conrad, 1991).

The process of accommodation by the RLDS to mainstream American Protestantism can be encapsulated most readily in a personal anecdote. In the summer of 1975 I was a student intern in the interpretive program at Nauvoo. During this experience, the first in my life where I had to interact with Latter-day Saints, we were forever trying to find effective ways to answer questions about the differences (identities) between the RLDS and the LDS. The traditional approach had long been to define the RLDS identity in relation to the LDS. Typically, we set this up by explaining what we thought the LDS believed about God, temples, baptism, missionary programs, organization, etc., and from that to launch into a discussion of what the RLDS believed about the same subject. Depending on the stridency of the individual making this analysis, there might or might not be some commentary on which of the two positions was true, correct, or appropriate.

The RLDS hierarchy wanted to move away from that traditional approach and made it known to the leadership at Nauvoo that it was now unacceptable at the church historic sites. Leaders tried to cast the change in the context of seeking to find a positive approach to evangelism, one that did not juxtapose the RLDS in any way with the LDS. The newer approach seemed to make sense to those of us involved in the interpretive program at church historic sites at the time and it helped pave the way for an interpretive program that was more even-handed, less polemical, and more mainstream. (I even possess an undated mimeographed booklet entitled *Positive Evangelistic Approaches to L.D.S. Doctrines* written by John W. Bradley and Eugene R. Chancey, both full-time appointee ministers in Utah in the 1960s. The book presents strategies that are indicative of the approach desired by the RLDS leadership and was written for the use of members seeking to convert Latter-day Saints.) At the same time, it fundamentally undercut the *raison d'être* of the entire historic site program as a mission tool, the supposed reason for undertaking the effort. That was a problem we wrestled with yet never resolved throughout my association with the sites. In the end we retreated into a kind of historical non-sectarianism about the church's past that sounded very much like the non-committal story one would hear at a state-run site about the Shakers, the Oneida Perfectionists, or the utopians of New Harmony. In retrospect, the revision of the traditional means of identity for the Reorganization manifested in something as simple as the historic sites program signaled a larger shift taking place in the church. It represented what observers have since come to realize was a fundamental desire on the part of many in the church's leadership quorums to move away from the traditional pattern of identity as the people in the middle in tension with Utah Mormonism and acceptable American Protestantism.

This move represented a conscious effort led by young men of influence in the church's hierarchy to reshape the church in response to the issues of modernity. Many of them were firmly imbued with middle-class values and had seminary education that had opened a whole new world of religious ideas to them. Like the frog who jumped from a well into the sea, they realized after a lifetime of experience limited to the Reorganization that a broader vision was possible and probably necessary for the advance of the church. A schism among the membership began to develop as educated elites began to press the church toward increasing openness to Protestant norms not understood by some of its full-time appointees and by many of its members.[2]

This dichotomy began to be seen very quickly within the church's appointee force. Many of the field ministers, especially members of the Quorum of Seventy, began to rebel against what they perceived as a de-emphasis of Restoration distinctives, the very things that made the

Reorganization what it was, and the resultant drift toward ecumenism. Al M. Pelletier, one of the most dynamic Seventies in the church during this period, was an old school Reorganization member. Most of his education and training had been independent or under one of the church's other appointee ministers. He had no use for the shift from exclusivity within the institutional church that he began to see in the 1960s. In 1967 he complained in an open letter to the Joint Council about 'several items in publications and church school materials which are unscriptural.' He continued:

> As far as the liberals, it is most unfortunate that we are divided into schools of opposition today. The church I joined years ago was comprised of Latter Day Saints. I still try to be one. I believe and teach and preach what is in our Church History, The Inspired Version, The Book of Mormon, and the Doctrine and Covenants. Every time I teach these things I'm speaking out against any liberal who denies the authenticity of some of these things. I cannot help this but can only follow the admonition given in scripture, to teach the fullness of the gospel as taught within the scriptures which are to be a 'law unto the church.' These teachings accompanied by my personal testimony will continue to consume my time and energy. I believe in this church and tell it to the world. I do not preach any doubts. I am sorry that some both preach and write about their doubts.[3]

Significantly, Pelletier left the church in the early 1970s, in part over the theological reformation taking place (Yarrington, 1990).

It would be inappropriate to suggest that the theological reformation of the RLDS was executed entirely by well-educated 'young Turks' who wanted to remake the Reorganization into a Protestant denomination, although such individuals were largely responsible for it. In part, however, it was fueled by the church's expanding missionary work in non-Christian cultures. Church leaders sent into those areas in the post World War II years determined that traditional Reorganization missionary techniques, as had been used at the historic sites, were ineffective. The usual missionary approach, they argued, was to demonstrate how the Restoration brought about by Joseph Smith, Jr, was correct and true to God's dictates and then to convince investigators that the RLDS was the 'true' successor to Smith's prophetic legacy. Several leaders asserted that these techniques were next to meaningless in societies where people were not already converted to Christianity.[4]

While the Reorganization's belief system was altered as a result of its contact with non-Western civilization, it was never a foregone conclusion that the Reorganization would be fundamentally altered because it moved into foreign missions. Other churches made similar moves and their bedrock religious distinctives remained intact. The most obvious example from the modern era would be the Utah Latter-day Saints who, while having their own difficulties on the international scene, have retained their distinctive identity in spite of interaction with other cultures. Many of the early converts to the RLDS in these new areas were already Christian and entered membership in the Reorganization because of the traditional 'true church' arguments made by the movement's missionaries. Indeed, many of the people joining the church in such places as Latin America and Asia during the reformation era were former Latter-day Saints who had become disenchanted with Mormonism. If the church changed fundamentally because of the conversion of non-Western members, as many members of the leading quorums have suggested, the numbers of converts have been so insignificant, only 2720 by 1970, that it raises a question about how such a small number could restructure the church so thoroughly. It seems, instead, that the church was already in the process of theological change as it entered the foreign mission field in a substantive way, and this missionary endeavor provided added impetus and a rationale for the changes already at work (Draper, 1982).

The 1984 World Conference marked the climax of the RLDS reformation and finalized the shift of the church far away from the middle ground between the Latter-day Saint movement and the larger Protestant position. At the meeting, the RLDS accepted in formal conference action the revelation now incorporated into the Book of Doctrine and Covenants as Section 156. This document represents the watershed in the RLDS' wrestling with the questions of modernity, providing for women's ordination, something that had been a sore point among liberal elements of the church for several years; a priesthood review process to validate orthodoxy; and a commitment to build a new temple in Independence.[5] The revelation, as well as the hierarchy's subsequent actions since 1984, sealed the shift of the RLDS away from being the people in the middle, between Mormonism and Protestantism, to closely identifying with the liberal element of mainstream Protestantism. The fallout from this shift forced outside the church many of its traditional members as something on the order of 20,000 to 30,000 members who could not accommodate to the thrust of the institution ceased their activity.

There have been attempts since the reformation to forge a new RLDS identity that no longer is based, even implicitly, on the concept of the people in the middle between Mormonism and Protestantism. Instead, it sits firmly within the camp of liberal Protestantism. Any new consensus has to overcome the traditional powerful paradigm that allowed the institution to accomplish worthwhile undertakings. While that traditional identity had never appealed to the mainstream from its place in the middle, it provided a spiritual home for those alienated from either side while being unable to accept either one in its totality. Accordingly, a long-standing source of converts to the RLDS had been among Utah Latter-day Saint defectors who rebelled against that organization's seemingly more authoritarian polity and esoteric religious conceptions while still accepting the general parameters of the Restoration ideal established by Joseph Smith. Few of those people will now find a home among the RLDS. Likewise, the RLDS often found converts among Protestants who were attracted to Mormonism for all kinds of reasons (the power of the Book of Mormon and the prophetic ministry of Joseph Smith were often cited), but who could not embrace some of its other concepts. Again, those people are less tempted by the Reorganization than previously since the church has abandoned many of the distinctive ideals that were earlier attractive.

This course by the RLDS away from Restoration ideals has been unaltered since the 1960s and seems to be accelerating at a rate no one could have predicted. Moves to shed the name 'Reorganized Church of Jesus Christ of Latter Day Saints' in favor of the more ecumenical 'Community of Christ' signals this continuing move toward Protestantism. A possible admission to full fellowship in the Reorganization of individuals baptized in other churches without rebaptism signals a similar shift. This raises all manner of questions about the nature of priesthood authority and the concept of Restoration that no one has yet been willing to tackle.

Parenthetically, how the baptism issue relates to LDS conversions to the RLDS will be interesting to watch. Would the Reorganization require their rebaptism while admitting others on the strength of baptism in another denomination? Not to do so violates the rationale behind the shift, but if they accept LDS baptisms it legitimates the priesthood authority of Brigham Young and his successors which would, even today, certainly cause a stir among many RLDS leaders. If this change takes place, it essentially means full-scale abandonment of the ideal of a Restoration accomplished through the prophetic leadership of Joseph Smith (Brown, 1994).

In abandoning its traditional place in the middle, the Reorganization has been trying to find a new set of features that will attract converts. The most promising of these is an effort to reform itself into a peace church. One of the most important aspects of the use of the new Independence Temple has been its dedication to the pursuit of peace (D&C 156:5). It is a singularly exciting proposal, but what does it mean? Peace is a term that means many things to many people, but how will it work in the temple? Is it a site for a 'Great Power' summit, a place of individual counseling, a center for study and reflection? It might legitimately be any one or all of these, as well as a location for other activities, but the real issue is that either no one knows or they are not telling, and it remains an especially troubling aspect of the potential uses of the temple as it has remained at the level of cliché. Understanding the evolutionary nature of this issue and especially appreciating the opportunity that it can provide as a worthwhile focus for the church in the future, it is troubling that the issue still rests at the level of cliché and the temple remains a building in search of a function. The emphasis on this aspect of the work of the church has reached significant proportions since 1984. In 1986, for instance, the church sponsored an international Peace Symposium at the Kirtland Temple to try to engage with some of these issues (Jones, 1987).

While this movement away from its Mormon heritage is taking place, the church has still not yet dealt with a wide variety of issues that prohibit it from being fully in the Protestant mainstream. The most important of these is the role of prophecy and the designation of an individual to serve as prophet/president of the church. As part of that role, the individual saddled with this position has traditionally brought written counsel to the church on a regular basis and this has been accepted as revelation and canonized in the Doctrine and Covenants. This has become increasingly infrequent in recent years and may virtually cease after the current prophet/president is replaced. Probably someone other than a member of the Smith family will fill this position after Wallace B. Smith retires, and the title of 'prophet, seer, and revelator' could be quietly dropped from the job description. There may continue to be a president, but not a person recognized as prophet. That might be a positive move, provided the church does not give up on the idea of divine revelation altogether and could accept the prophetic leadership of someone other than the president. To do so, however, raises all manner of questions about power and control that the hierarchy is loath to tackle.

Additionally, the RLDS has to deal with the Book of Mormon. To continue to accept it, even though it is essentially being ignored by the current leadership of the church, presents an enormous problem for the fashioning of a new identity. Its acceptance reflects the middle ground of identity between LDS and Protestants that had held sway until the mid-twentieth century and its continued acceptance represents something of a schizophrenia on the part of the organization.

Finally, questions about quorums, ecclesiastical offices, the idea of Zion and the millennium, and a host of other concerns will have to be dealt with in a meaningful way to forge a new identity that successfully transcends what had, traditionally, been a position neither Mormon nor Protestant. Failure to forge a new dynamic identity will spell the doom of the Reorganization. The theological confusion and thereby lack of identity that has been present for the last 20 years has enabled the church to enter a negative growth track, especially in North America where more than 90 per cent of its membership still reside. It is not impossible to view the RLDS of one hundred-plus years beyond as a small group of adherents linked mostly by kinship and revolving around the Independence Temple as the reason for their being. In that respect, they could become something akin to many of the other Mormon factions still in existence such as the Cutlerites, Bickertonites, and Hedrickites. They might be interesting and have worthwhile positions on many issues, but they would hardly represent major movements for good in the world.

At a fundamental level, being the people in the middle, neither Mormon nor Protestant, provided the RLDS with a useful means of identification that served it relatively well for more than a century. Abandonment of that traditional position has brought with it enormous challenges that have yet to be fully worked out. Perhaps it will fashion a new identity even more effective than earlier, but few are sanguine that such will be the case. In many ways the 1990s are the decade of decision for the RLDS on this issue. Its leaders must decide finally, after a generation of theological reformation and misunderstanding and resultant disruption, what its role in the world of the future is to be, and build a consensus for that role among both the membership and the larger society. At the same time, a complete divorce from the past is impossible and even undesirable. A new construct of past and present is necessary, one that will enable the Reorganization to define itself and its mission. I would hope that the institution can weather that crisis of identity and emerge as a stronger, more dynamic religious institution. I hope that the movement will recapture something of the experiential nature of the Restoration. I pray that it will find a trajectory, not necessarily the one formerly used, that links present with past and propels a people into the future.

Notes

1. RLDS Church (1970), *Report of the Commission on Education*, April: 64. Reorganized Church Library-Archives; *Information Please Almanac* (1980): 42. New York: Simon and Schuster; Walter N. Johnson Papers No. 67:6 'Appointee Compensation.' Reorganized Church Library-Archives.
2. *Report of the Commission on Education*: RLDS Church (1970): 116. Cf. Knapp (1982).
3. Al M. Pelletier to All Members of the Joint Council, May 29, 1967. Walter M. Johnson Papers, 1905–80. Reorganized Church Library-Archives.
4. Charles D. Neff (1972) The Church and culture. *Saints Herald* 119: 13–14; 51–2; (1974) The problem of becoming a world church. *Saints Herald* 121: 554–7; Clifford A. Cole (1971) Theological perspectives of world mission. *Saints Herald* 118: 11; (1960) The world-church: our mission in the 1980s and The Joseph Smith Saints. *Life*, May 2: 42, 63–6.
5. *Book of Doctrine and Covenants* (1986 edn, Section 156). Independence, MO: Herald Publishing House. *Guidelines for Priesthood* (1985). Independence, MO: Herald Publishing House.

Part II
The Expansion of Mormonism

7 Ethnic American Mormons
The development of a community

Jessie L. Embry

Scholars have often described the United States as a melting pot because, apart from the Native Americans, the settlers were all immigrants. Now, it is popular to refer to the country as a salad bowl because so many groups have remained segregated. Frequently these are 'people of color': Native Americans, African-Americans, Hispanic-Americans, Asian-Americans, and Polynesian-Americans. Through immigration and high birth rates, these ethnic groups have been growing rapidly during the last 35 years. If current rates continue, by 2020 Hispanic and non-white US residents will double, while the white population will remain the same. According to W. A. Henry, 'Once America was a microcosm of European nationalities ... Today America is a microcosm of the world' (1990: 28).

What experiences do these ethnic Americans have as members of the Church of Jesus Christ of Latter-day Saints, given that many of them do not speak English? Though membership records do not identify race or ethnic background, the number of foreign-language wards and branches in the United States and Canada illustrates the Church's growth among ethnic minorities. In 1994, for example, there were 138 ethnic branches in California, 28 in Utah, and 28 in Texas, with other ethnic congregations scattered across the country. In California, just over half the foreign-speaking units were Spanish, while three-quarters of those in Texas and just under half in Utah also spoke Spanish. Polynesian and Asian branches were the next largest groups, including a Chinese branch formed in Salt Lake City in the 1960s and Vietnamese and Cambodian branches organized in the 1980s for refugees. In the 1990s the Church organized a Tongan-speaking stake in the Salt Lake Valley.

The LDS Church has varied in its policies on ethnic branches. During the 1960s, Apostle Spencer W. Kimball directed Native American missions and congregations and also organized German, Japanese, and Chinese-speaking units in Salt Lake City. At the organization of the German branch, though, the General Authorities asked the immigrants to return to their geographical wards when they learned English. Church leaders viewed the separate units as temporary homes until the immigrants became part of the melting pot (Embry, 1992: 83).

Frequently the ethnic members did not blend in, either not learning English or wanting to study the gospel in their native language. Because it separated Church members, some general authorities questioned the value of having ethnic branches. As a result, the First Presidency sent a letter to all local leaders in 1972 asking members to be conscious of 'racial, language, or cultural groups.' Where language barriers existed, wards could organize special classes that would be taught in that tongue. However, stakes had to receive clearance from general Church leaders to create exclusive branches.

This move was not completely successful, and some ethnic members became inactive. As a result, in 1977 the Church reversed this policy and adapted a new basic unit plan which provided a model for restoring ethnic branches, and in 1980 Kimball, by then president of the Church, described the needs of these units. He told local leaders:

> Many challenges face all of us as we fellowship and teach the gospel to the cultural and minority groups living in our midst. . . . When special attention of some kind is not provided for these people, we lose them. (Embry, 1992: 84)

Like Church leaders, ethnic members disagree on the advantages and disadvantages of ethnic branches. Since 1985 the Charles Redd Center for Western Studies at Brigham Young University has conducted oral history interviews with 'people of color' who have joined the Mormon Church in the United States. One subject frequently discussed was how these people felt about separate congregations. Both recent immigrants from Japan and Native Americans related the same advantages and disadvantages.

Ethnic members liked to attend specialized wards and branches for the language. Kiyomi Patrick, a Japanese woman student who joined the Church in the United States, explained at the Asian branch in Provo, Utah, 'I can communicate easily.'[1] Branch members not only spoke Japanese but they understood the same culture. Patrick continued, 'I can just become friends with Japanese people because we know each other. We don't have to explain everything we feel. We can just communicate well without saying anything.'

These branches often held cultural parties. While Euro-American wards occasionally held *luaus*, they were common in Polynesian wards. Chinese and Asian branches celebrated New Year and mid-autumn festivals, Hispanic wards sponsored *Noche de Latina* (Latin Night). The interviewees commented that these social events helped the branch members remember their cultural identities and eased homesickness.

Interviewees felt that they were more likely to receive church positions in separate congregations. (Jane) Yin Yet Liu from Hong Kong attended a college ward at Ricks College and Brigham Young University. When her brother came to the United States to study, she decided to attend the Asian branch with him. 'When I was in the American ward, there was no chance that I would get a calling at all. Maybe the bishop would wonder, "I don't know if this girl can speak English very well, and I'm not sure she understands what I'm saying." ' In the Asian branch, she served as a Relief Society teacher and then a Sunday School teacher. Serving in these positions made her 'feel like I am more in to the Church than before.'[2]

But ethnic members also saw disadvantages in having ethnic branches. Some felt that since they were living in the United States, they needed to learn English and American culture. Yuriko Ikenoue, a Japanese student at BYU, had never been to an Asian ward because, as she put it, 'I want to get to know about American culture since I live here. I want to get to know American people, culture, and society.'[3] Ricardo Diaz, a Hispanic American BYU student, had a positive experience in the Spanish-speaking ward, but he said, 'It is a haven for people who don't want to learn English. . . . Also it doesn't force other people to become Americanized.'[4]

Interviewees also complained that converts did not always understand church procedures and doctrine. While new converts throughout the United States faced the same problems, cultural differences added to the obstacles. Esperanza Silva-Ayerdis served as a Relief Society president in a Spanish ward in California. One of her counsellors, an immigrant, frequently disagreed with her decisions and insisted, 'This is the way we do it in El Salvador.'[5] Susan L. Pham, a Vietnamese immigrant, complained that in her ethnic branch in California, 'Some [women in Relief Society] take advantage to teach false doctrine that belongs to [another] church.'[6] Quoch Anh Dinh, a Vietnamese American who came to the United States as a child and later served with Vietnamese immigrants, said the branches he worked with were 'so new and so struggling that it's hard to retain new converts. It's almost like trying to build a house without a foundation.'[7]

Some interviewees saw the stress on culture as negative. John F. Pham, a Vietnamese immigrant, served as a branch president when he was quite young. He explained that Vietnamese culture teaches respect for older people. Elders advise those who are younger and not the reverse. As a result, many members did not recognize Pham's authority and refused to accept his leadership.[8] Daniel Afualo, a Samoan, explained a similar leadership problem. In Samoa only high chiefs speak at certain ceremonies. They also make most of the decisions for a village or family group. Afualo attended a Samoan ward where only these chiefs held leadership positions.[9] Those types of questions frequently arose as cultural groups imposed their traditional values on a new religious tradition.

The interviewees also had problems with ethnic congregations because they allowed Euro-Americans to maintain their stereotypes about other groups. De Von Tu'ua, who is part Samoan and Tongan, attended a ward for single adults in the Salt Lake Valley. He commented, 'I think the reason why you have singles, Samoan, Spanish, and Laotian wards is because you don't have tolerance for the difference.'[10]

An even greater problem emerged when Euro-Americans assumed that because people were from the same geographical region they shared common experiences and friendship. For example, the Asian branch in Provo included people who spoke Korean, Cantonese, Mandarin, and Japanese. With so many language groups, sacrament meetings were in English. Each group had separate Sunday schools, but they frequently combined again for priesthood and Relief Society in English. This branch combined people like Japanese and Koreans who have been enemies for centuries.

Some members saw positive reasons for combining nationalities. Rhee Honam, a Korean who served as the Asian branch president, explained:

> The language is different; there are cultural differences. The feelings between Koreans and Japanese and the Chinese and the Japanese are not that harmonious outside the Church for political reasons. But in our ward, we have true unity, complete harmonious brother and sister relations.[11]

Others who attended the branch did not find the same unity. While they did not see open hostilities, neither did they see intermixing. One of my interviewers, a young Euro-Canadian woman who served a mission to Hong Kong, attended the branch. She explained that in sacrament meeting the Koreans sat with Koreans, the Japanese associated with Japanese, etc. Chao-Teh Wang, a Chinese woman who grew up in Taiwan, explained that in the Asian branch 'I don't interact with a lot of other Asian people. There are a lot of Chinese there who I can talk to and go do things with.'[12] Kaori Yanagida, a woman who grew up in Japan, went to an American branch because 'if I go to the Asian ward, my friends are going to be Japanese. I would always hang out with those people and just speak Japanese.'[13]

The Mormon Church teaches that all people on this earth are children of God. Some church leaders have argued, 'Do you think when we get to the other side of the veil the Lord is going to care whether you came from Tonga or New Zealand or Germany or America? . . . No. That's why we call each other brothers and sisters' (Embry, 1992: 83). On the other hand, other leaders have contended, 'Our prime role is not to teach people English or how to become American. Gospel principles . . . don't vary from language to language. We declare Christ, not English' (Florence, 1992: 36). With this attitude, local leaders believed ethnic groups 'learn[ed] better in their own language surrounded by other members who shared the same ethnic/cultural background' (Embry, 1992: 84–5). So while the ideal might be united congregations where all ethnic groups worship together, language and cultural differences prevent the utopia. Because the leaders and the members see strengths and weaknesses in having separate congregations, the LDS Church will continue to struggle on how to best serve its members of color.

Notes

1. Kiyomi Patrick, oral history interview by Arien Hamblin, August 15, 1994. Oral History Project, Charles Redd Center for Western Studies, Manuscript Division, Harold B. Lee Library, BYU, Provo, UT. (Referred to below as LDS Asian-American.)
2. Yin Yet Liu (Jane), oral history interview by Arien Hamblin, August 15, 1994. LDS Asian-American.

3. Yuriko Ikenoue, oral history interview by Matt Eyre, September 24, 1994. LDS Asian-American.
4. Ricardo Diaz, oral history interview by Esmeralda Meraz, March 13, 1991. LDS Hispanic-American Oral History Project, Charles Redd Center for Western Studies, Manuscript Division, Harold B. Lee Library, BYU, Provo, UT. (Referred to below as LDS Hispanic-American.)
5. Esperanza Silva-Ayerdis, oral history interview by Janean G. Barker, November 19, 1992. LDS Hispanic-American.
6. Susan L. Pham, oral history interview by Vonae Adams, October 23, 1994. LDS Asian-American.
7. Quoch Anh Dinh, oral history interview by Matt Eyre, October 3, 1994. LDS Asian-American.
8. John F. Pham, oral history interview by David H. Tanner, October 22, 1994, LDS Asian-American.
9. Daniel Afualo, oral history interview by Esmeralda Meraz, January 26, 1993. LDS Polynesian-American Oral History Project, Charles Redd Center for Western Studies, Manuscript Division, Harold B. Lee Library, BYU, Provo, UT. (Referred to below as LDS Polynesian-American.)
10. De Von Tu'ua, oral history interview by Alan Cherry, January 23, 1993. LDS Polynesian-American.
11. Rhee Homan, oral history interview by Steve Jenks, February 24, 1994. LDS Asian-American.
12. Chao-Teh Wang, oral history interview by Matt Eyre, September 22, 1994. LDS Asian-American.
13. Kaori Yanagida, oral history interview by Matt Eyre, September 22, 1994. LDS Asian-American.

8 Mormonism in Chile

David Clark Knowlton

The rapid growth of Mormonism, as part of a stupendous increase in non-Catholic religions, forms an important part of the transformations currently changing the face of Latin America. Much sociological work has explored this phenomenon, particularly in terms of Pentecostalism, the most numerically significant of the new religions (Garrard-Burnett and Stoll, 1993; Martin, 1990; Stoll, 1990). An open question remains, however, as to the place and role of Mormonism in this panorama, particularly when one takes into account its substantial institutional differences from Pentecostalism. In this paper we shall explore some of the social dynamics behind Mormonism in Chile as an attempt at answering this question.

Mormonism in Latin America

According to the most recently published figures, the Church of Jesus Christ of Latter-day Saints claims, for the end of 1993, some 2,749,000 adherents in Latin America.[1] If growth has continued at the same pace as that of 7.5 per cent between 1991 and 1993 in Latin America, it now has over 3,000,000 members there. According to some projections, Latin Mormons will become the majority of the Church's members within the next ten or fifteen years: already Latin America comprises 32 per cent of the total Church and has far and away the largest number of new members each year (Heaton, 1992: vol. 4: 1521). This is where actual growth in church institutions is taking place; outside its borders, excluding Anglo America, one finds a mere 15 per cent of members.

Three countries in Latin America have several hundred thousand members each: the giant countries Brazil and Mexico, where Mormons are a tiny minority of their huge populations, and Chile. Mexico claims the largest membership, 688,000 – 8 per cent of the total Church and 25 per cent of the total for Latin America. Brazil lies second with 474,000 members, 5.45 per cent of the total Church and 17.24 per cent of Latin America, while Chile is third with its 345,000 members. Chile thus represents almost 4 per cent of the total Church and 12.55 per cent of Latin America's Mormons.

Yet Chile is radically different from these others. First it is a small country when compared with the others. Its population of some 13,600,000, a mere 3 per cent of Latin America (Wilkie *et al.*, 1983: vol. 30, pt 1: xii), is not even half that of either Mexico City or São Paulo, Brazil. These other countries have additional large cities. In Mexico and Brazil the numbers of Mormons, large though they may be on a Mormon scale, represent a small percentage of their national population, 0.8 per cent for Mexico and 0.3 per cent for Brazil. Furthermore they are minimal when compared with the massive growth of other religions, such as Pentecostalism and Umbanda, for example. Chile, in contrast, at 2.6 per cent has the greatest percentage of its national population as Mormons of any country outside of Oceania, including the United States. Thus for Chile as a society, Mormonism is ten times more significant than for Brazil, if numbers are any indication. The Church of Jesus Christ of Latter-day Saints forms a significant presence in Chile, and Chile one for the Mormon Church.

Mormonism in Chile

Missionary work began in Chile in 1956 through the efforts of North American Mormons resident in Chile's capital, Santiago (Acevedo, 1990). Initially missionaries began work among the friends and peers of American families, as well as openly proselyting in neighborhoods of high, middle and low social classes (D. Palmer, 1979: 76). Among its early converts, many were members of Chile's professional and business upper middle classes.[2] The initial branch or congregation was established in the solidly bourgeois neighborhood of Nunoa, although soon a branch was founded in Santiago's working-class, industrial neighborhood of San Miguel. The church also spread south into the industrial city of Concepción and west into the twin port cities – the chic Viña del Mar and the working-class Valparaíso.[3]

Since this origin in Chile the Church of Jesus Christ of Latter-day Saints has been spatially segregated. In part this is due to the choices made by mission leaders about the use of resources and personnel, but in part it also reflects the kinds of relationships established between Chilean society and this foreign institution.

The latter concerns us more here because in this Mormonism differs substantially from Pentecostalism. The latter began in the rural south as part of an indigenous Pentecostal revival and only later spread to the urban neighborhoods of Santiago (Schlumberger and Herrera, 1987). Mormonism began there as a foreign import, closely connected with the colony of North Americans resident in Chile, many employed with US multinational corporations, such as Kodak, or with the US diplomatic mission. It penetrated Chilean society using a relatively large corps of foreign missionaries closely managed and co-ordinated by a Church bureaucracy intent on finding Chilean members who would fit the social and class profile of 'leaders' for the Church in that country.

At the start of 1960, after four years of missionary work, Mormonism claimed some 600 members.[4] We do not, at the moment, know much about the social origins of these early converts, but they included a corps of leaders who were educated, and relatively well off, even though not of Chile's elite. The first convert baptism, for example, was a civil servant with the Sociedad Nacional de Agricultura (Acevedo, 1990: 30). These nevertheless did form part of Chile's bourgeoisie as it has expanded, and served to locate Mormonism in Chile's social space. They gave it an institutional and class anchor within Chilean society, which when added to the American presence, made it capable of connecting people vertically through the strata of Chilean society.

Nevertheless, the Church also obtained a solid presence in the working-class neighborhoods of Santiago, that soon were to expand almost exponentially with massive immigration.

Within the next decade I estimate that Mormonism grew to more than 17,000 members, an increase of 2783 per cent. By 1980 it had 90,598 members, an increase of 426 per cent over the last decade and by 1990, some 290,500 members, an increase of 221 per cent. These estimates are based on *Deseret News Church Almanac*, October 1980.

Distribution of members

These converts are not evenly distributed through Chile, nor have rates of conversion been constant through time. For 1986, Acevedo lists the largest single concentrations of Mormons for metropolitan Santiago, followed by significant numbers in the cities of Valparaíso and Viña del Mar, as well as Concepción (1990: Appendix 2: 109–72). These form the majority of the Church in Chile. Yet in relationship to the total regional population, the areas with the greatest concentrations of Mormons are found in the far, desert north followed by the coastal city of Valparaíso.

Related to this issue of regional distribution is that of class. The data for this are limited but, nonetheless, important. Class is not merely a sociological variable, but has been active in separating and influencing the Chilean population in the historical changes of the last 30 years. It is, also, a conscious element in Mormon strategies of proselyting, manifested in the trope of 'leader.'

An internal report, prepared by Mormon General Authority Elder Teddy Brewerton in the mid-1980s, notes that in Chile while:

> 30 per cent of the population enjoys 70 per cent of total income . . . the majority of the members of the church come from a sector which perceives only 17 per cent of national income. A fourth of Chilenos (and here we have a large number of members) receives only 5 per cent. (Acevedo, 1990: 79)

Thus according to Elder Brewerton, the majority of Church membership comes from a lower middle class, including the industrial workers and *petite bourgeoisie*, those who obtain 17 per cent of the national income, while a substantial number also come from among the poor, those obtaining a scant 5 per cent of Chile's income, but who represent 25 per cent of its total population.

Rodolfo Acevedo gathered material on the occupation of male converts 18 years and older in the Santiago South mission in 1986 for his thesis at the Catholic University. He divides his sample of 707 men according to occupational category:

Table 8.1

No.	%	
69	10	unemployed
257	37	workers
127	18	employees
40	6	middle businessmen (who manage their own business)
11	2	members of armed forces, non-officers
106	15	professionals, those with professional degrees
57	8	students
29	4	retired
696	100	

Acevedo emphasizes that 45 per cent of the converts came from the ranks of laborers and unemployed. But I find it equally significant that 15 per cent are professionals and 26 per cent from the *petite bourgeoisie*. Thus, Mormonism, unlike Pentecostalism, tends to draw a significant sector from the *petit bourgeois* categories. What is lacking among these converts are members of the Chilean elite and the real *haute bourgeoisie*. To the degree that we can generalize these limited data over time and space, we find then a social profile for Mormonism as an institution that we can at least use as an hypothesis.

It is unfortunate that we cannot further segregate the membership according to other social indicators. For example it would be interesting to divide the category of laborers into skilled and unskilled, etc. Nevertheless, there are other measures we can employ. For historical reasons, neighborhoods in Santiago are highly significant indicators of historical and social processes and, since census material on social status is aggregated by neighborhoods, this allows investigators to profile them according to class.

Fortunately Mormon stakes and wards are geographically based and information on the construction of chapels and the formation of stakes is publicly available. Although the stakes do not correspond exactly to neighborhood boundaries, their naming gives us an idea of their location. The dating on the construction of chapels allows us further to locate the growth of Mormon membership by period, and perhaps establish a connection with historical social process.

To review the data rapidly I divide the city into four sectors. The eastern neighborhoods, against the mountains, are those with, generally, the highest social status, and the lowest indices of poverty. The north and south regions, stretching outward from the shell of old Santiago, are among the poorest. Those of the south contain more of the old industrial sectors, along with many new *poblaciones* and new neighborhoods, while those of the north contain perhaps the largest number of *poblaciones*. The east is somewhat similar to the north and south, but is increasingly bourgeois.

If we organize the data from the 1982 Chilean census to locate those *comunas* which have the highest percentages of indices of either poverty or working-class status we get the following distribution.[5] Of the twelve *comunas* with the highest illiteracy rates, i.e. above 5.8 per cent (the average for metropolitan Santiago was 5.2 per cent), we find six in the south and four in the north, with one (Penalolen) in the far east, in what is an anomalous neighborhood for that region (one that has nevertheless been much studied), and one in the north-east on the fringes of the upper-class neighborhoods. Similarly of the 15 with the highest percentage of their population unemployed, i.e. above 25 per cent, we get eight in the south and six in the north, with one (Penalolen) in the south-east. Furthermore, of the 23 with the highest percentages of blue-collar employees, i.e. 39.9 per cent and above, eleven are in the south and nine are in the north, while three are in the west. These form a swath slicing the city along the north–south corridor. Similarly, all the areas with high numbers of white-collar employees lie on the east of the city while a smaller aggregation is located in the centre and a couple of neighboring *comunas*. Thus the city is highly segregated according to class.

Of all the chapels constructed in Santiago between 1965 and 1986, 32 per cent are in the north, another 32 per cent in the south, 20 per cent in the west and 21 per cent in the centre of Santiago and the more upscale east. Thus 84 per cent of the chapels have been built in the poorer neighborhoods of the city, 64 per cent of these in our north–south corridor of extreme poverty, indicating a preponderance of members within those neighborhoods. And there is a strong concentration of them in the north, in the band of the poorest regions, those with combined totals of working class and unemployed near or above 70 per cent, centered on the extremely conflicted *comuna* of Conchali, while in the south a similar concentration is found in the equivalent band centered on La Cisterna.

In terms of stakes, as of 1986, a similar distribution holds. Of a total of 18, six are in the north, five in the south, three in the west, 14 of the 18, while one is in downtown Santiago and three are in the east.

If we plot this according to specific *comunas*, we notice, for example, a strong concentration of Mormon institutions, again, in some of the poorest neighborhoods of Santiago. This contrasts with the employment data gathered by Acevedo, and suggests that within these poor neighborhoods the membership of the Church is unequally distributed. Although the

Church is garnering a share of the poorest of the poor it suggests that the Mormons are, disproportionately, finding a niche among residents of very poor neighborhoods, but those of higher than average social standing. However, this requires further demonstration, given the vagaries of Acevedo's data.

Employment data are also available for stake leaders, since it is published in the official *Church News,* though their titles are sometimes difficult to classify due to the ambiguities of the editorial process. Nevertheless, they do furnish a rough idea of the social position of those who become leaders. Although these data are probably available for the last 20 years, they are presented in Table 8.2 only for 1993 and 1994.

Table 8.2 Summary of occupations of LDS stake presidencies, Chile 1993–94

Category	Santiago	%	Chile	%
Church employee	7	13	15	13
Military	–	–	4	3.5
Professionals	1	2	4	3.5
Educators	1	2	6	5
Business admin.	12	22	30	26
Business employee	6	11	11	10
Small business owner	5	9	7	6
Merchant	11	20	13	11
Government employee	1	2	1	1
Technicians	5	9	12	10
Unskilled labor	–	–	3	3
Farmers	–	–	1	1
Others	5	9	8	7
Totals	54	99	115	100

Several things immediately stand out. First, there is a relatively high percentage of Church employees, 13 per cent, although the figure is somewhat less than the 16 per cent obtained for the Church as a whole in Latin America. Second, business together (by this category I mean organized formal business, not small-scale enterprises nor informal activities) is 36 per cent, a substantial number, while for the Church as a whole in Latin America it is much larger, 50.1 per cent. Third, we find larger numbers of lower occupations here among stake leaders than we do for the Church as a whole. For example, merchants are 11 per cent, while in Latin America they are 2.8 per cent; laborers, including skilled, unskilled and technicians, constitute 20 per cent, while in Latin America as a whole they are half that at 9.2 per cent. Thus we find a higher representation of lower occupations than we do elsewhere in the Church, a tendency which follows that of the concentration of stakes in the poorest of Santiago's areas, if not for the whole of Chile, for which we do not yet have information.

Nevertheless, these lower occupations still are relatively high on the class ladder. They do not represent the large numbers of un- or semi-skilled labourers and the unemployed in Santiago. Merchants and small business owners are a substantial 16 per cent in Santiago, while skilled labour is a mere 5 per cent and unskilled labour is unrepresented.

This suggests that if Acevedo is correct and the Church tends to select 45 per cent of its male converts from the unemployed and the workers, they are represented here by only 5 per cent of the stake leaders. What happens to the other 40 per cent is an important question.

Synthesizing these two sets of data means that, given the abundance of stakes, and therefore members in the poorest neighborhoods of Santiago, the blue-collar and unemployed, i.e. the poor and the super-poor, to express it in related terms relevant to the literature on Chile, are less likely to become Mormon than they are to be represented in the population as a whole of the neighborhoods where the Church is numerically strong. Therefore, the Church in these neighborhoods is much more successful at attracting the minority of residents who claim white-collar status, and these are more likely to be represented among the Church's leadership than are blue-collar workers, even though they are the largest single sector of the adult male membership and even more the largest sector of the neighborhoods.

This means that there is an over-representation among the white-collar occupants of these neighborhoods in two senses, first in that they are more likely to convert than their lower-class neighbors and, second, that they are more likely to be represented among the hierarchy of leadership than their fellows. The higher we go in the hierarchy, to include mission presidents, regional representatives and general authorities, the more marked this difference becomes. Here we find a strong bias towards higher education in the form of university degrees, as represented in upper levels of management, either in business or church, and large business ownership. This is part of the formation of a corporate entity that links the popular classes vertically.

A useful contrast here is with Catholicism, which performs many of the same functions but whose recent imagery, outside the Opus Dei movement favored by many in the upper classes, stresses the lower-class character of the church. Its Base Ecclesial Communities have become forums for the celebration in the sacred space of lower-class culture and value. Mormonism contrasts with this, in that, in the same neighborhoods, it celebrates formal business and bourgeois values and society. Even though both institutions anchor vertically, the one stresses that and sacralizes it while the other emphasizes the option for the poor. In almost complete contrast, Pentecostalism organizes people primarily horizontally, with limited vertical engagement and thus involves a different set of social issues.

Pentecostalism

These same neighborhoods have also had larger numbers of their population become Pentecostal, numbers far larger than those for the Mormon congregations. They also have had strong participation in various forms of left Catholicism, at different times and places. Nevertheless, for the moment let us look at Pentecostalism. David Martin (1990) theorized that in Latin America as a whole, and Chile in particular, Pentecostalism represents a movement towards a more bourgeois society, but among sectors that are yet to obtain that status in society. By contrast we find a Mormon emphasis, in the same neighborhoods in which Pentecostalism is strong, attracting sectors which are attaining, or have already attained, what Martin thinks Pentecostals merely seek. If this is true elsewhere in Latin America, it would make a significant contribution toward our understanding of the social position and role of the new religions that are reshaping the continent.

Urban Santiago and social process

Early in this century the social structure of Chile was built on a rural order of large estates and a mining oligarchy, with a rather small urban elite and middle groups. However, with the politics of import substitution in the 1950s and 1960s, the Chilean industrial sector grew, recruiting workers who came to reside in the growing neighborhood of San Miguel and nearby, precisely where the second branch of the Church was organized in 1956. Thus Mormonism arrived at a time this neighborhood and its neighbors were expanding rapidly due to the growth of urban working-class employment. Emilio Willems (1967), in his classic study, identifies urban immigrants as one of the three social sectors most likely to make a religious change and identifies the religious organizations as filling important institutional functions within the cities to integrate this population into the new milieu.

The industrial workers were not the only people coming to San Miguel and surrounding neighborhoods. During this same period, transformations in Chilean agriculture, involving the collapse of the *latifundia* system, led to the massive migration of former agricultural workers, peasants, and rural townsmen with limited and *petit bourgeois* skills, to Santiago, provoking a huge urban growth, unprecedented in Chilean history, but resembling what was occurring elsewhere in Latin America. Migration was further motivated by rapid demographic growth during the same period, with limited opportunities for employment or education outside Santiago. Between 1960, shortly after missionary work had begun there, and 1990, metropolitan Santiago grew by some 132 per cent. In 1920 Santiago had a mere 14 per cent of the national population, by 1960, 27 per cent and by 1990 it claimed almost 40 per cent of the nation (Orteaga and Tironi, 1988).

So this period, from the arrival of the Church in Santiago, has, apart from the rise of Allende, been characterized by the subsequent Pinochet coup and massive repression, by the recent coming of democracy, by extreme urban growth along with severe shortages of housing, and by the development of an array of social organizations to meet the needs of the migrants and connect them to national society (Orteaga and Tironi, 1988; Oxhorn, 1967). The nature of these organizations shifts in relationship to the national political structure and its dynamics and in relationship to lower-class attempts at mobilization to obtain benefits from elite strata and to upper-class attempts to co-opt them.

As a result, the urban growth of Santiago, spreading out from the older working-class neighborhoods of the shell, has been a patchwork of relatively established middle and lower middle class, as well as large working-class and sub-working-class neighborhoods, along with organized and spontaneous *poblaciones* or shantytowns. These each have a different history of communal and political organizing as well as connections with different political parties, when such have been active (Schneider, 1967). They each have a history and a different fit into the national social structure, making them potentially relevant variables for the deferential attraction and impact of Mormonism.

Around San Miguel, and other similar working-class neighborhoods on the edge of the old urban core of Santiago, neighborhoods began to grow rapidly to meet the needs of this immigrant population that overtaxed Chile's urban system. Much of the development has been in the form of planned suburban growth, often directed by political parties and other organizations. This connects the immigrant population into the clientelist system of the parties and organizations. This has been a major force in Chilean history connecting the workers and poor to the elite sectors in society through patron–client relationships. Nevertheless much of the growth has also been in the form of the direct appropriation of land by organized groups of 'squatters,' who then would attempt to manipulate the judicial system to legalize their occupation of land (Schneider, 1967).

Mormon growth moved quickly from San Miguel and into this new population. Judging by the dates on the construction of chapels and the formation of stakes the strongest early growth of the Church came in the southern *comunas*, precisely at a time they were growing most quickly. In 1978 this began to shift, when substantial construction of chapels began in the northern areas of more recent rapid urban growth. This was particularly concentrated around the northern community of Conchali, and the neighboring *comunas* of Huechuraba, Recoleta, Independencia, Quinta Normal, Renca, and Quilicura.

The north is further different from the south in that San Miguel and neighboring areas had some of the strongest indices of labor union activism, and hence involvement in socialism and the events surrounding the rise and fall of Allende, in the late 1960s. This is about the time Mormon growth would have begun to shift to the north and suggests a negative relationship between socialism and union activities and Mormon growth during this period. These southern neighborhoods also suffered severe repression during the dictatorship, including the so-called *allanamientos*, the disappearance of political activists, and the destruction of any local political organizations and labor unions. They became relatively socially disorganized, although the underground socialist movements retained a certain vigor. Interestingly, during the later period of social disorganization, Mormon institutions also increased in number in these areas, although the correlation needs further substantiation. For the moment it is merely suggestive.

In contrast, the northern neighborhoods were relatively uninvolved in the events leading to the Pinochet dictatorship, but they were strongly involved in the massive 'protests' of the 1980s that disrupted the Pinochet government and led to another round of massive repression. It is estimated that as much as 15 per cent of the population was involved and this in turn led to severe repression of the entire area. However, this needs to be explored in relationship to the growth of Mormonism and the whole range of other voluntary organizations for the region, because the situation varied from *comuna* to *comuna* and from family to family.

Mormonism has obtained most of its membership since the brutal *coup d'état* of more than 20 years ago. Nevertheless, the periods of repression and their relationship to the growth of different forms of voluntary organizations, do relate strongly to Mormon growth rates. The boom in Mormon growth actually occurred during the period of relative repression and social disorganization of the popular neighborhoods. Between 1976 (three years after the coup) and 1980 the Church had its highest growth rates, besides those of its first decade when the overall numbers were rather small. During this period its membership would double almost every two years. At the peak of this period, in 1978, it grew by an amazing 45.49 per cent; then it began to decline into the early 1980s, only to rise somewhat between 1987 and 1988.

Because of an economic crisis, felt more heavily in the northern *comunas* than in the southern, both areas broke out into massive and spontaneous demonstrations which attracted massive and violent police intervention. Prior to this time the *comunas* were relatively disorganized, except by religious organizations. After the protests of 1983 these *comunas* exploded in a whole range of grassroots social organizations, many under the protection of the Catholic Church. They also re-established connection with national political organizations and, in 1983, witnessed a major shift in the Chilean left as two important guerrilla groups were formed which would soon begin attacking the Mormons. Both had strong followership in the popular *comunas* among the youth.

The LDS church had a spurt of growth just prior to the protests. During the time of the economic crisis it actually saw its rates decline. For example, in 1978 the Church had a peak rate of 45.49 per cent per year. This declined slowly to 11.2 per cent in 1982 and then to 9 per cent during the crisis and protests – a time when one normally would expect it to grow. This suggests that Mormon growth is somehow mediated by the lack of political avenues of expression and by the repressive force of the dictatorship. In the year following the protests we see a precipitous drop in numbers of converts in both the south and north Santiago missions. In the south they dropped that year by almost a quarter (23 per cent) while in the north they declined by 15 per cent. In contrast the number of conversions actually increased for the rest of Chile that year, since the total decline for these two missions is greater than the total decline for Chile as a whole. Furthermore, in 1986, as guerrilla attacks began against the Church in these areas, and as a range of social organizations sprung up to meet people's needs and to build towards the end of the dictatorship, the two continued to decline, while the numbers of conversions for the country as a whole rose significantly, by almost a fifth. Overall, the north mission had a dramatic 75 per cent decline while the south dropped by almost 45 per cent.

Conclusion

We do not know exactly why these declines took place, but their contextual relationship with the events of the protests and subsequent political florescence present us with a useful hypothesis that is substantiated by extensive ethnographic evidence about how the Church is understood by many in the popular neighborhoods. It is surrounded by substantial tension and conflict which are related to its involvement in Chile's social order and political system.

However we understand these events, this chapter presents an opening discussion in an ongoing project seeking to relate Mormon growth to broader Latin American events; removing it from the ghetto of 'Mormon Studies' *qua* celebratory navel gazing of an Anglo-Mormon intelligentsia, and shifting it to the domain of Latin American social history and sociology. To this end, much research is needed. Chile is but one story, and we have only begun to devise some of its potential outlines. Latin America, which soon will hold the majority of Mormons, is filled with many more tantalizing stories, where Mormonism will never be just what it hopes.

Notes

1. *Deseret News* 1995–96; *Church Almanac*, Salt Lake City, 1995. Since they do not aggregate membership figures for the entire region of Latin America, this calculation has been made by the author. It includes the membership listed for the following countries of Hispano- and Lusoamerica; Argentina, Bolivia, Brazil, Chile, Colombia, Costa Rica, Cuba, Dominican Republic, Ecuador, El Salvador, Guatemala, Honduras, Mexico, Nicaragua, Panama, Paraguay, Peru, Puerto Rico, Uruguay and Venezuela.
2. First Chilean joined Church twenty-four years ago. *Deseret News Church News*, October 4, 1980.
3. The initial branches were formed in the following neighborhoods of Santiago: Nunoa (July 1956), Providencia (July 1957), San Miguel (November 1958), and Parque Cousino (August 1956), as well as in the cities of Concepción (February 1957), Viña del Mar (May 1957), and Valparaíso (June 1959).
4. Acevedo (1990): 64. These figures vary somewhat from those listed by D. Palmer (1979). The former draws his numbers from mission records and

historian reports while the latter uses the statistical recapitulations at Church offices.
5. The items of illiteracy, unemployment and the percentage of blue-collar workers should, really, be kept separate since they make a great social difference, but, for now, they are left together because of the limitations of available data.

9 Mormonism in black Africa

E. Dale LeBaron

The Church of Jesus Christ of Latter-day Saints was established on the African continent relatively early in the Church's history when Brigham Young sent three missionaries to the white settlers of South Africa in 1853. At this time Mormon missionaries were not actively proselyting amongst blacks because the Church had an established policy, revealed through a pamphlet, that they were not to receive the priesthood. The Church existed in Africa for 125 years before missionaries proselyted among the blacks there.

However, many years before missionaries were sent to black Africa, thousands of Ghanaians and Nigerians learned about the teachings of the restored gospel, not directly from missionaries or members but from friends and family who obtained literature while travelling overseas. These investigators wrote countless letters to Church headquarters requesting more literature and asking for missionaries to teach and baptize them. They did receive the literature they requested but they also received a letter indicating that the time was not yet come for missionaries to come to black Africa. Establishing the Church in black Africa posed a serious problem since there would not be priesthood holders available to provide the necessary ordinances, such as the sacrament, unless there was a continual flow of missionaries to every area where the Church existed in Africa. They were told they must wait for baptism, and so they did, some for more than ten or twenty years, before they were able to receive the missionaries and join the Church. But, while they waited, they united with others in sharing their newly discovered religious beliefs and in worshipping together. As their numbers grew they organized themselves into congregations and named themselves 'The Church of Jesus Christ of Latter-day Saints.' Many of the letters sent from Nigeria and Ghana to Church headquarters in Salt Lake City, Utah, even bore a letterhead which read, 'The Church of Jesus Christ of Latter-day Saints.' From the 1950s through the 1970s there were many congregations so named, with tens of thousands of participants, yet not one person was an officially baptized member of the Church. During this time, they continued to seek support and help from Church headquarters. They even paid for promising young students to go to Church-owned Brigham Young University and the University of Utah, so that these students could join the Church and try to persuade Church leaders to send missionaries to Africa (interview with Edwin Q. Cannon Jr).

In 1960 Church President David O. McKay assigned Glen G. Fisher to visit Lagos, Nigeria, when returning from South Africa, where he served as mission president. Fisher was the first official Church representative to investigate these congregations of Africans seeking membership. He told the Church's First Presidency that he found them to be very sincere and devout in their convictions of the Book of Mormon, the Prophet Joseph Smith and the restoration of the gospel. He recommended that the Church consider sending missionary couples of husbands and wives to Africa to baptize those who were ready, and to organize the Church among them to providing the necessary ordinances for these faithful people (interview with Glen G. Fisher, August 1987).

The letters from African investigators increased in number and in fervor as shown in the following example from a leader of a Nigerian congregation dated July 29, 1961 (interview with LaMar Williams, February 1988):

I have to say that until I hear from you as promised, my heart will not rest; for it is made up. And there is no turning back to me until I achieve my objective to be a baptized member of the Church of Jesus Christ of Latter-day Saints and to receive the gift of the Holy Ghost by the laying on of hands by those in authority; and to be fully instructed in the gospel as restored in these modern days by our Savior, Jesus Christ, through his chosen Prophet, Joseph Smith, and others of his elect in order to be able to preach the true gospel to my people and to win for my Savior, hearts that should have otherwise perished in darkness ... I appeal through you to the Church in general, and especially to President David O. McKay and the presidency to help me and my feelings.

After some deliberation, the First Presidency decided to send missionaries to these people in Nigeria. Elder LaMar Williams, who had served as a secretary to the Missionary Department for several years and had been corresponding with these Africans, was assigned to make a preliminary trip to Nigeria and then to be the presiding elder in this area. He and his wife, along with four other couples, were called as missionaries to Nigeria. Elder Williams made three visits to Nigeria to prepare for the establishment of the Church there, but the Nigerian government would not grant them resident visas. For five years they tried to obtain the necessary visas, but when the Nigerian civil war broke out in 1966, the First Presidency abandoned their plans.

With Elder Williams's release from this assignment he turned over to the missionary department more than 15,000 names and addresses of Nigerians who were waiting anxiously to become members of the Mormon Church. For the next twelve years Church representatives made periodic contact with these faithful people (interview with LaMar Williams, February 1988, and with Lorry Rytting, September 1988).

In 1973, Spencer W. Kimball became the President of The Church of Jesus

Christ of Latter-day Saints and, as an apostle and President, travelled throughout the Church for more than 30 years. His sensitive spirit reached out in love to all people, especially to those deprived of priesthood and temple blessings because of lineage. He was aware of many all over the world who longed for full fellowship, but his particular concern seemed to be for those in Brazil and Africa. As the Lord's prophet and seer, he struggled mightily with this issue. He noted: 'This matter had been on my mind all these years. We have always considered it' (*The Church News*, January 6, 1979: 15). However, as the most distinguishing feature of The Church of Jesus Christ of Latter-day Saints is that of divine authority by direct revelation from God to His living prophet, matters dealing with Church doctrine and priesthood ordination must be determined by revelation (McKay, 1976: 98). When he became Church President, Spencer W. Kimball was asked about the position of the Church regarding the blacks and the priesthood. He answered:

> I am not sure that there will be a change, although there could be. We are under the dictates of our Heavenly Father, and this is not my policy or the Church's policy. It is the policy of the Lord who has established it, and I know of no change, although we are subject to revelations of the Lord in case he should ever wish to make a change. (Kimball, 1982: 448–9)

On September 30, 1978, at the 148th Semi-annual General Conference of the Church of Jesus Christ of Latter-day Saints, President N. Eldon Tanner, First Counselor in the First Presidency, presented the following statement regarding this revelation to the membership of the Church for their vote of acceptance.

> In early June of this year, the First Presidency announced that a revelation had been received by President Spencer W. Kimball extending priesthood and temple blessings to all worthy male members of the Church. President Kimball has asked that I advise the conference that after he had received this revelation, which came to him after extended meditation and prayer in the sacred rooms of the holy temple, he presented it to his counselors, who accepted it and approved it. It was then presented to the Quorum of the Twelve Apostles, who unanimously approved it, and was subsequently to all other General Authorities, who likewise approved it unanimously. President Kimball has asked that I now read this letter:
> June 8, 1978 To all general and local priesthood officers of The Church of Jesus Christ of Latter-day Saints throughout the world:
> Dear Brethren: As we have witnessed the expansion of the work of the Lord over the earth, we have been grateful that people of many nations have responded to the message of the restored gospel, and have joined the Church in ever-increasing numbers. This, in turn, has inspired us with a desire to extend to every worthy member of the Church all of the privileges and blessings which the gospel affords.
> Aware of the promises made by the prophets and presidents of the Church who have preceded us that at some time, in God's eternal plan, all of our brethren who are worthy may receive the priesthood, and witnessing the faith-

fulness of those from whom the priesthood has been withheld, we have pleaded long and earnestly in behalf of these, our faithful brethren, spending many hours in the Upper Room of the Temple supplicating the Lord for divine guidance.

He has heard our prayers, and by revelation has confirmed that the long-promised day has come when every faithful, worthy man in the Church may receive the holy priesthood, with power to exercise its divine authority, and enjoy with his loved ones every blessing that flows therefrom, including the blessings of the temple. Accordingly, all worthy male members of the Church may be ordained to the priesthood without regard for race or color. Priesthood leaders are instructed to follow the policy of carefully interviewing all candidates for ordination to either the Aaronic or the Melchizedek Priesthood to insure that they meet the established standards for worthiness.

We declare with soberness that the Lord has now made known his will for the blessing of all his children throughout the earth, who will hearken to the voices of his authorized servants, and prepare themselves to receive every blessing of the gospel. (Doctrine and Covenants, Official Declaration 2)

This revelation provided a powerful demonstration of the Church's ninth article of faith, which states: 'We believe all that God has revealed, all that He does now reveal, and we believe that He will yet reveal many great and important things pertaining to the Kingdom of God.' Elder Bruce R. McConkie, a Mormon Apostle who witnessed this revelation, observed:

It was a revelation of such tremendous significance and import; one which would reverse the whole direction of the Church, procedurally and administratively; one which would affect the living and the dead; one which would affect the total relationship that we have with the world; one, I say, of such significance that the Lord wanted independent witnesses who could bear record that the thing had happened . . . This affects what is going on in the spirit world . . . This is a revelation of tremendous significance. (1978a: 152)

President Gordon B. Hinckley, who became Church President in 1995, reflected on the impact which this revelation had:

I need not tell you of the electric effect that was felt both within the Church and without. There was much weeping, with tears of gratitude not only on the part of those who previously had been denied the priesthood and who became the immediate beneficiaries of this announcement, but also by men and women of the Church across the world.

Gone is every element of discrimination. Extended is every power of the priesthood of God . . . This has opened great areas of the world to the teaching of the everlasting gospel. (1988: 70–1)

Of those who wept and waited, surely there were none so patient for so long with so little gospel light as those in black Africa. Their story is one of the most unusual chapters in the history of the Mormon Church. They became pioneers for thousands of black Africans who joined the Church after 1978. In a church known for its pioneering heritage, the following three stories of African pioneers are uniquely inspiring.

One pioneer in Ghana is Joseph William Billy Johnson. In 1964, he prayerfully read the Book of Mormon for the first time. He relates:

> One early morning about 5.30 am, while about to prepare for my daily work, I saw the heavens open and angels with trumpets singing songs of praise unto God ... In the course of this I heard my name mentioned thrice, 'Johnson, Johnson, Johnson. If you will take up my work as I will command you, I will bless you and bless your land.' Trembling and in tears I replied, 'Lord with thy help I will do whatever you will command me.' From that day onward, I was constrained by that spirit to go from street to street ... to deliver the message which we had read from the Book of Mormon ... I did exactly as the Lord commanded me ... and immediately ... our persecution started. (Personal interview, Ghana, May 1988)

For the next 14 years, Brother Johnson preached in towns and villages within a 70-mile radius of his home in Cape Coast, Ghana. He organized twelve congregations which he named 'The Church of Jesus Christ of Latter-day Saints' and had 1400 followers. Those years were full of great personal sacrifice and service which caused him to become respected and recognized throughout the area. When the missionaries finally arrived 14 years later, there were hundreds of people who had knowledge and conviction of the Book of Mormon, the Prophet Joseph Smith, and the restoration of the Lord's Church. They were waiting and praying for baptism into that Church. Brother Johnson was an unusual pioneer (S. J. Palmer, 1979).

In Nigeria, Anthony Obinna was a faithful and persistent pioneer. As a life-long seeker of truth, he relates the following which occurred in the late 1960s:

> One night I was sleeping and a tall man came to me ... and took me to one of the most beautiful buildings and showed me all the rooms. At the end he showed himself in the crucified form. Then in 1970 I found this book to read. It was the September, 1958 *Reader's Digest*. There was an article entitled, 'The March of the Mormons' with a picture of the Salt Lake Temple. It was exactly the same building I had seen in my dreams. (Personal interview, Nigeria, June 1988)

Brother Obinna persistently wrote to Church headquarters and to Church missions, seeking Church literature and pleading for personal visits from Church representatives. After years of waiting and writing, he wrote the following to the Council of Twelve on September 28, 1978: 'Your long silence about the establishment of the Church in Nigeria is very embarrassing ... What could hinder this church from having a foothold here? Did Christ not say, "Go ye and teach all nations?" ' Unbeknown to Brother Obinna, at the time this letter was written the revelation had been received and missionaries were on their way to him. When the Obinna family learned this they wrote the following to the First Presidency:

> We are happy for the many hours in the upper room of the temple you spent supplicating the Lord to bring us into the fold. We thank our Heavenly Father

for hearing your prayers and ours and [that he] by revelation has confirmed the long promised day ... We thank you for extending the priesthood which has been withheld [from] us and to prepare us to receive every blessing of the gospel. (Personal interview, Nigeria, June 1988)

When the missionaries arrived in Nigeria they found many prepared for the gospel through the teaching and leadership of Anthony Obinna. Brother Obinna was the first to be baptized by the missionaries who arrived in West Africa in 1978. Sister Obinna was the first President of the Relief Society, the Church's women's organization, in black Africa. The first LDS chapel built in Nigeria is in Aboh Mbaise, near the home of the Obinna family.

A pioneer from South Africa is Moses Mahlangu. I first met Moses in 1976, soon after I arrived to preside over the South Africa Johannesburg Mission. As I met him he greeted me warmly, and said: 'So you are the new mission president.'

'Yes,' I replied, 'I am. Do you know any others?' He then named the mission presidents of the previous twelve years and told me his story. Moses lived in the township of Soweto, near Johannesburg. In 1964 he had obtained a copy of the Book of Mormon which he prayerfully read and knew it was true. He located the missionaries and was taught by them. The mission president in 1964 was so impressed with the faith and testimony of Moses that he wrote to the First Presidency requesting special permission to baptize Moses. The First Presidency advised the mission president that because of the conditions which existed in South Africa at that time under apartheid, they felt that Moses should wait. And so Moses waited for 14 years. During his wait, he regularly came to the mission home to obtain copies of the Book of Mormon and pamphlets, to share with his people. He also held regular meetings in his home where he taught his family and friends from the Book of Mormon. Fluent in nine languages, Moses shared his testimony with many people. His dedication and persistence in living gospel principles impressed many.

Shortly after the revelation on the priesthood in 1978, Moses was baptized a member of The Church of Jesus Christ of Latter-day Saints. While reflecting upon his long wait to join the Church, Moses compared himself to Cornelius, 'who was very good in waiting to receive the word of God or to be a member of the Church ... till the angels came and told him what to do.' In 1989, at age 63, Moses was a grounds keeper at the Johannesburg temple which he regularly attends. He also served in a leadership position as the elders' quorum president in the Soweto branch.

In conclusion, the following dream by a latter-day pioneer from Nigeria is significant and symbolic. Jude Inmpey is a convert to the Church of Jesus Christ of Latter-day Saints. One of the first to join the Church in his country, Brother Inmpey has held key leadership positions including district president and counsellor in the Nigeria Aba Mission Presidency. A few years after his baptism in 1979, Brother Inmpey had a dream which he later shared along with his explanation of its meaning.

It was just a dream. It happened around 1986.

I was at a very big party. It was high society. There were many whites. An organ was playing. It didn't seem very pleasant. Many people were shouting, 'What is wrong with your organ?' Then someone shouted, 'Look, he's only playing the white keys and not the black ones.' The person corrected this and started playing on the white and the black keys. The melody was restored. Everybody was happy.

At the time it happened it seemed as if it was the real thing, but then I woke up and found that it was all a dream. It was like a revelation. I was asked how I felt about the gospel and Church coming to my people in Nigeria. I told them my dream. The Lord's music within the Lord's Church is much sweeter and more fulfilling when both the black and the white keys are used. (Personal interview, Nigeria, June 1988)

The faithful Saints from Africa add strength and testimony to the Church as the gospel is spread to every nation, kindred, tongue and people. Jude Inmpey's dream has become reality. With the gospel blessings being extended to all God's children, 'the Lord's music within the Lord's Church *is* much sweeter.'

10 India
A synopsis of cultural challenges

Roger R. Keller

When the missionaries of The Church of Jesus Christ of Latter-day Saints entered India they found no spiritual vacuum but a country rich in religious history, inhabited by persons representing Hinduism, Jainism, Buddhism, Sikhism, Islam, and various forms of Christianity. Given the diversity of this religious environment, there is, as yet, no consensus among Latter-day Saints on what the church will or should ultimately look like in India. Consequently, the Latter-day Saints who believe they have a message that can give added meaning to the spiritual lives of their religiously diverse brothers and sisters are all walking into unknown territory. Some of the lessons of missionary work can be learned from those who have gone before. Many lives have been invested and even lost in the proclamation of the gospel to the peoples of India by both Catholics and Protestants. If there are lessons to be learned from these dedicated men and women, LDS should learn them and be grateful for them.

Perhaps the most critical lesson relates to culture. As Catholics and Protestants already know, and as LDS are discovering, Indian culture poses immense challenges to the proclamation of the Christian message. This is particularly true in the areas of language, ministry, music, and marriage. Because all LDS missionary work is currently conducted in English the missionaries work largely in the cities and amongst the fairly well educated. One clear reason for using English is the number of languages spoken in India. There are 14 major languages and probably more than 200 smaller language groups or distinct dialects (Crowther and Finlay, 1990: 53). Without English, even educated Indians often could not talk to one another (Tyler, 1973: 20). Thus, on the surface it seems sensible to conduct missionary work in English, especially if one seeks educated persons to be church leaders. The obvious problem, however, is that approximately 75 per cent of all Indians live in the villages. Is the LDS church in India, then, to be a church of the educated elite in the cities, or one reaching all Indian people? (Cf. Neill, 1984: 164.)

David Shuler, an anthropologist at Brigham Young University, believes that the missionary work will progress in India much as it did in the Philippines where the missionaries first taught in English amongst educated urban dwellers. At first the church grew relatively slowly, but once there was a cadre of native leaders, the fullness of the gospel was taken to the villages in the native languages, creating immense church growth. When interviewed, Shuler expressed the belief that, within 30 years, the language of India will be English because people even in the villages are realizing that they cannot get ahead if they do not know English (interview, Bangalore, July 1994). From his work with literacy programs Schuler reports that, even in remote villages, mothers want their children to learn to speak, read, and write English, not Tamil, Hindi, or Telugu (further interview at BYU, February 1995).

The need for a common language can be seen, for example, in a Bangalore sacrament meeting where church members speak as their first language either Tamil, Telugu, or Kannada but have only English as their common bond, and most seem relatively comfortable with it. However, there will come a day when the church is large enough to have branches conducted in each of these languages, for people worship most effectively in the language of their birth.

Gurcharan Singh Gill, President of the India-Bangalore mission, recognizes the vast challenge that language ultimately holds for the missionary effort and is already petitioning the church to send him missionaries trained in Hindi, Bengali, Telugu, and Tamil. With those four languages, he says he could teach 80 per cent of the people of India, most of whom live in the villages. As in the Philippines, it will be the poor in the villages who will be most open to the gospel, not the rich or the wise, for the eyes of the poor are not yet clouded by the distractions and trinkets of the world.

Concerning ministry, James A. Berquist and P. Kambar Manickam state:

> The churches can become the Church in India only when the Gospel is expressed and ministry undertaken in living dialogue with society. The only possible form of ministry adequate for the wider missiological task can be one involving the whole people of God, clergy and laity, each discovering its own form of service within the variety of Christ's ministries. (1976: 29–30)

From Berquist and Manickam's studies it would appear that the laity have too often been marginalized in clergy-centered churches. Within the LDS context, this is impossible, for the church works only when all persons are involved in ministry. Thus, the very kind of ministry that Berquist and Manickam espouse and seek is already present in the Church of Jesus Christ of Latter-day Saints.

There may be, however, one area in which Indian culture challenges the LDS, but in a way that can be met within the structure. When Jessie Ramjan, a female pastor in the Church of South India, was asked if there were any unique elements to being a woman in ministry, her answer was that she had access to the family and home in a way that a male pastor could never have. A man goes to a home and the men talk, while the women and the children remain in the kitchen or in other parts of the house. However, as a woman, Ramjan had access to the entire family. It was appropriate for her not only to talk to the husband, but also to invade the kitchen and to talk to the women and children there. Her experience had been that if ministers were close to the women, they were close to the families (interview, Bangalore, July 1994). If she is right, this poses an interesting question for strategies of ministry carried out by LDS with their patriarchal priesthood. Perhaps it will become essential in India for the male Branch President to lean more heavily on his female Relief Society President for information about his people than many Bishops may do in Western countries. Obviously, a Branch President would retain all priesthood responsibilities, but in many instances the culture denies him access to persons whom women can approach. It would thus seem that the office of Relief Society President may need to be more fully exploited in India to bridge this gap.

Music may not seem like a particularly important issue, but the way the music of worship is handled says a great deal about how well a culture is understood. In the mainline city churches of India, the liturgy, including the songs, is Western. The liturgy with its songs may be translated into the native language, but in form and harmonies everything is Western. Within the Catholic church, however, and in rural Protestant congregations, the words and the music of the hymns are often Indian. Music expresses the heart and soul of a culture. It is doubtful that Indians can worship as fully using Western harmonies and Western instruments as they can with their own scales and instruments. Thus, while initially it may be acceptable to translate some of the LDS Hymnbook into Hindi, Tamil, or Bengali, in the end there will only be a truly Indian expression of Mormonism when Indian members are permitted to write hymns with melodies from their own culture which are played on their own instruments. One of the most common means of worship in India is listening to the scriptures being sung. This is particularly true of the Sikhs where devotees sing from the sacred Guru Granth Sahib for hours during the day. Through the music, people are drawn into the message of the scriptures. If the door of music can be opened within the parameters of priesthood authority, a thoroughly vibrant and orthodox community of believers will emerge in India.

On the practical and personal level, marriage of LDS to LDS is currently difficult for young men and women in India. For example, an LDS woman, a medical doctor, had Christian parents who wanted to arrange a marriage for her with a doctor like herself. A Lutheran minister offered to help her find a 'Christian,' but first she would have to denounce her Mormon faith. What does a young LDS woman do in a situation like this? Socially acceptable marriages are still arranged in India, and Indian LDS church members will undoubtedly expect to continue this tradition. A woman who respects her parents will find it very hard to turn down a marriage arrangement; she would probably be cut off from the family. Yet, since a woman joins her husband's family, it would be almost impossible for an LDS woman to maintain her ties with the church were she to marry a Hindu or a Christian of another tradition. Latter-day Saint families express a willingness and a desire for their daughters to marry LDS men, even if they are not quite of the social station that the parents would have previously sought. But where are those men to be found? If the church cannot answer this question, suggested Gurcharan Singh Gill, it will be a barrier to women being willing to join the church; Gill asked what the church should do about this. He found a partial answer in the seminary and institute programs of church education which would provide a safe environment in which relationships between young LDS and their families may develop and lead ultimately to marriage (interview, Bangalore, July 1994).

In summary, Steven K. Iba, Zone Administrator of the Church Educational System for India, stated the challenges facing the LDS church best at a conference in Singapore telling the area directors that in Asia they must be prepared to 'play the *raga.*' A *raga* is a particular pattern in classical Indian music, but what turns that pattern into aesthetically pleasing music are the improvisations provided by the performer within the patterns (Schuler interview, February 1995). In Asia, Latter-day Saints enter a totally new and different world from that which their missionaries encountered in Western-influenced countries. The church has inspired patterns within which it must work, but perhaps it will be the church's ability to improvise within the patterns under the guidance of the Spirit that will determine the success or failure of the missionary work in India.

Part III
Emotional and Social Life

11 Childhood in early nineteenth-century Britain reflected in some LDS sources

Malcolm R. Thorp

Childhood in history has been a topic of considerable scholarly interest in recent years. The historiographic controversy has largely focused on the overall interpretation of childhood, beginning with Philippe Ariès's pioneering work which argued that French children lived under harsh conditions, not the least of which was the lack of parental affection (1962: 368). More recently, Linda Pollock has challenged this view by arguing that children were not only wanted but were basically well nurtured by parents in England and America from early modern times to 1900 (1983: 262–71; see also O'Day, 1994: 163ff.; Abbott, 1993: 140ff.). While basically the argument which follows shows considerable sympathy with Pollock's position, the main problem with her study, especially as it relates to the early nineteenth century, is the limited numbers of sources used, and the obvious fact that these sources invariably reflect middle-class conditions rather than the childhood experiences of common people. It might also be argued that Pollock's sources do not reveal the immense diversity of childhood experiences, which make generalizations about the totality of childhood hazardous, but still useful propositions.

One source for insight into childhood experience hitherto neglected by historians is the rather extensive numbers of diaries, journals and reminiscences that exist in various repositories interested in the LDS religious experience. Indeed, out of these extensive materials relating to the British Isles in the early nineteenth century, I have isolated some 158 accounts touching upon childhood, many of which are extremely brief, but nevertheless of some importance for some of the larger questions relating to childhood. Unfortunately, some topics explored by Pollock, such as breastfeeding, teething, toilet training, are not subjects of any interest to these writers. Virtually all of these accounts take the form of later autobiographical reflections, many extremely brief, which were typically written somewhere between ten to 50 years after emigration to America, which usually occurred in the 1840s and 1850s. Still, such descriptions, although often abbreviated by the passage of time, do give some revealing glimpses of what these autobiographers thought to be significant about their childhood. Moreover, most accounts were written from a working-class perspective, thus providing information that is not otherwise readily obtainable. The LDS sample might differ somewhat, however, from the mainstream of working-class life, in that families of these autobiographers were invariably described as being religiously inclined, and usually belonged to an organized religious group. Only a scant few stated that there were no religious influences in their homes.

Most studies on childhood focus on the question of parental sentiments towards children, and few delve into the equally important topic of whether or not children and early adolescents thought this time in their life to be one of happiness and relative tranquility. This is perhaps the most difficult question to answer, due to the complexity of the issue of what is meant by 'happiness,' as well as the fact that conditions inevitably would have changed in working-class families over a 15-year period. Thus there could have been momentary difficulties that briefly interrupted an otherwise normal childhood. To be sure, there does not appear to have been a general pattern of authoritarian child-rearing and abusive parental behavior that might have led to negative reflections. Still, the lack of uniformity in the childhood experience meant that each child was confronted with different problems and circumstances, some of which were not conducive to the promotion of happiness. Several such accounts lack the detail that we might want, but tell in cryptic language tales of hardship. Elizabeth Macdonald simply stated that her younger years were spent 'as a domestic slave.'[1] Peter Stubbs bluntly stated that 'the days of my childhood were not filled with happiness.'[2] William Lang summarized his entire childhood years in these brief words: 'My early youth was spent assisting my Parents, our family being large, nine children and my Father a laborer it was necessary that I should help him. What Education I received was at Sunday School when I learned to read and write. As soon as I was old enough, worked for myself hired to Farmers by the day, week, or month.'[3]

In some cases, however, memories of early years were filled with idyllic images of a simple and pleasant life long since lost.[4] Perhaps a handful of autobiographers viewed childhood in glowing terms – as a time when home was a happy place, and where children could enjoy friendship and play. Edwin Cox talked about such happy memories, including the Christmas season and the midsummer school holiday when he and other children engaged in various games and sports. 'We also had all kinds of out door Sports and finished up with Singing and music and a grand display of Fireworks . . . aye we used to have some happy times when I was a boy, and childhood seems all to short when the cares and anxieties of manhood overtake us.'[5] Joseph Gee lost his mother when he was about eight years old: 'I did not realize my loss then but I did realize the loss and what it was to be without a mother as years rolled by.' In spite of this hardship, he still recalled the hours spent rambling through the field and woods and playing down by the river amongst the 'pretty sweet primroses and daffodils and bluebells and wild roses and honey suckles, also the old house in which I was born and the garden and fruits and etc,' images which in later life in Utah were reminiscent of Merry Old England myths.[6] Likewise idyllic was the experience of Martha Yates who grew up in Rendlych, a small, peaceful country town in Wiltshire. 'At the edge of the town was a wild wood or game preserve. Everywhere was green grass and yellow buttercups.' Her father and mother were fond of each other. Unfortunately for her, however, this happy situation was reversed with the death of her mother when she was seven years old. This was followed by the death of her father three years later. One day, after her shopkeeper father's death, a bailiff came and foreclosed on the family home. Martha and her siblings were then raised by an aunt and uncle who were 'very good to them.'[7]

Jane Hindley wrote of her childhood: 'I received a pretty liberal Education and had a comfortable happy home in the Isle of Man with my Father who had married again and had a large family of Brothers and Sisters.'[8] Aaron Nelson relates that he was brought up in a family of twelve by kind and affectionate parents.[9] Fond memories, devoid of the tragedies of life, however, were the exception to the rule.

For some children, there was grinding poverty, early and arduous work, and poor circumstances with not enough food to eat.[10] There were often frequent moves in search of better economic circumstances. Still, in spite of all the hardships, James Thomas Wilson wrote, 'Taking all together we managed to make life somewhat bearable.'[11]

Perhaps the most recurring hardship was the large number of cases where there were reversals of family fortunes that led to subsequent family difficulties. Indeed, there were a number of diarists who came from prosperous middle-class homes, but saw their situation reversed by disastrous circumstances. Ann Harvey's father, for example, bought a cotton factory at Eaton Lane, and the family were well-to-do for about ten years. However, a fire broke out in the factory, the property was razed to the ground, and Ann's father was among the victims who lost their life fighting the blaze.[12] This disaster resulted in a significant loss of economic status, a reversal that was viewed in many accounts as the beginning of a train of events that was eventually to lead the family to Mormonism and resettlement in Utah.

The death of William Jex's father in 1839 left the family almost in a state of destitution. 'But,' Jex recorded, 'having many kind neighbors and friends the family was provided for, and mother taking in washing.'[13] In other cases the extended family provided some support in times of crisis. But, in many instances, particularly with the death of the father, the burden of providing for the family was passed on to children, who were forced to leave school and engage in menial employment. In all of these circumstances the family was undoubtedly driven to the margins of subsistence – keeping 'the wolf away from the door,' perhaps, but little more.

Disasters could lead families to a reassessment of values and beliefs. In the case of William Grant, his entire family was turned towards Christianity by a cholera epidemic in the early 1850s: 'I do not know of any of my relatives,' William recalled, 'ever making any profession of religion or belonging to any Political party.'[14] But this family crisis prompted his father to become a religious seeker, and eventually, this led to the family`s conversion to Mormonism.

In extreme cases, families were forced by economic reversals into the workhouse, the 'bastille' of the working class. Benjamin Perkins's parents joined the LDS church when he was about four months old in 1844. 'The people hated the Mormons and for two or three years my father could not get a day's work anywhere. At last we had to go to the poor house, and as nearly as I can remember we were there for about six months.'[15] Destitute children, such as George Watt, the first convert baptized at Preston in 1837, found their way into workhouses when there was no alternative to starvation. In Watt's case, his mother could not provide for young George, who apparently found conditions in the workhouse at least bearable.

As indicated in several examples above, the frequency of deaths of either one or both of the parents during childhood was a factor obviously affecting one's attitude and happiness. Nearly half of the sample group (72 out of 158) lost one or (in 15 cases) both parents during their childhood years. This figure might have been even higher had all of the writers commented on parental loses in a systematic way. While this high incidence of death might seem unusual, it is in keeping with the pattern of mortality found in early Victorian society. Michael Anderson, for example, found that about 10 per cent of children in Preston in 1851 had neither parent alive (1971: 54). The chances of at least one parent dying in years 1–15 of a child's life were relatively high. According to the adjusted figures in Wrigley and Schofield (1989: 711); the average death rate for men and women during the normal childbearing years (age 25 to 40) were as follows (per 1000 of population):

Table 11.1

Age	Death rate
25	47.8
30	52.6
35	58.4
40	66.2

This would mean that, according to adjusted death rates for the period, about 17.7 per cent of mothers and fathers in the population might be expected to die during the 15-year period of childhood. For either parent dying during these years, the probability would thus be 35.4 per cent, a figure only marginally lower than the 45.6 per cent in the sample from Mormon literary sources. Still, the fact that the LDS sample is somewhat above the national average is of some importance in understanding the turn to religion that occurred subsequent to the deaths of parents.

Joseph Gee lived a most unfortunate childhood. He said of his deceased mother: 'I was very young when my mother died (and oh I lost a friend) and I was very poor and my father was getting very old and I had no sister to help me and fix up and mend my old clothes and for a time my life was a sad and heavy one.'[16] Thomas Ashment likewise remembered the death of his mother in 1854. 'My faith,' he recalled, 'was somewhat tested a little she died the powers of darkness raged, and the trials of life appeared like unsurmountable mountains before me. I called upon the Lord in much weakness, for strength to overcome.' That night he had the following dream: 'I saw in my dream an angel of light standing at the foot of my bed having the cover of a coffin under his arm the cover was in a ruff state not having the smoothness of a plane there on. The angel held out his hand. I sat up in bead and shook hands with him and he gave me a sure promise, saying you shall overcome.' This was followed by a tender poem of farewell to his mother.[17]

A similar story of bereavement is related by James Bowler. While he was young his mother's health declined. On day the neighbors came to the home and pronounced her dead. While his grandmother was preparing the burial cloths, Bowler's mother rose from the bed and said: 'Mother I am not dead as you suppose.' She then told in detail many scenes she had witnessed in the spirit world, relating at the same time that she had been allowed to return for a short while in order to bring another child into the world, but in just one year she was to leave her family for the eternities. James concludes by stating that a year later (after giving birth to a daughter) she died.[18]

Given the frequency of remarriage following the death of a parent, it was a common occurrence for children to live with step-parents and other relatives. Living with step-parents could be a trial.[19] Robert Williams bluntly stated that his stepmother hated young children.[20] Robert Stoney relates that his father died when he was only a small child. For several years he lived with an uncle. But when his mother remarried, he returned to live in this new, but not happy home. 'The second husband,' he said, '(unlike my own father) was a course blunt Ignorant Man & consequently not very kind to me. He had driven me from house 2 or 3 times when my Mother having had to send me Vituals as best she could.' As a result, Stoney was forced into the market-place at an early age at 'very low wages.' His affection for his mother continued, however, and he stated that 'My mother who was then in good circumstances was very kind to me.'[21] Yet these instances of family dysfunctionality created by tensions between stepchildren and step-parents was not universally the case, and there are counter-examples of kind second parents who treated children with affection and respect.[22]

Few orphaned children were as fortunate as Mary Tyndale, who was taken in by a Mrs Reid while still in early infancy. In Mrs Reid's home, Mary grew up to feel that her foster parents and brothers and sisters were as close to her as her own blood relations. 'Mrs. Reid,' she recalled, 'was a good, kind mother and brought me up in the fear of the Lord. I was sent early to school, but my health was very bad until I was twelve years old . . .' It was not until years later that she learned that Mrs Reid was not her mother: 'when the truth of my parentage was told me, it was a source of great grief to me for I loved her and never knew any other and refused to leave her.'[23]

Orphans were not, however, numerous in this sample. But the impression received is that orphans usually encountered troublesome years until they reached maturity. William Gibson, one such an unfortunate youth, said: 'I have had to labor hard from my boyhood having been left without father, mother, brother, or sister. I have often tasted the "kindness" of the tyrant and oppressor. Some of them cared more for their horses and dogs than for their fellowman. The first cost them something, the latter, nothing.'[24]

The death of siblings was also an unsettling event during childhood. Perhaps the most unfortunate of all Mormon converts was James Godson Bleak, who was the third child in a family of six and the only one to reach manhood.[25] One sister and three brothers died in infancy. His brother John died aged 11, to make matters even worse, leaving him in a state of despondency that he could not soon overcome. Hannah Cornaby stated that the death of her younger sister, Lydia, when she was 14 had an impact on her religious thoughts. Not long after, Hannah decided to join the Congregationalists.[26] William Williams wrote about the death of his young sister, Rebecca: 'she lives near 1 year and then died from teething[.] Jesus took her to himself for said he on a certain occasion[,] In Heaven their angels are always in the Presence of my Father[.] Joseph Smith said on a like occasion They are too Pure and Holy to live here therefore God takes them to himself.'[27]

Given the high incidence of infant mortality (especially during the first five years of life) these tales of bereavement might have been expected. Because most of the Mormon sources used here are later reminiscences, however, there is no way to tabulate systematically the numbers of autobiographers who experienced the death of siblings. But it might be surmised that LDS sources fall into the general national pattern, which indicates a death rate for the first five years alone at around 20 per cent .[28]

There is a smaller but significant number of dysfunctional families, families troubled by such problems as chronic alcoholism, quarreling between parents, and the abandoning of family responsibilities, usually by the father. Incidents in which the father took to drinking and consequently neglected his occupation as well as family responsibilities were not uncommon.[29] Charles R. Bailey recalled that his father, a stonemason, was not an unpleasant man until he went on a drinking binge: 'he was one of those men who lacked fortitude and was very easy led by company to drink and many times he lost his manhood & would get drunk. It was then that he would be unkind and abuse his family, drinking up all his wages – and this made him very unpleasant.' When Charles was about eleven his father left home for about 13 weeks following an incident in which he physically abused his wife and broke household furnishings. The family eventually was forced to move to Birmingham and then Manchester to escape his wrath.[30] Thomas Beard reported that his father, a miner by profession, not only drank heavily, but played the fiddle and sang comic songs in public houses. His wayward lifestyle impoverished the family.[31]

In other cases fathers abandoned their families, leaving wife and children to fend for themselves. Henry Roper remembered his father leaving home when he was five years old. 'One Sunday night he offered to stay home with the children while mother attended church. After she had gone he packed his clothes and left early in the morning for Yorkshire.' Shortly afterwards he married another woman. The minister of the parish was an old acquaintance and recognized the father, who denied his identity in order to escape charges of bigamy. Two years later the father left his second wife and a small son.[32]

Mercy Keetch described her home life as not always happy because 'pa would drink.' There was also contention over religion because her father was not religious and prevented his wife from attending any religious services. While the father was at work, the mother would gather the children together and taught them that all places of worship were places that the Lord loved. In contrast, Mercy was taught that 'the Lord did not like houses and places where they sold beer and strong drink or places where they dance for all those places wear [sic] wicked places.' What comes out strongly here is the dysfunctional relationship between parents concerning religious and cultural issues, as well as the authoritarian control exercised by the father.[33]

Mathew Rowan's mother died in a cholera epidemic in the early 1830s. 'My father added to our wretchedness by becoming more gay and heedless than before. He drank a deal, which gave his children for their once neat and clean suits of cloths, bunches of literal rags.' The family became so destitute that Henry recalled gleaning potatoes after the harvest. To make matters worse, his father later remarried a woman who was both extravagant and an alcoholic.[34]

In several cases it was the mother who left. John Martin's mother abandoned her husband in the middle of the night, taking young John with her on travels of hardship, want, and even imprisonment for vagrancy. Young John was forced by necessity into the profession of chimney sweep, working for a 'hard cruel man' for six or seven years before he was able to escape. Still, in spite of these difficulties, there was a bond of affection that continued to exist between mother and son, and John would frequently visit his mother when circumstances permitted.[35]

There were also cases where parental rigidity, usually in matters of religion, was resented. Patience Loader indicated that her parents were 'very strict' with their 13 children.[36] Richard Kearsley remembered his Wesleyan father 'as the best man in the world' but a man that was 'too strict.' 'He did not seem to manifest that affection for me that my disposition desired and might say craved after.' Moreover, this lack of affection carried over into relations between parents. Kearsley described his mother 'though she was not a handsome woman her portrait is indelibly Photographed by affection on my Memory.' His father's abrupt mannerisms and authoritarian personality often brought his mother to tears. This was especially so on Saturday nights, as preparations were made for the Sabbath. 'I recalect [sic] it was mothers custom to strip and wash us children and put on us clean night gowns, and if we were not finished when father came home on Saturday nights there was always unpleasantness and mother would cry.'

Richard's mother died when he was twelve years old, and his father remarried soon after. Unlike some of the children in our sample, however, Richard remembered a fondness for his stepmother.

Ann Harvey recalled her father being 'very strict with his family and demanded prompt obedience from all.' Her mother was also strict, 'but more sympathetic toward her children than my father.' She then makes a most revealing comment about parental rigidity of the time: 'I think there are instance [sic] where homes have been made unpleasant by the strict and rigid laws and requirements that have been enforced by parents, where the children's inexperience and simplicity have not been considered much less made a study of as they should be.'[37]

Jane Robinson was raised by her father following the death of her mother when she was very young. 'My dear father was exceedingly kind and affectionate to me, more so than he was to my sister Anna, who was two years older.' The father later remarried, when Jane was five or six years old. The stepmother was kind and loved Jane as one of her own children.[38] On the other hand, Ellen Briget Gallager stated that she had a 'cruel stepfather' who deserted the family until she was in her teens.[39]

In spite of some examples of cruelty, still there seems to be a prevailing sentiment, as indicated by Pollack, that children were both wanted and cared for. There is little evidence that children were resented, although some cases of maltreatment might suggest this. And there are few cases of parents physically abusing children. Indeed, LDS sources suggest that family life was at least reasonably dynamic, although the role of the father was often more remote than the mother. For the majority, however, childhood was not a time of unmitigated happiness and fond memories. Indeed, accounts of the tribulations encountered during childhood were important to the larger story of a growing spiritual awareness that eventually led believers to the Latter-day Saint faith.

Notes

DUP Daughters of Utah Pioneers
HDC Historical Department, Church of Jesus Christ of LDS
WPA Works Progress Administration

1 Elizabeth Macdonald, autobiography: 1–6. HDC.
2. Peter Stubbs, autobiography. BYU, Margaret Steed, Hess Collection, Box 1, fd 3.
3. William Lang, autobiography: 1–2. BYU.
4. At least one account in this survey claimed a genteel upbringing. According to a later description of the life of Fredrick Walton: 'His mother, who was early left widow, belonged to the English Gentry class. Her family home was lovely old English estate and she grew up with wealth and culture that her station demanded. It was a household with servants to do every menial task, and . . . she was reared to be a lady with a knowledge of books, of fine embroidering, and music. In 1840 she married Edward Walton, son of the Walton's of Willinhall, a young man of her own class. Their new home was one of those

well-ordered homes of the English well-to-do people and to them were born Fredrick in 1841 and . . . daughter Mary Ann (1843). In 1848, when Fredrick was only seven years old, his father died and his mother was left with the responsibility of her home and her two small children. A few years later she met and married William Reeves . . . who was already a Latter-day saint.' History of Centerville: 262–5.

5. Edwin Cox, Record Book. BYU.
6. Joseph Gee HDC, Ms 1020.
7. Biographical sketch of Martha Mary Ann Peck Yates. Copy in author's possession.
8. Jane Hindley, journals, 1855–1905. HDC, Ms 1764.
9. Aaron Nelson, journal and reminiscences. BYU, Ms 534.
10. Edmund Hepworth as a young boy worked in the coalfields, along with other members of his family. He said: 'We went to work before daylight, we came out of the pit after dark, we only saw daylight on Sundays. William (his brother) and I worked together. Many the day we worked on a penny loaf of bread, nothin' to it, not even a drink of water to it. On Sunday there was a little meat for those who worked, the children never had meat to eat.' History of Edmund Hepworth (1841–1915). Unpublished Ms, BYU.
11. Life of James Thomas Wilson. BYU.
12. Ann Harvey, autobiography. HDC, Ms 10483.
13. William Jex, autobiography. HDC, Ms 4864.
14. Life of William Grant, Histories of Utah Pioneers of Adams Camp. DUP, BYU.
15. WPA Project, 9. BYU.
16. Joseph Gee. HDC, Ms. 1020.
17. Thomas Ashment. HDC.
18. James Bowler, Diary. BYU.
19. See 'Ellen Briget Gallager Cottam.' *Our Pioneer Heritage*, 6: 481.
20. Robert Williams, autobiography. HDC.
21. Robert Stoney, reminiscence and diary. HDC, Ms 3872.
22. William Jex, autobiography. HDC, Ms 4864.
23. Mary Tyndale (Ferguson) Baxter. *Our Pioneer Heritage*, 6: 500–1.
24. 'Carter.' *Our Pioneer Heritage* 6: 22–3.
25. James Godson Bleak, autobiography. HDC.
26. Hannah Cornaby, *Autobiography and Poems*: 16. Salt Lake City: J. C. Graham & Co., 1881.
27. William Williams, reminiscences. HDC, Ms 9132.
28. Infant and child mortality figures in Wrigley and Schofield (1989: 249) indicate a combined death rate for females to age five (per 1000) as 199 for females and 222 for males for years 1750–99.
29. See William Adams. HDC.
30. Charles Bailey, autobiography. BYU.
31. J. Kenneth Davies, *George Beard*: 1.
32. 'Henry Roper.' *Our Pioneer Heritage*, 15: 131–2.
33. Mary Keetch, reminiscences. HDC, Ms 4855.
34. Mathew Rowan: 1–9. HDC.
35. John Martin: 1–17. HDC.
36. Diary of Patience Loader Rosa Archer: 1. BYU.
37. Ann Harvey, autobiography. HDC, Ms 10483.
38. Jane Robinson. *Our Pioneer Heritage*, 16: 529–31.
39. Ellen Briget Gallager. *Our Pioneer Heritage*, 6: 481.

12 Guilt, fear, anxiety and love Disciplinary councils among Latter-day Saints today

Melvyn Hammarberg

On Saturday afternoon, December 3, 1994, Sam Weller's Zion's book-store in Salt Lake City held an author's signing for D. Michael Quinn and Richard Van Wagoner, who had each recently published important books in Latter-day Saint history. The two authors spoke briefly about their research experiences, fielded questions from the hundred or so persons who crowded into the store's outer hallway, and then sat at a pair of tables to autograph their volumes for the faithful. I stood in line like the rest, clutching my copy of *The Mormon Hierarchy: Origins of Power* (Quinn, 1994), waiting to congratulate Mike.

A young woman in the parallel line moved close to the man behind me and said, 'Oh, I'm so sorry that they've called you in. When's the hearing?' 'Tomorrow morning,' the man behind me said. 'It's kind of a relief. But I'll be glad when it's finally over.' I couldn't help overhearing this exchange and so introduced myself. The young man said, 'I'm Brent Metcalfe,' and mentally I put the picture together. A week or ten days earlier, I had read an article in the Salt Lake *Tribune* reporting Metcalfe's call to appear before an impending church disciplinary council. The likely charge was apostasy for contributing to and editing *New Approaches to the Book of Mormon* (Metcalfe, 1993). We talked briefly about critical approaches to the Old and New Testaments, and the extension of these scientific methods to questions of the human origins of the Book of Mormon, and then got the autographs for which we had come, and went our separate ways.

A week later in the *Tribune*'s 'Religion' section, under a headline that read, 'LDS Church Excommunicates Author, Researcher,' the Associated Press reported:

> An author and private researcher has been excommunicated from the Mormon Church after compiling a book of essays that question the historicity of the Book of Mormon. Brent Metcalfe, 36, was excommunicated Sunday after a disciplinary council before leaders of the church's Brighton Stake.

This exchange and set of newspaper reports was my introduction to the use of disciplinary councils in the Church of Jesus Christ of Latter-day Saints, and prompted my reflections upon them as emotionally potent identity-defining and boundary-maintaining instruments. The charge against Metcalfe was apostasy, a failure to obey priesthood authority within the Church. What I soon discovered, of course, was that most disciplinary councils concerned another great set of sins, sexual immorality. The pages of the Salt Lake *Tribune* reported several cases of ward or stake officials who were involved in sexual offenses, and in some instances sought to explore the underlying issues through confidential interviews using pseudonyms (e.g. Jorgensen, 1994). Apostasy and sexual immorality are among the more extreme cases, the limiting cases, that establish the Church's outer boundaries of inclusion, making clear to members and non-members alike that crossing those boundaries means risking the loss of membership in the community of Latter-day Saints (Barth, 1969).

Church disciplinary councils have had an important role in what Mauss (1994: 196–201) has described as 'retrenchment' within the Church during the last several decades, clarifying how the Church's normative structure differs from the wider society while the Church itself has borrowed modern secular features and many 'ideas and practices characteristic of Protestant fundamentalism.' But disciplinary councils also deal with issues of group identity in personal, categorical and evaluative terms, not only what it means to be a Latter-day Saint, but what it means to be a 'good' Latter-day Saint, where self-appraisal and appraisal by others is made in terms of feared, ideal and actual actions that are defined in cultural terms (Wallace, 1967; see also Hallowell, 1967).

Psychologically, disciplinary councils give rise to a variety of emotional responses that are linked to different kinds of cognitive/situational appraisals (Beck, 1976). Feelings of guilt, for instance, arise in relation to self/situational appraisals involving the violation of internalized normative standards. Fear is felt in relation to realistic appraisals of danger to one's personal domain. Anxiety is manifest when personal coping resources seem inadequate to potential threats. Feelings of brotherly and sisterly love arise when a person feels accepted just as they are. Clearly, other feelings, like shame, sorrow, or remorse, are also linked to cognitive/situational appraisals in content-specific ways that require a close, personal, culturally-sensitive 'reading' of disciplinary reports, usually from the person-in-question's point of view or as inferred from a particular situation defined from the point of view of the Church's belief system.

My purpose in this chapter is to explore briefly the role of church disciplinary councils from the point of view of the Church, and to examine some of their emotional impacts and effects on a member's own sense of personal identity. These are topics that have not received much attention, but are central to some of the current tensions within the Church, and to the personal identities of individuals as members of the Church.

Church disciplinary councils

Church discipline may involve informal private counsel, cautionary instruction, or informal probation if a transgression of Church norms is relatively minor, confession voluntary, and repentance clear. Formal disciplinary councils are mandatory only in the cases of serious transgressions. A listing of serious transgressions subject to discipline

> includes (but is not limited to) attempted murder, rape, forcible sexual abuse, intentionally inflicting serious physical injuries on others, adultery, fornication, homosexual relations, child abuse (sexual or physical), spouse abuse, deliberate abandonment of family responsibilities, robbery, burglary, embezzlement, theft, sale of illegal drugs, fraud, perjury, or false swearing. (*General Handbook of Instruction*, 1989: 10–4)

Most formal Church discipline is administered locally within the wards of the Church by the Bishopric group of a bishop and his two counselors, though the stake presidency has general responsibility among all wards within a stake, and specific responsibility if excommunication of a member holding the Melchizedek priesthood appears to be the likely outcome. In the latter case, the stake High Council of twelve members, together with the stake president and his two counselors, participate in the disciplinary council. Only members of the all-male priesthood administer Church discipline. The official view is that these councils are 'councils of love,' and as one former Bishop suggested, they serve as 'emergency clinics where the most extreme soul-saving measures are taken to help individuals who are in serious jeopardy of losing their spiritual life' (Bishop B, 1995b: see Notes at end of chapter). Possible decisions include 'no action,' where the case is to be handled informally; 'formal probation,' which 'restricts or suspends a member's privileges in designated ways until he or she shows specified progress or meets prescribed conditions'; 'disfellowshipment,' which means a member is 'no longer in good standing, may not hold a temple recommend, serve in a Church position, or exercise the priesthood in any way,' among other restrictions, but is encouraged 'to pay tithes and offerings, to continue to wear temple garments if endowed, and to seek a return to fellowship in the Church through sincere repentance and righteous living.' Finally, 'excommunication' involves a formal severance of Church membership, 'an exceptional, ultimate penalty reserved for those circumstances in which it is mandatory or clearly directed by the Spirit' (*General Handbook of Instruction*, 1989: 10–5).

Obedience to righteous authority versus free agency

One area of tension within the Church today is between obedience to spiritual authority through the priesthood, and 'free agency' as the spiritual birthright of every person descended from Heavenly Father. This tension sometimes leads to anxiety over what can be advocated in the name of free agency, and may result in fear of actual disciplinary action and excommunication if ideas and actions do not conform to higher priesthood authority.

I attended a meeting of the B. H. Roberts Society in November 1994 during which Lavina Fielding Anderson recounted the previous year's series of disfellowshipments, excommunications, discontinuance of status among some BYU faculty, and resignations from the Church. She called these events 'the orthodoxy wars.'

Lynne Whitesides had been disfellowshiped. Avraham Gileadi, Paul Toscano, Maxine Hanks, Michael Quinn, and I were excommunicated. That was in September 1993. Also that month, John Beck, who had withdrawn in June from BYU's faculty along with his wife, Martha Nibley Beck, resigned from the Church. In June, David Knowlton and Cecilia Konchar Farr had been notified that BYU would not grant them continuing status. In October Steve Benson, the Pulitzer-prize winning cartoonist for the *Arizona Republic*, and his wife Mary Ann Benson resigned from the Church. David Wright, a scholar of ancient scriptures at Brandeis, was excommunicated in April 1994 after a year of increasingly tense meetings with his bishop and stake president. Within the week, Michael Barrett, counsel for the Central Intelligence Agency, was also excommunicated in Washington, DC, for writing letters to the editor providing historical and doctrinal information to correct incomplete or inaccurate news stories (L. F. Anderson, 1994).

In response to the six disciplinary councils in Utah, which received national media attention (see *Time*, June 13, 1993), the First Presidency and the Quorum of the Twelve in November 1993 issued a statement regarding disciplinary councils. It read, in part:

> We have the responsibility to preserve the doctrinal purity of the Church. We are united in this objective. The Prophet Joseph Smith taught an eternal principle when he explained: 'That man who rises up to condemn others, finding fault with the Church, saying that they are out of the way, while he himself is righteous, then know assuredly, that [that] man is in the high road to apostasy.' (*Teachings of the Prophet Joseph Smith*: 56) . . .
> Faithful members of the Church can distinguish between mere differences of opinion and those activities formally defined as apostasy. Apostasy refers to Church members who '(1) repeatedly act in clear, open, and deliberate public opposition to the Church or its leaders; or (2) persist in teaching as Church doctrine information that is not Church doctrine after being corrected by their bishops or higher authority; or (3) continue to follow the teachings of apostate cults (such as those that advocate plural marriage) after being corrected by their bishops or higher authority.' (*General Handbook of Instruction*, 1989: 10–3) (First Presidency, 1993)

Most members most of the time are not concerned with the possibility of Church discipline over doctrinal issues, and generally there appears to be wide latitude in what individuals may believe as long as they do not advocate their individual beliefs as having normative application to the Church. Still, one evening I arrived at the home of Jim Barker (pseudonym) for an interview about how ideas may be explored in the Church, only to discover that the First Counselor in the Bishopric had just preceded me in response to a father's concern that Jim, in his role as a Sunday School teacher, was teaching from materials written by someone who recently had been excommunicated. The father's son had brought the matter to the father's attention, and the father carried it to the Bishopric. Needless to say, Jim was somewhat anxious that evening, even though the matter had been amicably resolved (Barker, 1994: see Notes).

Anxiety was reported to have run high also in the spring of 1993 as a group of women prepared for a conference called 'Counterpoint,' intended to discuss the many different voices of LDS women in the Church. Many of those who had originally indicated their desire to help plan and participate withdrew, purportedly in response to various official pressures within the Church. A reorganized planning committee nonetheless convened the conference, which drew nearly three times the expected attendance. Lavina Fielding Anderson was one of those who helped plan this conference, and who shortly after was called in by her stake president in relation to an article she had published in *Dialogue* (Anderson, 1993a) concerning ecclesiastical or spiritual abuse in the Church.

In response to the frequent question, 'Aren't you afraid?' she wrote:

> What do we have to fear from our Church, the institution into which we were voluntarily baptized, whose meetings we attend, in whose temples we marry and worship, whose classes we teach, of whose divine origin we bear testimony? How can we say we're afraid of an institution that exists to bring us to Christ? How can we say we fear priesthood leaders who only want what is best for us? All of these goals and purposes are true. I know them. I believe them. But the fear is real, too. (Anderson, 1993b)

She then suggested that women are afraid of losing their jobs if they are employed by the Church, and so are men, of social stigma and scolding in their wards, of what will happen to their children, of reflecting badly on their spouses, of losing their temple recommends as a sign of worthiness before God.

In appealing her subsequent excommunication for apostasy to the First Presidency, she wrote:

> I still love the Church and wish to be part of it. I am still attending my meetings, reading the scriptures, holding family prayers, and participating in daily family devotional. I do not feel angry or bitter. My hope is for reconciliation and a healing of this breach. (Anderson, 1993c)

These 'orthodoxy wars,' as Anderson called them, suggest that despite great leeway there are some 'defining beliefs' that are not to be questioned within the Church, and that among these are the role of the prophet and priesthood in the life of the Church and the historicity of the Book of

Mormon. The first are questions of institutional and spiritual authority, while the second is a question of historical events and the spiritual meaning of a document. As long as the Book of Mormon is taken to ground its spiritual power in certain events claimed to have occurred in the historical past, then the occurrence of those events will be subject to historical, archaeological and cultural scrutiny as a matter of scientific interest, the results of which will be held as true or false as matters of degrees of probability. The evidential status of the Book of Mormon will be treated similarly to the evidential status of any other artifacts that are claimed to be evidence for a cultural past of a certain construction.

The question of institutional spiritual authority is of a different order, and suggests why charges of apostasy rather than heresy are brought against members. For it is as much a matter of claims to personal authority and its public meaning in the spiritual realm as of aberrant ideas that is at issue. Clearly, the priesthood under the living prophet, who is the President of the Church, is taken to mediate the Church's understanding of spiritual relationships against all public individual claims, whether made on the basis of scientific evidence, conscience, new revelation, older practice and tradition or any other basis. Free agency, therefore, has certain limits in relation to the priesthood and the prophet as part of obedience to Church authority. When obedience is made the issue in a disciplinary council, the only choices are to obey, or leave the church, or be asked to leave it, as in the case of the September Six.

Lavina Anderson's heartfelt appeal to the First Presidency confirms how personal identity as a Latter-day Saint survives even against the institution's severance of membership. Actually, it survives on both sides of this relationship, not only because some of those who have been excommunicated often continue their spirituality in belief and practice, but also because the Church will continue to reach out in an effort to reincorporate and restore the apostate to full membership under explicitly defined conditions, gently and eloquently phrased in the President Howard W. Hunter's plea 'to those who have transgressed or been offended to "come back" ' (Hunter, 1994). The voices of other general authorities have not always been so benevolent.

Violations of Church sexual standards and the ideal of unconditional love

A second tension within the Church today is between the ideal of 'unconditional love' as a popular understanding of Christ's atonement and the actual exercise of Church discipline that excludes members from the central blessing of the Church in sacrament meetings and temple covenants. It is a tension that suggests a 'tough love' model of conditional acceptance as the true operative basis for community acceptance, especially in the area of sexual sins. Essentially, the Church's normative position today is that sexual relations are acceptable only within a covenant of marriage between persons of opposite genders, either sealed in a civil ceremony for time or in a temple ceremony for time and eternity which is the preferred form. Premarital sex, adultery, fornication, and homosexual sex are all forbidden (First Presidency, 1991). Yet, one former bishop estimated that 90–95 per cent of his involvement in Church discipline involved responding to sexual sins, and that over the four-and-a-half years of his service as bishop he averaged about one such disciplinary hearing per month (Bishop B, 1995a; see Notes at end of chapter). As he stated elsewhere: 'Sexual immorality in all its varieties seems to be the overwhelming "sin du jour" (sic) in Mormonism, far outweighing in numbers and complexity, the instances of apostasy, crime and other grounds for formal discipline, despite the attention of the media' (Bishop B, 1995b; see Notes at end of chapter).

Members are told by Church authorities that violations of Church standards call into jeopardy all of a person's efforts to achieve the highest degree of glory in the celestial kingdom, and impede relationships with Heavenly Father, Jesus Christ, the prophets, one's ancestors and descendants, as well as with one's family and members of the Church. A violation therefore can provoke a self-consuming spiritual crisis, born of guilt, of considerable magnitude.

Consider the case of Ann White (pseudonym), today a woman in her early fifties who is contemplating remarrying in the Church. As an active teenager in Young Women's Mutual, she thought of herself as a 'little bit of a rebel' in regard to Church standards, because she dated boys outside the Church and fell in love with one. In her words:

> I was in love with a non-Mormon fellow, and that's the whole reason for not dating non-Mormon fellows, and I wanted to marry him. Of course, that met with strong opposition from my parents and my friends in the Church, and my leaders, and so I broke it off with him, and ended up marrying the good Mormon boy that I was not in love with, thinking that I would settle down and live the Mormon life and be blessed with children, that everything would work out and I would grow to love him. And it kind of backfired on me. For all of my young married years, I lived an ideal family life with this husband who was very good, a good provider, kindly, but on his career path and me on my path of raising the children and being a very active LDS woman. But deep inside was a feeling I was never quite good enough because I wasn't happy with the plan. I was putting on an act and I knew it. (White, 1995, for this and the following quotations; see Notes)

Ann was encouraged by her husband to marry in the temple, which added to her sense of disenchantment. She had not really wanted to be married to this man for time, let alone for eternity. She was torn inside, and felt she was putting on a false front. She said:

> I just didn't have integrity. I was not an integrated person because I was feeling different feelings inside than I was expressing outwardly . . . I was not telling the

truth. I was putting up this image that I was a happy little Mormon wife and I wasn't.

Vulnerable, she became sexually involved with a younger man. When she could no longer stand the guilt, she turned to her bishop:

> It was extremely emotional for me. I felt really inferior. [My Bishop] was very kind, as I remember. He suggested that I tell my husband, which I did. It was a pretty terrible, traumatic time. The Bishop asked me to do some reading to see if I couldn't strengthen my own testimony, and suggested that [my husband and I] might have counseling. But we didn't because my husband wasn't interested.

The bishop put her on probation for six months and encouraged her to seek counseling. Five years passed, and she again found herself emotionally involved with another man. This time she spoke both to the bishop and the stake president, who told her she could not leave her marriage for the sake of the children and that she simply had to adjust to her situation. She was disfellowshiped for a year, which meant she could not take the sacrament, or hold a Church position, or pray publicly if called upon. She said:

> People pretty much knew that there was a problem. [My husband] was pretty condescending. It seemed to me that the male authorities and my husband were in cahoots, kind of condescending to the point of [implying] 'this poor, little neurotic, emotional woman who really can't live the way she should, we really have to help her; we really have to give her another chance.' First I talked to the Bishop, then I talked to the Stake President, and then they sent me a letter requesting that I come to a Bishopric's meeting. I went in and the Bishop asked me questions and each member of the Bishopric, the three of them, had a chance to ask me questions. They asked me, not a lot of details, but how this happened. All that I remember is that I cried and that it was very difficult and embarrassing, intimidating – humiliating actually – not pleasant, and certainly I felt that I was probably a woman with a scarlet letter. That's how I felt – [like] an outcast among the good Relief Society sisters.

She became depressed and experienced an emotional breakdown. Then five years later she again fell in love with another man, but stopped short of sexual involvement. And she said to herself:

> Forget it, I can't do the marriage anymore and I can't do the Church anymore. So, I left. I felt that I needed less judgment, and that I just couldn't measure up. I did get divorced against the wishes of my husband . . . The Stake President was the kindest in recognizing my own needs, but still maintained that I not get divorced. So I felt that in order to get a divorce, I had to go against the authorities of the church. And I felt that if I was going to go against their advice, then I didn't want to be there. I was in counseling at the time, and I felt that if I had not done that, that I would have lost my real self.
>
> When I didn't go to church anymore, I felt very free. Freedom became an obsession with me – freedom to be who I was – and I swore to myself that I would never again be something inside and not be the same outside. That became one of my strongest values. During the eight years of relative inactivity,

the thing that I missed [most] was the friendship, the sense of community, the loving support from other members. When you're used to that on a weekly basis, when your whole life is your neighborhood and your church, and then suddenly you strike out by yourself, you miss it. I don't believe in church courts. I don't see the need for excommunication unless someone is teaching something or doing something that is really detrimental to the group as a whole, the church as a whole. But for particular failings, I'm not so sure it serves a [useful] purpose. It wasn't a deterrent to me; it only made my problems worse. There's a difference between receiving help in counseling and receiving discipline.

This is an interesting case for many reasons, the foremost of which is Ann's own inner sense that she had not followed her own heart in choosing her mate initially, because of pressures of mate selection within the Church. But the case also illustrates how guilt over the violation of marriage covenants, made in the temple with God, drove her to confession with her bishop. In the several stake and general conferences I attended, one theme was repeated often: if there has been sexual sin, seek out your bishop immediately, and take those steps necessary for repentance and restitution to restore your standing before Heavenly Father. As Bishop Bradlee Watson of Lynnewood, Washington, told me: 'In cases of worthiness, the Bishop is the common judge, and he's the only one who can help with those things.' He went on to say:

> The first time I was ever involved with any disciplinary action was when I was serving on the high council, and it was a very emotional time, because there's such an outpouring of love and desire to help and to lift, to bless, and yet, a very real realization that it's the Savior that's going to make the difference. He's the one that's going to be able to heal; we're just the instruments, the ones who are there to help. So, there's a real reliance upon the inspiration that comes from prayer. And I've found that to be true [in my role] as a Bishop. It's become a real joy to see the change that comes into [some]one's life as they go through those steps that the Savior has outlined in the scriptures, confessing and repenting, making a change of heart.

In the case of Ann White, she recognized in retrospect that an effort had been made to understand her need, and that the role of the bishop, or stake president, was one which expressed the community's love as well as its discipline. This did not, however, prevent her from raising questions about the role of fear as a whip to keep people in line, or about differences between what she experienced in counseling over against Church discipline.

Conclusion

Church disciplinary councils are boundary-defining instruments for determining who may or may not claim a formal personal identity as a Latter-day Saint. These councils act in regard to Church norms across a range of transgressions, with charges of apostasy and sexual immorality as limiting cases. Both kinds of behavior call into question, from the viewpoint of the Church's beliefs, an individual's status within the kingdom of God on earth. And while they complement each other as involving different forms of self-control and both boundaries can be crossed incrementally, they also contrast with one another in important ways. As one former bishop wrote:

> [T]here is less gray area in the realm of sexual sin than in the realm of apostasy. The formal definition of the latter ... allows for (even requires) a formal warning by an ecclesiastical leader before a member can be considered guilty ... No such latitude exists for sexual sin. In short, the line of apostasy seems to be established by ecclesiastical leaders on a case by case basis, with public, persistent, and belligerent opposition to church authority being the defining criterion. Sexual sin is unequivocal and need not be publicly known, formally warned, or even indisputably proven.

The only mitigating circumstance seems to be the moral responsibility and spiritual status of the offender, e.g. single, unendowed teenagers experimenting with newly-discovered sexual drives and opportunities are generally dealt with less harshly than are endowed, married adults who should have more knowledge and self-control (Bishop B, 1995b; see Notes below).

The psychological ramifications of disciplinary councils are also important, both in terms of self-appraisal and the evaluations of others, and also in terms of the cognitive-emotional effects they generate. Guilt, fear, anxiety and love are only a few of these effects. A fuller understanding of the cognitive/emotional dynamics would require a detailed interactional analysis of particular cases, which is beyond the scope of this paper. This initial incursion, however, suggests something of the rich and multi-leveled cultural and psychological meanings that disciplinary councils among the Latter-day Saints encode.

Notes

Barker, J. (pseudonym) (1994), personal interview, December 6.
Bishop B (pseudonym) (1995a), personal interview, March 22.
Bishop B (pseudonym) (1995b), personal communication, May 31.
White, A. (pseudonym) (1995), personal interview, February 2.

13 An overview of Mormonism and mental health

Daniel K. Judd

The relationship of religion and mental health has long been an issue in the social sciences and its sometimes controversial nature applies as much to the relationship of mental health to religion in general as to Mormonism in particular. Many have argued for the positive influence of religion while others have argued the opposite. William James wrote the following:

> We and God have business with each other; and in opening ourselves to His influence our deepest destiny is fulfilled. The universe, and those parts of it which our personal being constitutes, takes a turn genuinely for the worse or the better in proportion as each one of us fulfills or evades God's commands. (1929: 516–17)

Psychologist Albert Ellis represents those who argue for the negative influence of religiosity on mental health:

> Religiosity is in many respects equivalent to irrational thinking and emotional disturbance . . . The elegant therapeutic solution to emotional problems is to be quite unreligious . . . the less religious they are, the more emotionally healthy they will be. (1980: 637)

The apparent conflict between the assertions represented by the statements of James and Ellis has served as an invitation for many researchers to examine these statements in the light of scientific evidence.

Previous reviews of religiosity and mental health

Lea (1982), Bergin (1983), and this author (Judd, 1986) have published literature reviews concerning the relationship of religiosity and mental health through 1977, 1979, and 1985 respectively. Levin and Vanderpool (1987), Gartner, Larson, and Allen (1991), as well as Larson *et al.* (1992) have also published non-comprehensive reviews (cf. Sauna, 1969; Stark, 1971; Gorsuch and Aleshire, 1974).

This author is presently completing a major research project which will update the religiosity and mental health literature through March of 1995. This chapter is a brief overview of the preliminary findings of all research concerning the relationship of religiosity and mental health as well as a specific focus on various descriptions of Mormons.

In a previous literature review of religiosity and mental health research (Judd, 1986), I reported the outcomes of a total of 167 studies (182 outcomes). This initial study was a review of the research conducted in the 62-year period between January of 1923 and March 1985. This study represented data gathered from over 200,000 subjects. Some 30 per cent of the studies reviewed indicated a negative relationship where religion facilitated mental problems, 32 per cent a positive relationship with religion conducive to positive mental health, 33 per cent a neutral relationship, and 5 per cent a curvilinear relationship.

Figure 13.1 is a graphic illustration of these percentages. All outcome symbols have been adjusted. 'Positive' represents a relationship where religiosity is facilitative of mental health. 'Negative' represents an unhealthy relationship, etc.

For
the

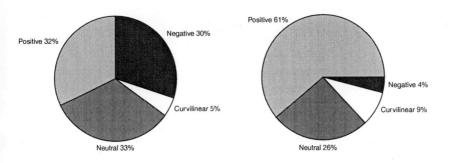

Figure 13.1 Religiosity and mental health: 1928–85

Figure 13.2 Religiosity and mental health: 1980–85

most part, these data are ambiguous as to the support or refutation of either a positive or negative relationship of religion and mental health. However, in the process of completing this initial study, I noted a positive trend in the research beginning in the late 1970s and continuing through the 1980s. Out of 23 studies conducted between 1980 and 1985, 61 per cent (14 studies) reported a positive relationship between religiosity and mental health, 26 per cent (six studies) a neutral relationship, 9 per cent (two studies) a curvilinear relationship, and 4 per cent (one study) a negative relationship. These data are represented in Figure 13.2.

A decade review (1985–95)

My initial literature review of the research published between March of 1985 and March of 1995 generated 373 specific studies which focused on the relationship between religiosity and mental health. A preliminary examination of the 373 studies (529 outcomes) published between 1985 and 1995 revealed that 59 per cent (311 outcomes) of the outcomes showed a positive relationship between religiosity and mental health, 13 per cent (67 outcomes) a negative relationship, and 26 per cent (138 outcomes) a neutral relationship. These data are summarized in Figure 13.3.

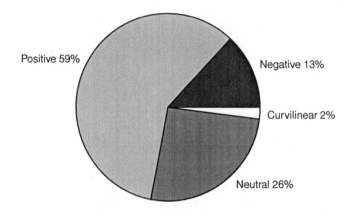

Figure 13.3 Religiosity and mental health 1985–95

Positive trend

The positive trend noted in my earlier study (Judd, 1986) is validated in the analysis of the present data. There continues to be little support for the assertion that religiosity is antithetical to mental health. Eighty-five per cent of the outcomes reviewed in this present investigation (1985–95) indicated either a positive (59 per cent) or neutral (26 per cent) relationship between religiosity and mental health, thus contradicting the negative assertions made by Ellis and others. Not only is there little support for the assertion of a negative relationship between religiosity and mental health, but the research evidence is supportive of a positive relationship. These statistics appear to be much less ambiguous than the 'mixed and even contradictory findings' reported by Gartner, Larson, and Allen (1991: 6). The conclusions based on the analysis of the data in the present study are consistent with the study of Larson *et al.* (1992: 557), which reported a 'positive relationship between religious commitment and mental health' in the 'great majority' of the 139 studies reviewed in the *American Journal of Psychiatry* and the *Archives of General Psychiatry* between the years of 1978 and 1989.

Specific outcomes (1985–95)

This most recent analysis of data (1985–95) indicates that high scores on measures of religiosity (activity, attitude, affiliation, and belief) are facilitative of marital and family stability, adjustment, and personal well-being. This most recent analysis also indicates that those who score high on measures of religiosity (activity, attitude, and belief) show the highest positive correlation with measures of mental health. Also, those who score higher on scales of 'intrinsic' religiosity score better on measures of mental health than those of an 'extrinsic' religious orientation. Allport and Ross (1967) suggest extrinsically religious people use religion as a means of obtaining status while intrinsics live their religious beliefs regardless of external circumstance. Here there also appears to be little difference in measures of mental pathology with respect to religious affiliation.

The 13 per cent of the total studies which indicated negative relationships between religiosity and mental health were observed in a random pattern across various mental health variables. The only possible significant pattern of a negative relationship between religiosity and mental health was observed in the area of prejudice. A possible explanation for this result could be the fact that many religions have strong opinions concerning such issues as alcohol/drug use and abuse, premarital sexual relations, homosexuality, and some gender issues.

The mental health of the Mormons

Of the 540 studies published between the years 1923 and 1995 this author was able to locate 55 studies that dealt specifically with Mormon samples. Of these 55 studies (73 outcomes), 67 per cent of the outcomes indicated a positive relationship between religiosity and mental health variables, 5 per cent negative, and 20 per cent neutral. A comparison of these data is illustrated in Figure 13.4 overleaf.

This overview of research concerning Mormonism and mental health represents responses from over 96,000 Latter-day Saints from a period of years from 1960 to 1995. Religious variables were classified specifically (or in combination) as religious affiliation, activity, attitude, or belief. Mental health variables were defined in terms ranging from anxiety, depression, and schizophrenia to marital satisfaction, self-esteem, and irrational beliefs; a complete list of studies is available from the author. General themes which were observed from an analysis of the data are as follows.

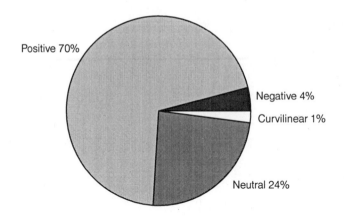

Figure 13.4 Religiosity and mental health: the Mormons

Mormonism and prejudice

Three of the 55 studies focusing on Mormonism and mental health indicated a negative relationship. Two of the three studies reporting negative results were in the areas of dogmatism and social distance. Emery (1992: 1) found that 'Mormons were significantly more dogmatic and more traditional in their attitudes toward women than were Protestants.'

Gender issues

An analysis of this study reveals that two of the specific reasons for Mormons scoring higher on the dogmatism scale than Protestants has to do with Latter-day Saint beliefs concerning women working outside the home and birth control. Leaders of the LDS Church have counseled Mormon couples not to restrict unduly the size of their families and for mothers not to work outside the home except in extenuating circumstances (see Benson, 1987: 1–13). While some claim that the Mormon lifestyle limits women's freedom and happiness, research evidence suggests otherwise.

Johnson *et al.* (1988) examined the impact of women's employment on the marital happiness of 313 Mormon couples. Their study indicated that while Mormon men were happiest when their wives were working full-time, the response from Mormon women was different:

> [For wives] there was a significant difference in global marital happiness with traditional homemakers being the most happy, followed by full-time employed wives. Wives working part time were the least happy. When wives identified themselves as strong Church members and the age of their children was added as a variable, results showed traditional homemakers with preschool children

had higher global marital happiness, consensus, and sexual satisfaction. (1988: 259)

Racial issues

Kunz and Yaw (1989) also used the Borgardus Social Distance Scale to show that Mormons' 'social distance' scores decreased dramatically after a revelation was announced in 1979 extending black members the priesthood on equal basis with whites. Their study also indicated that the decrease in social distance scores was maintained over a ten-year period. These studies support the assertion that 'prejudice' among Mormons is more a matter of theology than bigoted intolerance.

Affiliation and prejudice

Brinkerhoff and Mackie (1986) in a comparative study, found Protestant subjects scored the lowest on the Bogardus Social Distance Scale. Mormons and those reporting 'no affiliation' showed the next lowest social distance scores followed by conservative Christians and then by members of the Catholic faith.

Mormonism and the MMPI

In a previous paper, this author (Judd, 1986) combined and graphically illustrated mean scores from all MMPI research dealing with specific religious denominations. Included in the data set were scores for 2560 Mormons. Tables 13.1 and 13.2 on p. 118, first for males and second for females, contain the mean scores for the denominations surveyed. Inasmuch as the MMPI is normalized separately for males and females, respective summaries are reported.

All MMPI data relative to Mormon samples have been found to be either positive or neutral (see Judd, 1986; Rose, 1986). While Masters *et al.* (1991) reported partially negative results on four of 13 scales, the data were mean change scores which were judged to still be within normal limits. The MMPI scores for all denominations were found to be within normal limits with the exception of the Hare Krishna. One of 13 scales (paranoia) was found to be above average for Hare Krishna females. It is the author's opionion that this may be more a function of small sample size than psychopathology.

Mormonism and depression

In 1858 a writer from *Harper's Weekly* traveled to the state of Utah and made the observation that the Latter-day lifestyle turned Mormon women into

Table 13.1 Mean MMPI scores for respective religious affiliations (male, corrected for K)

Scale	LDS N= 1280	RC 469	Protestant 994	Jews 283	None 105	Krishna 29
Hs	12.5	12.6	12.5	12.6	12.9	12.2
D	17.4	18.9	19.1	20.9	20.6	18.3
Hy	19.7	19.9	19.7	20.7	21.0	21.2
Pd	22.9	22.8	21.9	22.8	23.1	24.5
Mf	25.0	24.9	25.6	27.9	28.6	28.2
Pa	10.5	10.0	10.0	9.8	10.2	9.1
Pt	26.6	27.8	27.4	27.4	27.4	24.5
Sc	25.7	27.7	27.3	27.5	28.7	25.1
Ma	19.8	20.5	20.5	21.0	20.8	21.4
Si	26.5	27.4	27.8	25.5	28.7	21.0
F	4.7	5.2	5.0	5.6	6.7	3.5
L	3.9	3.2	3.2	3.1	3.8	6.8
K	15.2	14.2	13.9	14.3	14.7	19.6

Table 13.2 Mean MMPI scores for respective religious affiliations (female)

Scale N=	LDS 1280	Catholic 469	Protestant 994	Jews 283	None 105	Krishna 29
Hs	13.8	13.5	13.3	13.4	13.6	16.1
D	19.6	20.5	20.2	22.6	23.1	20.5
Hy	22.3	21.3	21.9	22.1	22.7	21.8
Pd	22.4	21.5	21.2	21.7	22.6	23.1
Mf	37.7	36.5	37.3	38.4	39.0	36.5
Pa	10.8	9.9	10.0	9.7	10.9	17.0
Pt	29.6	28.8	28.7	29.0	29.1	25.0
Sc	27.0	27.1	27.0	27.2	30.0	24.5
Ma	19.2	20.3	20.2	20.5	20.7	18.5
Si	24.9	27.7	26.3	26.8	29.1	24.5
F	4.3	4.0	3.9	4.7	6.3	4.2
L	4.3	3.4	3.4	3.6	3.7	7.2
K	15.8	14.5	14.8	14.1	13.9	19.7

'haggard, weary, slatternly women, with lackluster eyes and wan, shapeless faces, hanging listlessly over their gates, or sitting idly in the sunlight, perhaps nursing their yelling babies – all such women looking alike depressed, degraded, miserable, hopeless, soulless' (G. L. Bunker and D. Binton, as cited in Judd, 1987: 150). In 1860, Dr Robert Bartholomew, the assistant surgeon of the United States Army, visited Utah and described Mormon men as having 'an expression of compounded sensuality, cunning suspicion, and a smirking self-conceit' (G. L. Bunker and D. Binton, as cited in Judd, 1987: 150).

While many anecdotal descriptions, such as the one above, and essays (cf. Burgoyne and Burgoyne, 1977) and media specials have discussed the detrimental effects of the Mormon lifestyle on mental health, especially the mental health of Mormon women, few have any grounding in research evidence. None of the studies included in this analysis, that included depression as one of its variables, indicated support for an unhealthy relationship of Mormonism and depression. Masters *et al.* (1991), in a three-year follow-up study of young adult Mormons, reported a three-point increase on the depression scale of the MMPI, but the score of 50 is considered well within normal limits.

Spendlove, West, and Stanish (1984: 491) looked specifically at Mormon women and depression. In a comparison of Mormon and non-Mormon women living in Salt Lake City, Utah, they concluded that 'no difference in the prevalence of depression was noted.' Table 13.3 graphically illustrates some comparisons within the LDS sample:

Table 13.3 Depression in LDS women

Variable	Risk group	% Depressed	Ratio
Employment	Yes	34.3	1.6
	No	20.4	1.2
Church attendance	Infrequent	41.7	2.3
	Frequent	17.8	
Temple attendance	Infrequent	19.0	1.2
	Frequent	29.7	
Prayer	Infrequent	37.5	1.8
	Frequent	20.5	
Mixed marriage	Yes	45.5	2.1
	No	21.5	
Motivation	Extrinsic	34.9	1.8
	Intrinsic	19.0	
Children	2 or less	28.2	1.1
	3 or more	19.4	
Age	>25	34.4	1.1
	<25	20.7	
Life events	>200	29.0	1.0
	<200	22.3	

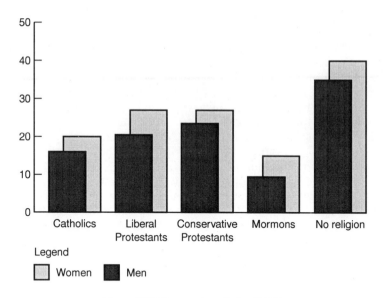

Figure 13.5 Divorces by religion (1985)

In a comparison of 3835 Catholic, Protestant and Mormon University students, Jensen, Jensen, and Wiederhold (1993: 1158) reported that 'Women in the LDS denomination reported less depression than women in the other denominations, but scores for LDS men were similar to those of Catholics and Protestants.'

Mormonism and family life

Fifteen of the 55 studies reviewed in this analysis looked at factors related to the Mormon family. Ten of these 15 studies reported positive scores on scales of marital satisfaction while five indicated neutral results. Wilkinson and Tanner (1980) reported Mormon samples to have positive scores on scales of family affection.

Heaton and Goodman (1985: 343) reported that when compared to those of no religious preference 'Catholics, Protestants, and Mormons are more likely to marry, less likely to divorce, more likely to marry following divorce, and they have larger families.' A comparison between the religious groups revealed that 'Mormons tend to have the highest rate of marriage and fertility, but the lowest rates of divorce.' Note Figure 13.5 for a comparison of Catholics, Protestants, Mormons, and those indicating 'No religious preference' with respect to divorce.

Mormons who marry in a temple ceremony are less likely to divorce than those married outside the temple in a civil ceremony (Thomas, 1983). Heaton (1988) reports that among men and women who were married in

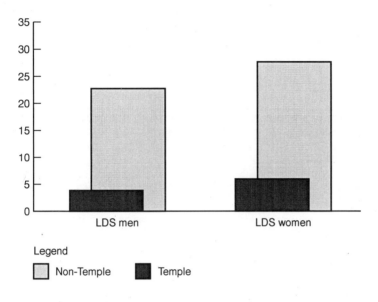

Figure 13.6 Temple marriage and divorce (1985)

the temple, 6 per cent of the men and 7 per cent of the women have been divorced. Among men and women not married in the temple, the data indicate that 28 per cent of the men and 33 per cent of the women had been divorced. Figure 13.6 illustrates the comparison between Mormons married in the temple and Mormons who marry out of the temple who later divorce.

Premarital sex

Miller and others (1987, 1988) found the prevalence of premarital sexual intercourse to be less with Mormon than with non-Mormon teenagers. Beck, Cole, and Hammond (1991) found young adult Mormons, along with young adult Pentecostals and Jehovah's Witnesses, to have the 'lowest likelihoods of premarital sex' when compared with mainline Protestant youth.

Delinquency

Chadwick and Top (1993: 51) found Mormon religiosity to be a significant deterrent to delinquency. Interestingly, this statistic held true for Latter-day Saint youth even when they were not in a 'highly religious climate.' In this study, religiosity was measured in terms of belief, attitude, and activity while delinquency was measured in terms of 'acts against others,' 'victimless delinquency behavior' (i.e. premarital sex), and 'delinquency against property' (ibid.: 57).

Mormonism and substance abuse

Of the 55 studies in this review, seven dealt with religiosity and substance abuse. Of these seven studies, four concluded that Mormon belief, attitude or activity contributed to lower rates of substance abuse than among non-Mormons. The remaining three of the seven studies indicated no significant relationship between Mormonism and substance abuse. Hawks and Bahr (1992: 1) concluded that 'for all religions except Jews, a lower percentage of Utahns [Mormons living in Utah] used alcohol than their national counterparts.' Figure 13.7 is a summarization of these data.

While Mormons differed from their religious counterparts in the use of alcohol, they did not differ in the quantity of alcohol consumed if they did drink.

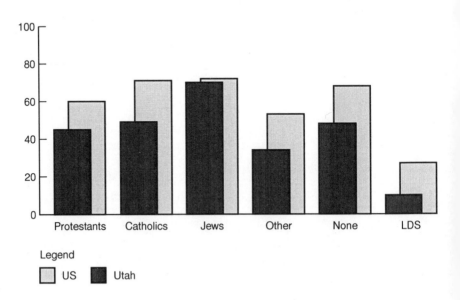

Figure 13.7 Adult use of alcohol by religion (1992)

Mormonism and well-being

Nine of the 55 studies dealing with Mormonism and mental health focused on various dimensions of well-being (six positive outcomes/three neutral). Ellison (1991: 80) reports that 'individuals with strong religious faith report higher levels of life satisfaction, greater personal happiness, and fewer negative psychosocial consequences of traumatic life events.' Denominational comparisons suggest Protestants, Jehovah's Witnesses and Mormons report greater 'life satisfaction than do their non-affiliated counterparts' (ibid.). Ellison also reports that religious faith appears to buffer the negative effects of trauma on well-being.

Duke and Johnson (1981b: 16) compared Mormon and national samples and concluded that 'Mormon respondents, on the whole, have a higher level of overall happiness than the American populace.' Within the Mormon sample, Duke and Johnson (ibid.: 23) noted that 'the greater the religiosity the greater the happiness.' The measures of religiosity which best demonstrated their conclusion were the 'beatitudes factor' (a measure of virtues like patience, kindness, etc.) and the factor they termed 'knowledge of the scriptures.'

Conclusions

This study has provided a brief overview of research concerning the relationship of religion and mental health from 1923 to 1995. Specifically, this study has focused on the mental health of the members of the Church of Jesus Christ of Latter-day Saints. General analysis of the studies for the relationship of mental health with religion in general and Mormonism in particular supports the following conclusions:

1. There is little support for the assertion that religiosity is antithetical to mental health. This conclusion holds true for non-Mormon as well as Mormon samples.

2. The data indicated that individuals who live their lives consistent with their religious beliefs experience greater general well-being, marital and family stability, and less delinquency, depression, anxiety, and substance abuse.

3. There are few differences in measures of mental pathology with respect to religious affiliation.

4. There exists a change in the number of positive and negative studies over time. Earlier studies show a greater incidence of negative studies while more recent studies report more positive relationships.

5. While a positive trend is noted, there are still some studies where negative results are reported. While some of these negative outcomes can indeed be a result of research bias, there is such a phenomenon as unhealthy forms of religious devotion. More research needs to be done identifying healthy and unhealthy forms of religious devotion.

Though the author recognizes the importance of objectivity, he is enthused with the most recent (1985–95) findings supporting a positive relationship between religiosity and mental health. The author concurs with James (1929: 516–17):

> We and God have business with each other; and in opening ourselves to His influence our deepest destiny is fulfilled. The universe, and those parts of it which our personal being constitutes, takes a turn genuinely for the worse or the better in proportion as each one of us fulfills or evades God's commands.

14 Commitment making
Mate selection processes among active Mormon American couples

Thomas B. Holman

A number of scholars have discussed Mormons' assimilation to the larger culture (Mauss, 1994; Heaton, Goodman, and Holman, 1994). Indeed, in many respects, American Mormons appear to be little different from other Americans, but as Heaton *et al.* point out, such comparisons may be inappropriate because of the unique meanings Mormons may attach to some aspects of social life and because religiously active Mormons may be different from inactive Mormons.

Two questions were addressed in this research. First, how do members of a minority religious group, a group with strongly held teachings about marriage, family life, and sexuality, move through the mate selection process? Further, where do these active Mormon young adults adapt to normative American mate selection processes, and where and how do they add uniquely Mormon notions to the process?

What emerged from my analysis of the data was what I have called a process of 'commitment making.' This category describes a fundamental part of an active Mormon's world-view, and demonstrates a fundamental difference between active Mormons and most non-Mormons and inactive Mormons.

The Mormon context for mate selection

Mormonism has a number of distinctive emphases, and some unique doctrines and practices, as compared with mainstream Christianity. Several of these relate to the area of interest here, mate selection processes.

A marriage performed in Mormon temples is a sacred event and is reserved only for religiously active couples. The ceremony centers on covenants the couple make with God and the promises God extends to the couple. The most important promise that couples receive is the assurance that if they keep their covenants with God they are sealed together for time and eternity, to become 'kings and queens and priests and priestesses to the Lord' to reign with Him in His kingdom forever (Taylor, 1987).

Temple marriage is taught in church classes, over the pulpit, and even prayed for by parents and children in family settings. Children are raised knowing that marriage in the temple is a critical and expected part of being a Mormon, but not all nine million Mormons marry in the temple or participate fully in Mormonism. Mormons often divide themselves into the categories 'active' and 'inactive.' Active Mormons are those who observe 'a full religious lifestyle of attendance, devotion, service, and learning' (Cunningham, 1992). Active Mormons also believe in and practice sexual abstinence except in heterosexual marriage. This means that one of the issues an active Mormon has to deal with is the wider American culture, given that some normative American practices of individuals in the mate selection stage seem to contradict the expected behaviors of active Mormons in this stage.

The mate selection process in American culture

Mate selection is generally viewed as a developmental process involving ever greater interpersonal interdependency. For most Americans, mate selection follows a predictable process of acquaintance, build-up and continuation leading to legal marriage (Levinger, 1983). This process is characterized by personal choice based on mutual physical attraction, growing interpersonal involvement, and interdependence, followed by commitment to marriage and actual marriage during the period of greatest relationship satisfaction (Cate and Loyd, 1992). This happens within the changing social context of late twentieth-century America. Some of the demographic trends characterizing the mate selection process at this time are a postponement of marriage, almost universal premarital sexual intimacy, and heterosexual cohabitation by many, if not most, couples (Surra, 1990; Whyte, 1991).

My purpose in this study was to understand how being an active Mormon 'played out' in the mate selection process in late twentieth-century America. More specifically, I wanted to investigate the heterosexual mate selection process of active Mormon young adults to see if they generally conform to the typical American model or if they deviate in uniquely Mormon ways.

Method

Data were derived from a longitudinal study of 56 Mormon couples over a nine-year period. The couples were contacted at three points in their relationship and asked to complete survey questionnaires, before marriage, at one year of marriage, and at eight years of marriage. In-depth interviews done with the participants at the eight-year mark were the primary data analyzed in this study. The analysis was primarily qualitative.

The informants were all never-married young adults when they completed an initial survey in 1978–79. All 112 were members of the Mormon Church and by most standards would be considered active members. Their average age was 21 years with a range of 18 to 26. All 56 couples were married in an LDS temple where they were sealed to one another for eternity.

The interview data were collected by me in the summer of 1987. The couples knew I was a professor at Brigham Young University and an active Mormon. This knowledge may have allowed the couples to speak freely and easily about their religion, using Mormon terminology. Conversely, that knowledge of my professional affiliation and personal orthodoxy may have stifled criticism of LDS doctrine or leaders.

Results

The most fundamental conclusion of my research is that active Mormon young adults travel this developmental path to marriage in ways that are both very American and uniquely Mormon. Furthermore, it is my contention that the unique Mormon twists to the mate selection process are indicators of a way of being and a way of thinking about the world, about the meaning of life, and about who they are and can become that is part and parcel of Mormon identity.

Like other young Americans, these religiously active Latter-day Saint young adults develop heterosexual relationships that culminate in marriage much as contemporary models suggest they would. There is a period of initial acquaintance, followed by increasing interaction and interdependence, and then a deepening connection that leads to the commitment of marriage. However, each phase is uniquely Mormon in ways that affect how they progress through the phase and what constitutes transition into another phase. Most importantly, how they constructed the process demonstrates aspects of their underlying world-view. The conceptual label I have chosen to describe what they do is *commitment making*. They tended to see themselves as continuing in and embedded in a long-term process of making commitments. Because of their shared value of commitment to marriage, these Mormon couples understand the process differently than do many other Americans. They see themselves in the process of making a commitment, not simply or even primarily in the process of assessing compatibility. For these couples it was not a matter of needing to get to know each other better, but rather a matter of being committed to marriage. One wife put it this way:

> Every person carries things that you are not going to know about them until you get married . . . If you want to prepare you prepare yourself that you are going to have a few surprises and accept that. But the key thing is that you love the person and you are committed; committed that you are going to make it work.

The sense of commitment making is demonstrated in who they include in their field of eligibles, what traits they are looking for in a mate, how they conduct the courtship and engagement, the criteria they use to decide finally to marry a particular person, and the stability of the resultant marriages.

Desired traits and initial attraction

When asked what they were looking for in a mate, every person mentioned that the prospective mate had to be a devoted member of the LDS church. One husband put it this way:

> First and foremost, they had to be LDS, which really means that they had to be LDS and had to be a strong member with a testimony and were active.

Most of the other traits mentioned by both men and women were phrased in terms of Mormon ideals including home, parenthood, and family, rather than in terms of their individual needs. There was little mention of wanting someone who would respect their autonomy, not interfere with their career aspirations, or provide need gratification. In fact, when asked what needs the partner had filled the majority had trouble answering the question, as if they had never thought about the process that way.

Physical attractiveness, which is so prominent in American courtship, certainly entered in and was often mentioned. It was a particularly important initial attractor for the males. However, physical attraction was generally seen as less important than the above mentioned traits. For example:

> I wanted someone with a good sense of humour and someone that was strong in the Church and liked sports and physical activities. Reasonably good looking I guess. Physical appearance would figure in there somewhere.

One husband summed up the importance of church and other traits such as physical attractiveness succinctly:

> The only thing really was that I wanted to marry a girl who was an active member of the Church who I liked. I got both of those.

Rapidity of movement

The most prominent feature of the build-up phase for these active Mormons was the rapidity of movement from acquaintance to a commitment to marriage. The time between first acquaintance and engagement was as short as two weeks and seldom more than four or five months. The mean length of engagement was five months, the modal month being four (41 per cent).

Reasons for rapidity of movement

This raises an interesting question: given the importance of the decision, that the marriage was to be eternal, why do they have such short courtships and engagements? The couples gave several reasons why they moved so quickly. First, they were ready and they were tired of playing the dating game. 'I felt ready. I didn't want to go and play the dating game for a long time. I wanted to settle down and have a more permanent type of thing.' Another couple said: 'We were both ready to get married. We were dating to marry.'

Another reason for the short acquaintance to marriage period was certainly related to the goal of sexual abstinence before marriage. A long courtship or engagement is 'a longer time for temptation.' As one young man stated about their four-month engagement:

> Any longer than that would be hard, because frankly, when you're 22 years old you have waited a long time to have sex and you are a little rambunctious!

Since within the Mormon context being together has eternal significance and requires moral purity, the couples could not, or at least would not, cohabit, so marriage was the natural thing to do.

Lastly, most of the couples received almost immediate parental support and even active encouragement to move along briskly. Note one son's recollection of a conversation with his parents:

> My parents talked to me and they wanted to know my intentions and I told them that I would like to get married but I could never do it because we will starve to death . . . so they talked to me and said that if I was in love I should get married and that things would work out.

Another son recalls his mother's reaction:

> I called her [his mom] up and said 'I'm going to marry Cheryl' and she said 'Great, I think you're supposed to marry her. Get going.'

Those parents who were concerned were usually concerned about their daughters' young age, but even these parents, except in one case, did not fight hard against the marriage.

Evaluation of rapidity of movement

Because the interviews were conducted at about eight years into marriage, I was able to ask the couples to evaluate the shortness of the mate selection process. Looking back, most of the respondents felt the process was about right. A few felt the process was too long. Only one individual said that the whole process was too short, and that was one of the wives who ended up getting a divorce. The ex-husband, however, did not believe that a longer courtship or engagement would have made any difference. Furthermore, only two, less than 4 per cent, of the 56 marriages had ended in divorce. The rapidity of movement did not appear to set them up for unstable marriages.

Individual choice

Like other Americans, the decision to marry was clearly an individual one. Parents, friends, and others may be consulted, although they frequently are not, but the decision of who to date, whether to continue the relationship, and whether to marry the partner is made by the individual, not by a parent, matchmaker, or other member of society. Interestingly, while parents were occasionally concerned about the timing of a marriage, no parents expressed concern in not being consulted about who to date, nor were they concerned about their young child having the right to make the choice of who to marry. Thus, these parents and young adult children seem very American, accepting the contemporary norm of personal choice.

This is especially interesting given the monumental nature of the decision. For active Mormons, the eternal family is not a nuclear family, but a generational family stretching eternally into the past and the future. Yet these young adults' parents did not feel they should have a major say in who was dated and who was married.

Again, this sounds very twentieth-century American. But it also conforms to LDS theology. In LDS theology the doctrine of agency is fundamental. Agency implies that each person has a God-given right and ability to choose good or evil. Furthermore, attempts to obstruct or prevent the exercise of this moral agency are to be resisted. Thus, parents understand that this choice is the right and responsibility of their offspring.

However, there is a clear expectation that one should seek spiritual input, indeed confirmation, of one's choice. Here we see the unique twist active Mormons add to the concept of personal choice. One can and should make the choice of an eternal companion. Parents, friends, and church leaders can be, and frequently are, consulted, but it is primarily a personal choice. However, the personal choice should be confirmed by a 'spiritual manifestation' of the rightness of the choice. These confirmations vary widely by individual.

Spiritual confirmation

Most couples talked of having received a spiritual confirmation from God about the marriage. One wife discussed the importance of receiving this kind of confirmation:

I know that I would never, never have gotten married had I not really strongly felt that that was what Heavenly Father knew was the right thing for me. So I think that really helped a lot and when you are thinking about eternity you really can't make that decision without help. At least I couldn't.

An important aspect of the confirmation was the anchor it provided in times of trouble:

He was talking about what he wanted to do with his life and I felt like . . . I had this feeling come over me that I wanted to be part of it and from there I felt like it was right, even though I had my ups and downs. I relied a lot on that feeling when I had questions or doubts.

In fact, the confirmation aspect of an active Mormon's mate selection process led, on occasion, to commitment to marriage before there was a strong physical attraction or a sense of being in love.

It just kind of came over both of us [that we should get married], that was the thing that happened, and all we needed to do was work on it, our emotional feelings towards each other.

This reminds one of what Levinger (1983) called the 'commitment before personal involvement' that characterized arranged marriages. Here again, however, the Mormons add a unique spin to the idea of commitment before extensive interpersonal involvement, the 'arrangement' is done by God, not by parents or some other societal agent.

The importance of commitment making

The importance of a commitment making view of life is illustrated even by the one divorced couple I interviewed. The wife had only been a member of the Mormon Church for one year when they married and was, in her words, 'real green' when it came to understanding LDS teachings. As the husband said:

I had thought, naively I guess, that someone who accepts the church will [accept and] live its principle and I guess I always had a feeling that problems can always be worked out. So I kind of glossed over [her commitment to LDS values]. The thought didn't enter my mind that she didn't have that kind of commitment.

That she had not internalized the value of commitment to marriage above individual need fulfillment is clear in her statement:

I think now looking back, I think that I should have come back and we should have gone through marriage counseling or whatever. I don't think I fought to keep the marriage together . . . And I think if I had come back and said to Stephen, this is what had happened, this is what . . . how I'm feeling. If I came home, I want to go to school. I want to do things, I need this. Then he would have realized the importance of it. Then it would have been different . . . I gave up so easily . . . I remember thinking that I was so young and that I was missing out on so many things, not so much men, just things . . . and so I think I should have come back.

Discussion

Certainly my informants do not represent all the varieties of courtship and engagement patterns possible among religiously active LDS young adults. For one thing, most of them were attending Brigham Young University at the time they met and were therefore in the highest concentration of active LDS young adults in the world.

But what I have noted is the unique ways these active Mormons manage and navigate the American courtship process. They are embedded in a cultural context that allows mate selection options antithetical to some of the basic tenets of Mormonism. Despite these American cultural versus Mormon sub-cultural differences, most were able to navigate a course that has resulted in stable, meaningful, fulfilling long-term relationships.

Thus, while these Latter-day Saint young adults were very American, and a simple checklist or survey of perceived attitudes that did not allow the meaning of the events to be expressed might suggest great similarity to other Americans, my findings imply that active Mormons are indeed different. This difference is a core, fundamental paradigmatic difference. The world-view of these LDS young adults is fundamentally different from most of their American peers. An aspect of this world-view that emerged was a sense of commitment making. This commitment making was a process that had begun in childhood as they were instructed in the importance of temple marriage and the eternal family. Making commitments is core to what it means to be a believing Mormon and the mate selection process demonstrates the salience of this core process to Latter-day Saints. It affects every aspect of the mate selection process, from what kind of person they look for, what they think of as necessary traits in a mate, how they proceed through courtship and engagement, how they finally decide whom to marry, and how important and final they perceive that decision to be.

Note

This research was supported by grants from the College of Family, Home and Social Sciences and the Women's Research Institute, both at Brigham Young University.

Part IV
Early Mormonism

15 Mormons and the millennial world-view

Grant Underwood

Scholars tell us that millennialism was a later, predominantly Christian, development growing out of Jewish apocalypticism (Hanson, 1979; Kromminga, 1945; Ball, 1975; Oliver, 1978). Its novelty was the expectation of a future 'golden age' on earth *before* the final, apocalyptic transformation at the end of time. As various versions of the millennial dream developed over the centuries, some retained the vivid and dramatic spirit of their eschatological progenitor, lashing out against contemporary society and promising imminent vindication for the beleaguered faithful. Others drifted toward a more irenic view of the world around them and interpreted the prophecies figuratively. By the nineteenth century, there were basically two rival millennial visions of the future. What is often labeled 'postmillennialism' constituted one approach. What most accurately should be called 'millenarian apocalypticism,' but more commonly is simply designated 'millenarianism' or 'premillennialism' (the two are used interchangeably), represented the other.

Simplistic differentiations about whether Christ will come before (pre-) or after (post-) the millennium are hardly sufficient to distinguish these two schools of thought. 'The distinctions involve a great deal more than the time of Christ's return,' explained historian Robert Clouse (1977: 7):

> The kingdom expected by the premillennialist is quite different from the kingdom anticipated by the postmillennialist, not only with respect to the time and manner in which it will be established but also in regard to its nature and the way Christ will exercise control over it.

As the prefix implies, however, the postmillennialists felt that these events would conclude the millennium, that is, that there would be only one general resurrection of all mankind and one Day of Judgment, and that both would coincide with Christ's return to earth at the end of the thousand years.

On the other hand, premillennialists believed that there would be *two* comings, two physical resurrections, and two judgments. The first resurrection would occur at the time of Christ's premillennial advent and would involve only the faithful dead. The rest of humanity would come forth after the millennium as the second resurrection. Like their postmillennialist counterparts, millenarians believed that Christ would come after the millennium to execute Final Judgment, but they also felt that there would be a kind of preliminary judgment, primarily the destruction of the wicked, that would accompany his appearance to inaugurate the millennium. On these matters, Mormon millennial views coincide with premillennialism.

Regarding the nature of the millennium itself, the most helpful distinction to make pertains to the way in which each group approached the interpretation of scripture. 'As a general rule,' premillennialists were 'literalists [who] stressed the discontinuities between the [present] world and the future,' while postmillennialists were 'allegorists' who emphasized 'the continuities, with respect to both the means of change and the result of change' (Oliver, 1978: 18–19). This distinction was plainly manifest in their differing perceptions of the millennial age. For the millenarian, the lamb really would lie down with the lion, immortal beings really would mingle freely with mortals, and Christ indeed would reign personally over the earth from some terrestrial capital. To all of these prophetic promises the postmillennialists gave a spiritualized interpretation. The scene of the lamb and the lion was just a pastoral metaphor to describe an age of peace and cooperation; the resurrection was the process of burying the old sinful self and 'rising' to a new spiritual life in Christ; and it was Christ's spirit, not his body, that would do the reigning during the millennium. One scholar has observed, 'The premillennialists are clearly closer to the meaning of the texts both accepted . . . Pre-millennialism is the basic stance; postmillennialism a compromise in the form of a metaphor' (ibid.: 21). As will be shown, Latter-day Saints tended to approach the prophecies quite literally and, therefore, articulated a view of the millennium consistent with premillennialism.

In the 1800s, however, postmillennialism reigned supreme. For the first three-quarters of the century, postmillennialism 'dominated the popular denominational magazines as well as the weighty theological quarterlies,' and 'it commanded allegiance in leading seminaries and pulpits alike' (Moorhead, 1984: 524–42). Thus was the eschatology of the nineteenth-century revivals collectively designated the Second Great Awakening, and of the various religious reform organizations sometimes known as the 'Benevolent Empire.'

Still, not everyone shared this vision of a rapidly Christianizing America, and the premillennial Mormons were among them. The Saints acknowledged the impressive impetus to evangelical activity that postmillennialism provided their contemporaries, but felt it was misguided. One Church leader wrote:

> Many are flattering themselves with the expectation that all the world is going to be converted, and . . . thus the great millennium, in their opinion, is to be established. Vain, delusive expectation! The Savior said to his disciples, explained one apostle, that 'as it was in the days of Noah, so shall it be also in the days of the coming of the Son of Man.' Query. Were all the people converted

in the days of Noah, or mostly destroyed?

In short, wrote another, 'The ignorance of the religious teachers of the day never appeared more glaring in any thing, than in an attempt to create a Millennium by converting this generation.'[1] Only a relative handful were expected to respond to the restored (Mormon) gospel prior to the millennium, and though they would be drawn from all the peoples of the earth, prophecy taught them that relative to the domain of worldliness, the Saints' 'dominions' would be 'small' 'upon the face of the earth' (1 Nephi 14:12).

On the other hand, the Saints also had their quibbles with standard premillennialism. Responding to a series of articles written by premillennialist Samuel McCorkle for Alexander Campbell's *Millennial Harbinger*, Sidney Rigdon, Joseph Smith's 'Aaron,' remarked:

> what a difference between a man of God, and a self authorized and self constituted messenger! The man of God will no sooner cry, Destruction, desolation, and judgment than he will tell them of an ark, a Zoar, a Palla, a Mount Zion, a Jerusalem, or some other place which God has provided for them who will hear his voice. But Mr. M'Corkle, like every other messenger that God has never sent [and like standard premillennialism], can cry, Destruction, desolation, fire, and judgment, and write very ingeniously about it, but there it ends. (*Star*, January 1834: 126)

It served little purpose in Rigdon's mind to proclaim a message of doom and gloom and then offer 'no way for escape! no hiding place! no city of refuge!' (ibid.).

Here was what was distinctive about Mormon premillennialism. Similar to how the doctrine of the 'rapture' would come to function for Darbyite dispensationalists in later decades, the Mormon doctrine of the 'gathering' served to provide a means of escape from much of the anticipated tribulation of the last days (Sandeen, 1970; Weber, 1979). At the same time, it produced a concentration of Saints who could be properly prepared for the coming of the Lord. The call to gather to a wilderness Zion where the Saints could establish the Kingdom as a sort of prelibation of paradise was compelling indeed, especially for English converts. Typical premillennialists might be hard put to know how best to wait in patience and purity for the coming of the Lord, but with Mormonism they could think they were actively preparing for the Advent if they paid their money and took passage to America. The gathering '[added] to the disembodied outline of the millennial dream the firm contours of America, the fresh start, the second chance, the new society. No British prophet,' wrote W. H. Oliver, 'produced a millennial vision as complete, as compelling, or as concrete as Joseph Smith's' and none 'enjoyed a success comparable to that of the Mormons' (1978: 238).

The gathering also involved more than just European and American converts. The end times were to be Israel's great day. In fact, the gathering and restoration of Israel was a prerequisite to the Savior's return. In order to be restored, though, Israel would first have to be identified. Through revelation to the Prophet Joseph Smith it was learned that not only were the Jews and the lost Ten Tribes of the Israelite race, but so were the American Indians.

The Saints' literalist hermeneutics helped them to discern in scripture two basic places of gathering. Isaiah 24:23 speaks of a day 'when the Lord of hosts shall reign in mount Zion, and in Jerusalem, and before his ancients gloriously.' Edward Partridge, the first Bishop of the Church, was typical of Latter-day Saints in his exegesis of this passage when he commented: 'Thus we see that the Lord is not only to reign in Jerusalem, but in mount Zion, also, which shows that Jerusalem and Zion are two places' (*Messenger and Advocate* 1, January 1835: 57). Isaiah 2:3 announces that 'out of Zion shall go forth the law, and the word of the Lord from Jerusalem.' Joseph Smith interpreted 'Zion' and 'Jerusalem' as two *different* places, rather than viewing the passage as a manifestation of Hebrew poetic parallelism which would make the terms synonymous. This meant that nearly every mention of Zion in Old Testament prophecy was understood as having reference to the New, for which we may read 'other,' Jerusalem to be built in America. Thus, the Saints believed that Zion and Jerusalem were two distinct holy cities located in two distinct hemispheres.

'Zion' was the designated gathering spot for Euro-American converts and their Indian neighbors, while Jerusalem was for the Jews. Understandably, most LDS interest focused on the American gathering place, Zion. Since an American Israel had been identified for gathering, Advent-anxious Saints did not have to wait, as did other Christian millenarians, for dramatic happenings within world Jewry in order to witness the restoration of Israel. Rather, they were able to see in their own missionary labors among the Native Americans, as well as in the US government's Indian-removal policies of the 1830s, Gentile 'nursing fathers' at work gathering the Lord's covenant people. Even more immediate was their own need, as part of Israel also, to gather to Zion.

In 1833, Joseph Smith composed his first description of the LDS faith for public consumption in a letter to the *American Revivalist and Rochester Observer*. The doctrine of the gathering was central. Referring to Isaiah 11:11, Smith announced that:

> the time has at last arrived when the God of Abraham of Isaac and of Jacob has set his hand again the second time to recover the remnants of his people which have been left from Assyria, and from Egypt and from Pathros &c. and from the Islands of the Sea and with them to bring in the fullness of the Gentiles and establish that covenant with them which was promised when their sins should be taken away. (Jessee, 1984: 271)

With the gathering and the restoration of Israel underway, there were only two choices: to join the Church and gather to Zion: or to face certain and imminent destruction. As the Prophet expressed it: 'Repent ye Repent ye, and embrace the everlasting Covenant and flee to Zion before the overflowing scourge [alluding to Isaiah 28:15, 18] overtake you' (ibid.: 274).

Because the Day of the Lord, as a day of judgment, was at hand, the elders were to traverse the earth to warn the wicked and gather the elect, preaching 'nothing but repentance,' for truly it was 'a day of warning, and not a day of many words' (D&C 63:58).

Elder Freeman Nickerson's proclamation to the Bostonians, as recorded in *Times and Seasons* (3, May 1842: 798), the LDS periodical in Nauvoo, Illinois, is typical:

> I request the citizens and authorities of the city of Boston to open a house for the servant of the people, that the Lord hath sent to this city to warn the people of the destruction which will take place in this generation, that is now on the earth, and teach them how they may escape, and come through and abide the day of the second coming of Christ to reign on the earth a thousand years.

Though neither Joseph Smith nor his followers were given to date-setting, many of their expressions evidence an acute expectation of the impending Advent. The early years were heady times for the Saints. Revelations were announced at a breathtaking rate, many of which contained expressions that the Lord would 'come quickly' and that his return was 'nigh' or 'at hand.'[2] Many Saints were told in prayers pronounced upon them that they would live to see the Savior come or build the New Jerusalem or that they would live to participate in other end-time activities. In short, the drama of unfolding events convinced many Mormons that they were living in the shadow of the Second Coming.

If their views about the last days and the inauguration of the millennium place them in the premillennial camp, so did their ideas about the nature of the millennium. Contrary to popular postmillennialist notions of Christ reigning in the hearts of the regenerate, early Latter-day Saints looked forward to the day when the 'King of Kings' would physically reign as supreme terrestrial monarch. 'Not,' remarked Rigdon, 'as some have said, a spiritual (which might be more properly called imaginary) reign; but literal, and personal, as much so as David's reign over Israel, or the reign of any king on earth.'

Especially gratifying was to be the Saints' millennial co-regency with Christ. Early Mormons basked in John's promise of being made 'kings and priests' to rule and reign with Christ during the thousand years.[3] Toward the end of his life, Joseph Smith began stressing the eternal implications of this concept, but before that, the Saints projected all their enthusiasm and expectations for the afterlife on the millennium, rather than on the far-off future state. It was the millennium, not 'heaven' to which the editor of the *Messenger and Advocate* (3, April 1837: 482) was referring when he wrote: 'The sure promise of such ravishing bliss enabled the Saints anciently to endure such great tribulations ... with more than manly fortitude.' Whereas modern Mormons anxiously await the day in which they will be crowned with an inheritance in the 'Celestial Kingdom,' early Saints longed for their millennial inheritance. For them, the millennium was the anticipated day of triumph and glory.

And it was to be Paradise regained. The link between primordium and millennium, between primitivism and millennialism, is well illustrated in Mormonism. An early Mormon apostle and publicist, Parley Pratt, wrote:

> Now we can never understand precisely what is meant by restoration unless we understand what is lost or taken away . . . First, then, it becomes necessary for us to take a view of creation, as it rolled in purity from the hand of its creator, and if we can discover the true state in which it then existed, and understand the changes that have taken place since, then we shall be able to understand what is to be restored. (1837: 89)

Put succinctly, the earth would be 'renewed and receive its paradisiacal glory' (Pearl of Great Price, 1989 edn: 61). Therefore, Pratt explained, 'man and beast' will become 'perfectly harmless, as they were in the beginning, and feed on vegetable food only' (1837: 160) and the earth will become again like it was before it was divided, with continental landmasses united to become a sort of millennial Pangaea. In the end, renewing the earth to its paradisiacal glory would take longer than enthusiastic Latter-day Saints first expected. Nonetheless, it is impossible to understand the dynamics of early Mormonism without acknowledging the pervasive way in which millenarianism helped the Saints to make sense of the world around them and their place in it.

A proper consideration of Mormon millenarianism would be incomplete without updating the story from the early period. One of the great themes in modern religious history has been the confrontation with modernity, suggesting the importance of exploring the relationship between modernity and millenarianism within the Mormon community. At the outset, it is important to distinguish institutional and intellectual modernization. The former has been described as the 'permeation of religious institutions by techniques and procedures developed in other sectors of [modern] society' that seem institutionally advantageous yet intellectually innocuous (Wilson, 1988: 17–22). From statistical reports and time management to telecommunications and computerization, from the bureaucratic rationalism symbolized by its now insufficient 26-storey headquarters building to its public relations typified by BYU athletics and the Mormon Tabernacle Choir, Mormonism, as an institution, has taken on the coloration of modernity.[4]

When it comes to the world of thought, to beliefs and values, however, modernity has been met with a different mind-set. In important ways, this has been due to the mutually reinforcing persistence of millenarianism and primitivism which stand in opposition to modernism. Two important dimensions of modernism are particularly contested: secularism and the emergence of 'scientific' history. 'Modernization is in many ways a secularizing process,' writes Peter Williams, 'and generally results in what we might call the "desacralization" of the world.' Its impact on religion is that 'the role of the supernatural as a direct, tangible force is downplayed considerably' (1980: 12). A second and related ramification is that a sense of profane time supplants the mythic realm of sacred time (Eliade, 1954, 1957, 1963; Segal, 1978: 159). Catholic historian John Dwyer has noted that 'the subjection of man to [non-mythical] history is the insight which, more than any other, characterizes the modern age' (1985: 352). Such subjection, however, is precisely what is absent in the 'historylessness' of primitivism and millenarianism. While the more celebrated clashes between modernism and traditionalism have dealt with conceptions of creation, compared to the social sciences, the challenge presented by the physical sciences has been 'relatively mild' (Berger, 1969: 39–40). Notions of doctrinal rather than biological evolution, and of cultural and ethical relativism have been far more threatening to primitivist millenarians (Garrison, 1988).

Latter-day Saints have responded, and continue to respond, to these influences in much the same way that conservative religionists do generally, by rejecting them for a universe thoroughly grounded in absolutes and the supernatural. As much as any other factor, what makes this possible for Mormons today is their core conviction that they are led by a living prophet and living apostles. Admittedly, their modern Moses may be dressed in a three-piece suit, but he still provides a symbolic connection with the mythic world of the sacred past. Through a living prophet and continuing revelation, Mormonism is prepared to respond to change without succumbing to desacralization. The overarching issue from the LDS perspective is not whether the church is abandoning traditional ways for modern ideas, but whether God's hand is in it.

While current prophets may theoretically supersede their predecessors, ancient or modern, in reality they are restrained by a primitivist respect for an additional primordium, the corpus of modern prophetic pronouncement. The speeches and writings of apostles and prophets throughout the history of the church provide a large body of material generally regarded as on par with Scripture. Where particular comments stray too far, their non-canonical status can be invoked, but by and large Latter-day Saints, leader and layman alike, are as loath to contradict what an apostle in the 1800s declared as they are to challenge the writings of Paul.

Thus, the millenarianism of earlier years tends to be preserved by respect for previous prophetic declarations. During the 1980s, LDS apostle and theologian Bruce R. McConkie published the longest work ever written by a Latter-day Saint on eschatological matters. What is striking is how little McConkie's millennial treatise differs from those written during Mormonism's first generation. The same supernatural biological and geological changes anticipated then are expected today, including the abolishment of infant mortality, the herbivorization of carnivores, the unification of continental landmasses, and the commingling of mortals and resurrected immortals. That such views seemed plausible in the early nineteenth century is perhaps not surprising. That they are still maintained today provides dramatic testimony of the degree to which LDS millenarianism in particular and Mormonism in general have resisted the encroachments of modernity.

The pendulum, however, should not be swung too far in the opposite

direction. A study of leaders' discourses at the Church's general conferences over the past 150 years reveals that millenarian rhetoric 'diminished
drastically after 1920.' Thus, 'even though an apocalyptic scenario of the
last days is still a central Mormon doctrine, it is no longer enunciated by
modern conference speakers with anything like the emphatic fervor of
nineteenth-century leaders' (Shepherd and Shepherd, 1984: 196). Though
Latter-day Saints still talk about the end times, for many Mormons these
doctrines have a detached and textbookish quality. The social ramifications
of their eschatology are rarely if ever discussed today, and soteriological
dualism is disparaged. The term 'wicked,' for instance, no longer refers to
all unbelievers. Today, it is applied only to the morally corrupt, and the
good and honorable of all religions are expected to be alive during the
millennium. As people make their peace with the world, the apocalyptic
dream of the 'great reversal' diminishes. In short, the more abrasive
features of millenarianism which served their needs in an earlier period
have been quietly, perhaps unwittingly, laid aside in recent years.

Still, on the eve of the twenty-first century, though Mormonism has
acquired the institutional accouterments of modernization, it remains intellectually insulated from the acids of modernity by an essential core of
supernaturalism. It has gone far towards modernizing without becoming
secularized. Key is the LDS conviction of continuing revelation.
Primitivism produced living prophets and, in turn, has been preserved by
them. So has millenarianism. But the door is always open to change.
Shrouded in the 'sacred canopy' of modern revelation, Mormons are free
to pick and choose their way into modernity. Inspired guidance from living
prophets gives them the confidence to feel that they can truly live 'in' the
modern world and yet be 'of' it only to a degree not harmful to their sacred
enterprise. Whichever path they are counseled to pursue, Latter-day Saints
continue to expect that it will lead them to an actual thousand years of
paradisiacal peace and prosperity which they call 'the millennium.'

Notes

1. *Star*, 2, June 1834: 163. The *Star* (full title *The Evening and Morning Star*) was the
   first LDS periodical.
2. The phrase 'come quickly' is found in D&C 33:18, 34:12, 35:27, 41:4, 49:28, 51:20,
   54:10, 68:35, 87:8, 88:126, 99:5, 112:34. Expressions that the end is 'nigh' or 'at
   hand' can be found in D&C 1:12, 1:35, 29:9–10, 33:10, 34:7, 35:15–16, 35:26,
   39:19, 39:21, 42:7, 43:17, 45:37–39, 49:6, 58:4, 63:53, 104:59, 106:4, 128:24, 133:17.
3. The scriptural reference is Rev 5:9–12. Some examples of their exegesis of this
   passage include *Star*, 1, June 1832: 8; 2, April 1834: 146; Pratt (1837): 85. A more
   developed understanding of this promise came during the early 1840s when the
   LDS temple liturgy known as 'the endowment' was first revealed. See Ehat
   (1982); Buerger (1987).
4. For twentieth-century Mormonism, see Alexander (1986b); Shepherd and
   Shepherd (1984); Cowan (1985); Arrington and Bitton (1979); Allen and Leonard
   (1976).

16 Magic and Mormon religion

Douglas J. Davies

There is, perhaps, no more appropriate title than 'Magic and Mormon religion' for an anthropologist interested in contemporary Latter-day Saint culture and its internal debates concerning the life-world of early nineteenth-century Mormons. Though intriguing historical debates in anthropological theory are conjured up by the word 'magic,' this chapter's purpose remains pragmatically contemporary in highlighting the place of the magical world-view in recent Mormon debates about early Mormon culture.

Magic as a distancing category

Although 'magic' is, quite obviously, a term embracing numerous phenomena, often involving power brokerage both in the world of scholarship and in the life of religious groups, here we consider it as a member of the category of what we might call 'distancing phenomena.' Terms of this type distance the user from the phenomenon described for a particular purpose of self-interest.

The British social anthropologist Ioan Lewis describes this for religious phenomena when he refers to 'the well documented process by which today's religion (or ideology) reduces yesterday's religion to the status of magic, each successive religious vogue marginalizing its predecessor' (1986: 96). This particular form of reductionism involves an act of distancing and can work both for academics and religious devotees as they engage in a process of status reduction of some other concept, person, or age.

My concern here is to raise the profile of this process as one through which one superior-minded group may designate some other group as relatively inferior in some way. The notions of witchcraft and cannibalism also belong to this category of descriptions (Douglas, 1970; Arens, 1979). Just as witchcraft accusations give the moral high ground to the accuser, and just as a group seeks to denature some other by accusing them of cannibalism, so with magic. Those on the self-defined high ground, whether of morality, religion, or intellectual status, accuse the moral lowlanders of magic. In a lighter vein, one might also include the word 'academic' in this category of derogatory descriptions, as in the phrase that something is 'merely academic.' Even the word 'theology' can be used in some religious groups to distance the true believer from those specialists who merely play with religious ideas. The *Encyclopedia of Mormonism* makes this abundantly clear under its entry on 'Theology': 'Not having what has traditionally been understood as theology Latter-day Saints instead have texts that describe theophanies' (Ludlow, 1992). Indeed, within Mormon life the word 'theology' occupies something of an ambiguous position as far as this sense of sincerity is concerned, so it is no wonder that magic will be an even more sensitive term.

One important caveat to be entered here is that the word 'magic' is regularly used anthropologically to describe a particular attitude to the world which, historically, has been associated with the notion of animism (Tylor, 1958) or pre-logical mentality (Lévy-Bruhl, 1965) and, more recently to account for other aspects of human behavior (Evans-Pritchard, 1937; Malinowski, 1948; Douglas, 1970). This is not what I am disputing. What I draw attention to is the fact that the word 'magic' can be used in what can only be called a morally evaluative fashion not only within traditional societies but also in contemporary academic discourse. And this moral evaluation is likely to have broader connotations for those engaged in it, not least in the wider world of Mormon studies.

Our concern, then, is with the distancing of a speaker from the subject matter concerned, a distancing which suits the speaker's purpose of establishing an identity as different, and probably better in some way, from that of those whose life-world, whose tension of consciousness, is deemed to be magical.

An analogy from English Anglicanism may help depict the scene I have in mind. Some years ago I explored the distinction between orthodox Christianity and folk-religion when speaking of Anglican priests as engaging, metaphorically, in self-absolution for dealing in the mixed-motive rituals of infrequent church attenders by defining the religiosity of these peripheral parishioners as being folk-religion. As representatives of a historical tradition of Christianity with core doctrines and a sense of commitment they were also, inevitably, engaged in performing rites such as marriages, baptisms, and funerals for people with very little obvious Christian knowledge or commitment. These occasional church attenders were viewed as different from the core congregation, often the central eucharistic congregation. I argued that many clergy felt more justified with this situation by invoking the notion of folk-religion to describe this lower order of religiosity. Their real priestly function focused on the eucharist and the core-faithful while their status as parish priests also demanded servicing the less committed through the occasional offices with their folk-religious penumbra (Davies, 1983).

This Anglican distinction between pure faith and folk-religion resembles, in certain respects, the distinction between religion and magic in some discussions of Mormon religiosity. An important framework for this distinction is provided by the idea of history. Speaking of earlier days Richard L. Bushman asserts that: 'Mormonism was history, not philosophy' (1984: 188). This familiar emphasis upon history suggests that, for Mormons, there are several notions of time, perhaps unclearly differentiated, which provide a mixed medium for understanding categories of truth. This is why the debate about the magical world-view of early Mormonism is so poignant, involving as it does several undifferentiated issues. For while it obviously embraces matters of origin, of revelation, and of truth, the magical world-view also, though less obviously, concerns the fact of distance and change between cultural life now and in the founding decades. For most traditional Mormons, time, interpreted as the historical flow of events, is the medium through which truth is revealed. This is why history and truth are closely juxtaposed in LDS thought and this is also why, I assume, a Mormon History Association exists rather than a Mormon Theological Association. And this makes the debate about the magical world-view of early Mormonism so poignant, as obvious matters of origin jostle with contemporary experience, making it important to explore both the fact of historical distance and the perceived relationships between the present and the founding decades.

As an analogy we might say, in terms of symbolic theology and folk-belief, that questions of seer-stones and gold digging assume in Mormon reflection the place occupied in devotional Catholicism by the Shroud of Turin. In other words, the formal Catholic preoccupation with the historicity of the incarnation means that less formal and popular ideas can focus on pragmatic issues like the shroud just as the Mormon preoccupation with the Restoration focuses on the pragmatic arena in which Joseph Smith received revelation.

But to use the idea of magic of that early period is not simply to speak descriptively, for it is hard to have a simply neutral category of magic. Magic is a term which often seems to be as evaluative as it is descriptive. A very similar argument exists in Protestant Christianity in the debate on myth and demythologizing. For Rudolph Bultmann, for example, myth refers to the life-world of New Testament times and demythologizing speaks of taking the elements of myth and reorganizing them in a rational scheme of contemporary faith. Myth and reason match magic and religion as pairs set within our distancing and bounding categories and, in the Bultmann context, raise the crucial question of whether the idea of the incarnation belonged to a mythical mode of thinking or whether it denoted a historical event.

In hermeneutical terms the historicity of Mormonism's founding events resembles the historicity of the incarnation within discussions of contemporary belief in wider Christendom. There are those who would argue that real faith in God is not necessarily tied to a belief in Jesus as incarnate deity and to the network of supporting doctrines such as that of the Virgin birth. Others, by sharp contrast, see that cluster of beliefs as truly foundational for Christianity and would oppose the attempted process of demythologizing.

Commitment to the founding era

These are important issues, but are not my concern in this chapter. What I want to argue is that there is something about the early phase of a religion which serves as a focus for commitment and which seems to serve as a source for that emotion which empowers commitment in subsequent generations. If this is an accurate representation of religious dynamics it means that 'magic' in the Mormon case may well be one driving force behind what may come to be accepted and defined as religion.

While some modern critical Mormons may want to distance themselves from the seer-stones they may still want to affirm the essence of faith which took its shape through the seer. The Mormon testimony underlying this desire to affirm the prophet and his ensuing church is born today but is set within a cultural complex which affirms its roots in yesterday. This is what makes the interpretation of the past so hard for many Mormon scholars. Ideal type Mormons see their contemporary faith as authentic and spirit inspired, it is real religion. They also see its origin as related to Joseph Smith, a real prophet. But then, if that prophet is set amidst what is called magic, a problem emerges. For magic in the present would be inauthentic, and the ordinary interpretation following from that is that magic in the past must also be inauthentic. Contemporary Mormons would, obviously, not want to distance themselves from the prophet but might well wish to set a distance from magic. Hence the double-bind of historical definition and perhaps, also, of historical awareness. Here Mark Leone's fascinating and provocative description of the uses of history may be useful as he argues that Mormons use history to control their identity and yet seem to lack any precise means of speaking about their own sense of the passing of time except in terms of genealogical work (1979: 208). The paradox he presents sets the possession of an extensive documentary history alongside a kind of personal memorylessness. There is, obviously, something of a conceptual problem here.

Let me approach this impasse from the realm of the history and phenomenology of religions with Mircea Eliade's idea that the 'sacred is an element of the structure of consciousness and not a moment in the history of consciousness' (1977: 313). This idea can be applied directly to Mormon life, especially if we utilize it in the light of another notion borrowed from the anthropologist Maurice Bloch (1992: 127ff.). Bloch is worried when a people cannot recognize themselves in a description of them given by an anthropologist, and I suspect that might be true for some Mormons reading Leone's work. When such interpretative blindness occurs it is, argues Bloch, because the anthropologist's description is logic-sentential, over-systematized, and language-like while life, as it is lived, is quite different.

Bloch describes daily life as lived in and through networks of beliefs and clumps of signification rather than by means of an integrated systematic ideology. Bloch explores these networks and clumps through the psychological notion of connectionism (1992: 130). This is a very apt theoretical way of interpreting Leone's description of Mormonism as a 'panoply of words, thoughts, maxims, elaborated clichés, explicit beliefs, sacred texts, traditions and values which are the symbolic inheritance of members,' constituting overlapping notions which 'lack either precision or specificity, taking on usable and precise meaning only in context.' 'Mormonism,' says Leone, 'has meaning only in context' (1979: 168). The problem with the debate over magic and truth within Mormon life is that the proper context of each is not always established.

Studies of religion which seek to render such mixed experiences in a logical way, whether in the history of a religion or in a systematic theology, thus contradict the experience of life, making descriptive accounts unrecognizable to the native even though they may please the theoretician. This process is reminiscent of Cantwell Smith's distinction between cumulative tradition and faith (1963). Cumulative tradition represents the experience of a culture rendered into some kind of systematic scheme of order, often through a theory of history or divine providence, while faith describes the inner and personal sense of the presence of power.

For Mormons, faith in Cantwell Smith's sense, or the sacred in Eliade's terms, lies in the experiential domain expressed in what Mormons call a 'testimony' gained in the present. In 'clump-terms' it is, of course, linked to Joseph Smith as a prophet and to the church as the true Church but the reference is to these phenomena as presented in the present and not in the past, they are encountered emotionally as part of the structure of today's church life and not through formal history. This might also be argued for genealogical work, that major dimension of Mormon life which, on the face of it, would seem to be profoundly historical and yet is probably of significance because of the contemporary sense of acting towards and on behalf of the dead, perhaps even gaining some sense of their contemporary presence.

Testimonies of the prophet or of the church do, in a profound sense, bring the past to the present just as it takes the present to the past. Religions do that sort of thing even though historians like to spend their time charting influences and differences in the process of the transition of values. The whole point about broad Christian doctrines of the Mass, Eucharist or Lord's Supper is to take the participant from now to the Last Supper or from now to the Crucifixion.

The ritually interesting thing about Mormonism is that its doctrine of the Sacrament Service has its emotional roots very firmly in the present, for it is in the here and now, through the Spirit, that members are to remember the historical life of Christ. Here, truly, the sacred refers to an element of the structure of Mormon consciousness and not to a moment in the history of Mormon consciousness.

These reflections bring me back to magic and to the past. My basic argument here is that the magical world-view of early Mormonism possesses two deeply intertwined dimensions. One concerns ideology and causality and the other ethos, emotion, or affect.

The first dimension takes an ideological perspective on the actual ideas of the early magic world-view, explaining how Joseph Smith caught the spirit of the age before transforming it into his own spell-binding new religion. On this line it is easy to argue that this early magical Mormonism became transformed into a rational theology encapsulated in a bureaucracy of strongly controlled charisma, rather along the lines of John Brooke's *The Refiner's Fire* (1994). To engage in this interpretation is to take magic as a distancing category, one that makes contemporary Mormon identity easier to accept.

The second dimension sees that magic world as an expression of desire. The emphasis is not upon the content of belief but on the emotional drive which came to frame an ethos. Richard Bushman could be taken to exemplify something of this when talking about early magic in terms of a 'yearning for contact with powers beyond this world' (1984: 79). This yearning he contrasted rather sharply, too sharply I suspect, with what he calls rational Christianity. Be that as it may, the important point I want to stress is that contemporary Mormonism bears a strong affinity with early magic in its desire for emotional affect. The sincerity of a testimony, the changed character of a Mormon, all depends on an emotional tone (D. J. Davies, 1987: 131ff.).

Because these two dimensions are seldom differentiated it is quite understandable that some contemporary Mormons might well be ambivalent over critical studies of early magical Mormonism. Were I an academic Mormon I might want to speak of Joseph Smith and his peers as living in a magical world not simply to offer an apt description of that life-world but as a means of describing my own life-world as different from theirs. My present world of religion as opposed to that world of magic. Yet, at the same time I would probably not be totally happy with that distinction because my own religious yearning would find something of a home in Joseph Smith's life and teaching as, most certainly, in the life of the church derived from him. While the Restoration might well have, as it were, been symbolized in magic seer-stones in 1830, in 1990 it is focused on a prophet of quite a different type. In other words the mood of religious truth, and from Clifford Geertz (1966) we have long learned the importance of such mood in defining religion, was reflected in magic in the 1830s but in religion in the 1990s. The focus of the emotion differs but the sense of a sacred focus remains central.

But, still speaking as a hypothetical Mormon academic, I could hardly expect non-Mormon academics to feel things like this. For them the early magical world-view and the present day rational administration of spirit would present two different scenarios. This issue of ethos, personal faith and church membership is a phenomenological fact which must simply be described and left to stand. It is, I suspect, one which academic Church members find as problematic as do non-Mormons, albeit for rather different reasons.

I conclude by referring to the Patriarchs of the Church and to their blessings. I do so because I wonder whether this particular phenomenon does not focus the issue of this paper by expressing the magical world-view in the present day.

In terms of social anthropology it is possible to examine the role of the Presiding Patriarch of the Church in terms of Rodney Needham's (1980: 63ff.) important distinction between jural and mystical authority (D. J. Davies, 1995). Just as the First Presidency and the hierarchy beneath him represent jural or legal authority over doctrine and Church practice, so the Presiding Patriarch, counting him apart from the General Authorities for this purpose, represents mystical power in the church. And it is this mystical power which, I would argue, significantly expresses something of the meaning of the magical world-view of early Mormonism. Symbolically speaking, the Mormon attitude towards both Stake Presidents and Patriarchs reflects the division of jural and mystical power in the contemporary Church but, historically speaking, it also reflects the emergence and increased development of a bureaucracy juxtaposed to a perpetuation of the earlier mystical view of life.

17 'Companions and forerunners' English Romantics and the Restoration

Gordon K. Thomas

By the end of 1819, the great English poets we generally lump together as 'the Romantics' had all achieved very notable success. William Blake, the oldest of the group, his best known writings long since finished, was at work on *Jerusalem*, the last of his 'prophetic' pieces. William Wordsworth, well known to the literary public ever since the publication, more than 20 years before, of *Lyrical Ballads*, continued to be very productive; in 1819 he published such famous poems as *Peter Bell* and *The Waggoner* and was hard at work on the *River Duddon* sonnets. By 1819, Samuel Taylor Coleridge had published all of his greatest poetry and was now established in a new career as a highly respected public lecturer on literature and philosophy. In 1819, George Gordon, Lord Byron, having already achieved enormous fame as perhaps the most popular poet who ever lived, published Cantos I and II of his masterpiece, *Don Juan*. In that year, the young John Keats turned 24, and in the same year he wrote his greatest Odes along with *The Eve of St Agnes* and 'La Belle Dame sans Merci.' And 1819 was for Percy Bysshe Shelley the year of his greatest poetic achievements: *Prometheus Unbound*, *The Cenci*, 'Ode to the West Wind,' *The Mask of Anarchy* and other works. Lesser poets of the period had either already ended their careers – Robert Burns had died in 1796 – or had gone on to other interests. Robert Southey wrote little significant poetry after becoming Poet Laureate in 1813 but had become a fine biographer and writer of histories; in 1819 he was at work on his *Life of Wesley*. Among novelists, Jane Austen's brilliant career had ended with her death two years earlier, in 1817. Walter Scott was in the midst of his series of very popular Waverley novels; both *Rob Roy* and *The Heart of Midlothian* were published in 1819, and *The Legend of Montrose* was completed. And Mary Shelley had just written *Frankenstein* in 1818.

But if 1819 was a time of astonishingly great literary production and achievement, it was a troubled time socially, politically, and religiously. In his sonnet 'England in 1819,' Percy Shelley wrote of his native land having hit rock bottom, a land ruled by 'an old, mad, blind, despised, and dying king,' and characterized by 'public scorn' and 'leech-like' rulers, 'liberticide' and 'Religion, Christless, Godless – a book sealed.' But these problems, paradoxically, represented for Shelley an opportunity: they were, he said, 'graves, from which a glorious Phantom may / Burst, to illumine our tempestuous day' (Cameron, 1969: 51–2). Similarly, surveying the conditions prevailing in 1819 in his 'Ode to the West Wind,' Shelley predicted that when things get *this* bad they *have* to get better; he concludes the poem by offering

> to unawakened earth
> The trumpet of a prophecy! O, Wind,
> If Winter comes, can Spring be far behind?

In his greatest work, *Prometheus Unbound*, another product of 1819, Shelley focuses specifically on religion, on religious error and tyranny. He predicts that what has till then passed as orthodox Christianity, 'a dark yet mighty faith' based on 'the pride of kings and priests' (Cameron, 1969: 366), is about to be reduced to the status of a dusty museum relic, 'not o'erthrown, but unregarded now, . . . abhorred by God and man.'

It is clear from these and many other passages that Shelley regarded both himself and each of the other great Romantics, with all of whom he had various kinds of personal connections and whose works he knew and relied on, as persons actuated, in his words, by 'a passion for reforming the world' (Preface to *Prometheus Unbound*). Each of them in 1819 had shown himself to be in his own way just what Joseph Smith would later describe himself to have been at the time: one 'destined to prove a disturber and an annoyer' of the kingdoms of this world and of 'the powers of darkness' (Joseph Smith, 1964: 1:20).

Shelley was much aware of what was indeed an ongoing process of reform and gradual improvement, in which the Reformation, 'which shook to dust the oldest and most oppressive form of the Christian religion,' he says, had had its part, as had 'the progress and development of the same spirit' in subsequent centuries. But now, by 1819, he insists, the period of gradual change is over, and the time of abrupt transformation has arrived: the Romantic poets, that is, 'the great writers of our own age,' he writes in an outburst of almost breathtaking prophecy,

> are, we have reason to suppose, the companions and forerunners of some unimagined change in our social condition or the opinions which cement it. The cloud of mind is discharging its collected lightning, and the equilibrium between institutions and opinions is now restoring, or is about to be restored. (Shelley, 1969: 302)

Shelley scholars have never known quite what to make of all this. They are not aware of any imminent and genuine transformation in the spiritual order for which Shelley may have had some private hopes; and they are certainly not aware of any historical event in the weeks or months following his writing of these words which showed any fulfilment of his prophecy of this 'unimagined change,' this 'restoring.' How could *they* know of what was to be the fundamental event in the latter-day Restoration, the First Vision of Joseph Smith, that which occurred 'on the morning of a beautiful, clear day, early in the spring of eighteen hundred and twenty' (Joseph Smith, 1964: 1:14) in a grove of trees on a farm outside the village of Palmyra in upstate New York? Yet of all the religious thinkers who seem to have anticipated, by inspiration, the Restoration which Mormonism proclaims to the world, such men as George Fox and Roger Williams and Thomas Jefferson, no one seems to have envisioned both its characteristics, its timing, and its universal effect so well as Percy Bysshe Shelley.

I credit Shelley, then, and, as he says, the other 'great writers of [his] age,' with being inspired visionaries, 'companions and forerunners' of the Restoration. Certainly they were not direct participants in the advent of Mormonism, except in the general and unmeasurable way of having helped to prepare people's minds for the great change, the rebirth. Nor am I suggesting, clearly, that poorly educated, 14-year-old Joseph Smith had been reading Shelley before he went to the woods that day. And there is certainly no way, no earthly way, that in 1819 Shelley and the others could have been aware of Joseph Smith. Shelley drowned off the coast of Italy in 1822, long before Mormonism began to be preached to the world. I am suggesting, rather, a very specific and personal application to the English Romantic poets of the principle enunciated by Brigham Young: 'I . . . believe positively that there is nothing known except by the revelation of the Lord Jesus Christ, whether in Theology, science, or art' (1869: 12: 207).

Somehow, Shelley has not yet had much of an audience among Mormon readers, despite his surely qualifying as being among one of the writers of the 'best books' out of which Latter-day Saints are twice commanded in the Doctrine and Covenants to 'seek . . . words of wisdom' and 'seek learning' (88:118 and 109:7). But I sense Shelley's presence, along with the other Romantics, in the great summation of the nineteenth century and its achievements offered by Lorenzo Snow, fifth President of the Church of Jesus Christ of Latter-day Saints, when he presided in a special meeting in the Salt Lake Tabernacle to commemorate the just-ended century, on January 1, 1901:

> As a servant of God I bear witness to the revelation of His will in the nineteenth century. It came by His own voice from the heaven, by the personal manifestation of His Son, and by the ministration of holy angels. He commands all people everywhere to repent, to turn from their evil ways and unrighteous desires, to be baptized for the remission of their sins, that they may receive the work of redemption spoken of by all the holy prophets, sages, and seers of all the ages and all the races of mankind. He will assuredly accomplish His work, and the twentieth century will make its advancement towards the great consummation. Every unfoldment of the nineteenth century in science, in art, in mechanism, in music, in literature, in poetic fancy, in philosophical thought, was prompted by His Spirit, which before long will be poured out upon all flesh that will receive it. He is the Father of us all, and He desires to save and exalt us all. (Snow, 1901: 31)

Though Shelley has not yet caught on among wide numbers of Latter-day Saints readers, his great contemporary, William Wordsworth, has, in some ways at least, fared spectacularly better. I know of nothing in the world of organized religion to compare with the phenomenon represented in Mormonism by Wordsworth's Ode 'Intimations of Immortality,' a work of unquestionably inspired poetic wisdom, written by someone not a member of the Church, which holds a place of authority and honor very much akin to favorite passages of scripture. Indeed, almost no scriptural passages, other than, perhaps, James 1:5 or Moroni 10:4, are so often cited by Latter-day Saints in their efforts to instruct each other and also to teach their beliefs to the world, as the familiar lines from stanza 5 of Wordsworth's Intimations Ode:

> Our birth is but a sleep and a forgetting:
> The Soul that rises with us, our life's Star,
> Hath had elsewhere its setting.

The film *Man's Search for Happiness* (now out in a new version), much used in the Church's visitors' centers and all over the world by the Church's missionaries, opens, as did the older version, with these lines of Wordsworth, and the poem is frequently cited in Church literature and sermons. Two or three decades ago, hundreds of thousands of women in the Church's Relief Society program studied together for a number of years a series of volumes constituting a massive literary anthology entitled *Out of the Best Books*. I cannot help but think of Shelley and his claim that he and his contemporaries were 'companions and forerunners' of great doctrinal and institutional changes when I find the editors of these volumes calling Wordsworth 'an inspired forerunner of the Gospel' (Clark and Thomas, 1964: I: 61).

In those same volumes, Wordsworth's poetry appears more frequently than the works of any other writer, and his Intimations Ode is given the place of honor right at the beginning of volume I. And why? Because, according to the editors, Wordsworth as a poet speaks 'with a voice of divine authority' (ibid.: 53), and, specifically, his Intimations Ode, say the editors, is the 'fullest and most beautiful expression in all literature harmonious with ... Latter-day Saint doctrine.' Others of Wordsworth's poems are also cited in these volumes for their inspired teachings. His masterpiece, the vast epical autobiography, *The Prelude*, is appropriately praised as an illustration in great literature of what is perhaps the most basic of all Mormon doctrines, in the editors' words, that 'man can move toward the potentiality of godliness that is his' (ibid.: 65). The same writers, in fact, surveying Wordsworth's works, finally pronounce the judgment that the only statement of a code of ethics higher or nobler than that presented by this poet is in Christ's Sermon on the Mount! (ibid.: 70).

Despite Shelley's envisioning a major role in the great rebirth of human society and religion for all 'the great writers' of his day, I must note that other Romantic writers and poets have gained little attention in Mormon teachings compared to the place occupied by Wordsworth. Robert Burns was unquestionably the favorite poet of Church president David O. McKay, who very often quoted Burns in his sermons. And a little attention has begun to be given among Mormon writers to Lord Byron as the author of the immensely popular and influential *Hebrew Melodies*, which played so important a role in the rise of the Zionist movement in nineteenth-century England and Europe, with its advocacy of a homeland in Palestine for the Jews (Thomas, 1993: 56), an advocacy again paralleling Mormon teachings on one aspect of 'the literal gathering of Israel' (Article of Faith 10). And Blake, Keats, Coleridge, Scott, Shelley, Byron, even Leigh Hunt, all occupy at least a few pages in those Relief Society volumes, *Out of the Best Books*, the volumes so dominated by Wordsworth.

I would not want to overstate any sense of linkage between Romantic poets and the rise of Mormonism. These poets are just what Shelley called them, 'companions and forerunners,' not active leaders of the Restoration but cultivators of the spiritual terrain into which others would plant the seeds of true fruition, prophets, at most, of preparation, not of Restoration. Joseph Smith certainly neither needed nor used these or any other literary figures in his work as the Prophet of the Restoration. And the Romantic poets, though they sometimes seem to be writing out of the effects of a very clear sense of vision, never even mention Mormonism by name.

Well, almost never. All but one of the greatest English Romantic poets died before the first missionaries arrived in their country in 1837. Blake, Coleridge, Byron, Shelley, Keats, Burns, Scott, all were dead by 1834 at the latest. But Wordsworth lived on, and he actually did have something like an encounter with Mormonism near the end of his life. This encounter is little known, even among Mormons. Clark and Thomas (1964: I: 61) write that Wordsworth 'perhaps never heard of "Mormonism".' In a letter written near the end of his long life, dated February 3, 1846, and addressed to Henry Reed, Wordsworth's American editor in Philadelphia, the poet appeals a little desperately for help from that side of the Atlantic: 'Do you know any thing of a wretched set of Religionists in your Country, *Superstitionists* I ought to say, called Mormonites or Latter-day saints?' (Wordsworth and Wordsworth, 1988: 756). So is Wordsworth investigating Mormonism in his old age? Well, the query is not exactly couched in the terms Latter-day Saint missionaries prefer to hear: 'Tell me about your Church.' In fact, the motive for inquiry was a family matter, for Wordsworth's letter to Reed continues:

> Would you believe it, a niece of Mrs W's has just embarked, we believe at Liverpool, with a set of the deluded Followers of that wretch, in an attempt to join their society. Her name is Margaret Hutchinson, a young woman of good abilities and well educated, but early in life she took from her Mother and *her* connections, a Methodistical turn and has gone on in a course of what she supposes to be piety till she has come to this miserable close. If you should by chance hear any thing about her pray let us know.

The following month came Reed's reply; he speaks of Joseph Smith, murdered nearly two years before, as 'the Prime Impostor,' but also says, 'I know nothing of those wretched and wicked fanatics' (Wordsworth and Wordsworth, 1988: 756n.).

In fact, Margaret Hutchinson had gone to Nauvoo, and she died during the Mormon Exodus the following year and was buried at Winter Quarters. Wordsworth's own search for further information about the Mormons was cut short by his own quite feeble old age and by his death in 1850.

But the story doesn't end there. In his journal for August 21, 1877, Wilford Woodruff tells of his experience in the St George Temple on that date. He himself, he writes, was baptized on behalf of a hundred eminent persons, with some of his associates serving as proxies in the baptism of yet others, including such great female writers of the Romantic period as Hannah More, Maria Edgeworth, and Jane Austen. The names of most of the women do not appear in Wilford Woodruff's *Journal* but have been gathered from St George Temple records. Among the persons for whom Wilford Woodruff was baptized that day are Columbus and Napoleon Bonaparte, Thomas Jefferson and Stonewall Jackson, and several major literary figures, including the great German writers Schiller and Goethe, and then this list of names: Robert Burns, Sir Walter Scott, George Gordon Lord Byron, William Wordsworth, and also members of their families (Woodruff, 1983–85: 7: 367–9). According to his recollections, many, at least, of the persons for whom Wilford Woodruff performed these baptisms, and then directed other ordinances to be performed also, had appeared to him in vision and had requested the temple ordinances (Alexander, 1991: 231).

If Wordsworth's attitude, for one, had thus shifted from indignation in 1846 to asking for and receiving the blessing of baptism in 1877, it would seem that he and his niece must have had some interesting discussions once they met beyond the grave. And in later times, Latter-day Saint temple ordinances have been performed for the other great English Romantics, including Samuel Taylor Coleridge, William Blake, John Keats, Charles and Mary Lamb, Percy Bysshe Shelley and his famous novelist wife Mary Godwin Shelley, and other members of their families.

Here is the point of all this. In his journal entry, following his list of names, Wilford Woodruff adds this brief note, acknowledging his own sense of having been in the temple among 'companions and forerunners' in the work of bringing about what will yet be seen as the greatest social and spiritual transformation of modern times: 'I felt thankful that we had the privilege and the power to administer for the[se] worthy dead ... that we could do as much for them as they had done for us' (Woodruff, 1983–85: 7: 367–9). What 'they have done for us' deserves much wider recognition, both among Latter-day Saints and among all who seek to understand just what happened to the world in the nineteenth century as a result of the still too largely 'unimagined change' in ideas and institutions which came as accompaniments to the Restoration.

Part V
Female Factors

18 Issues in contemporary Mormon feminism

Lynn Matthews Anderson

To comprehend the significance of the questions of women, divinity, and priesthood authority, it is essential to understand that Mormons believe God is a glorified human being; that we are literally spirit offspring of God; and that it is God's own selfless will that we become gods ourselves.

In the late twentieth-century Mormon church, all worthy males from the age of twelve and older are ordained to various offices in a lay priesthood that not only provides the governing structure of the church, but is also the means by which men can become like God. Women's place in Mormon theology, however, is fraught with uncertainty and ambiguity, which is nowhere more evident nor more poignant than in the consideration of the Mormon doctrine of a Mother in Heaven.

This doctrine was first enunciated in a hymn written by Eliza R. Snow, a prominent leader in nineteenth-century Mormon women's organizations. Numerous male church leaders have endorsed the doctrine; the most authoritative confirmation was an official statement of the church's First Presidency in 1909: 'all men and women are in the similitude of the universal Father and Mother, and are literally the sons and daughters of Deity' (Smith, Winder, and Lund, 1966: 516).

However, the doctrine has not been canonized nor expanded beyond the vaguest of inferences, that there simply 'is' a mother in heaven. Not only is the Mother not worshiped, she is scarcely discussed, sung about, or included in the general church curriculum. Most Mormons do not pray to her, particularly now that such prayer to her has been officially proscribed on the grounds that, unsurprisingly, there is no scriptural precedent for doing so (Hinckley, 1991: 3–4). What kind of a mother cannot speak to her children, nor be spoken to?

'Maternal deism' best describes our Heavenly Mother's relationship to us here in mortality: she co-created us spiritually, but to all appearances has since left us alone. This is particularly ironic, in that Mormon women are constantly told that women are nurturers by nature, but our Heavenly Mother, ostensibly what all worthy Mormon women are destined to become, is not on the scene to provide nurturing to her mortal children. Is this what awaits women in the life hereafter?

The thought of an aloof, distant, or otherwise occupied Mother has been so painful to some Mormons that they have diligently searched for ways to prove that she has been actively involved in this sphere. Some have postulated that the Mother is the Holy Ghost; others believe that when the scriptures speak of 'God,' they are speaking of both the Father and the Mother as a single unit. Yet even the most egalitarian of these speculative ideas do not satisfactorily address the gender-based inequity found in God's Church on earth, but instead raise the specter of a heavenly basis for sexism.

This question, then, is crucial for most Mormon feminists. Is the anthropomorphic Mormon God a divine couple, a dyad composed of both a Father and a Mother, co-equal in might, majesty, and power, or is the Mother simply God's wife, or one of his wives, a subordinated consort lacking authority in and responsibility for the temporal salvation of her children? Is the Mother a passive onlooker or an active participant in what Mormon scriptures call God's work and glory? (Cf. PGP, Moses 1:33.) In fine, does our Mother hold, and actively exercise, the priesthood, which Mormon apostle Bruce R. McConkie defined as:

> the power and authority of Deity by which all things exist; by which they are created, governed, and controlled; by which the universe and worlds without number have come rolling into existence; by which the great plan of creation, redemption, and exaltation operates throughout immensity. (1966: 594)

If Mormon women are to take our cues from what we experience and are taught in church, our future is one of silence and obscurity. What Mormons believe about being exalted is almost entirely male-oriented. Our scriptures speak in androcentric language about male deity creating this world and thus we believe that exalted men will build worlds and rule over them. We know from experience that we pray to a male God and thus infer that male gods will be prayed to. The possibility of women's equal participation is downplayed; even though, in the Mormon temple ceremony called the endowment, Mormon women wear the same robes of the priesthood and say the very same explicitly priesthood-related words that men do in order to pass into 'heaven' at the final stage of the ceremony, the significance of our doing so is never discussed in or out of the temple. If temple-endowed Mormon women do hold the priesthood, as some have asserted (Quinn, 1992: 356–409), most are completely unaware of the fact.

At least some contemporary church authorities hold the same highly dichotomized view of the sexes as Church leaders of earlier generations. This view is exemplified by apostle Boyd K. Packer's assertion that:

> There are basic things that a man needs that a woman does not need. There are things that a man feels that a woman never does feel. There are basic things that a woman needs that a man never needs, and there are things that a woman feels that a man never feels, nor should he. These differences make women, in basic needs, literally opposite from men. (1977: 7)

Apart from certain very specific biological constraints, it is hard to imagine that members of the same species would not hold most basic needs in common, and indeed Elder Packer does not give any specific examples to back up his assertions. Mormon feminists acknowledge the gross biological distinctions between women and men, but we also point out that throughout history, the facts of biological maternity have been historically used to deny women property rights, suffrage, equal opportunities for education and employment, fair compensation, and equal standing under the law. But because many church leaders concur with Elder Packer's radical differentiation between women and men, the structure of the church itself continues to reflect this sex-based dichotomy in myriad ways. Indeed, men's and women's experiences in church are so different as to lead one to think we belong to two churches, one for women, and one for men, rather than to one church headed by Christ Jesus.

I believe leaders' erroneous views hamper their ability to relate to and work well with women. It does not help that most top leaders have little or no recent experience in working with women as peers in the day-to-day world. But until circumstances and culturally-founded ideas about women change such that church authorities can perceive women as more than just potential or real mothers, just as men are more than just potential or real fathers, or priesthood-holders, until the truth becomes evident to them that women are full human beings with the same kinds of aspirations, intelligence, talents, and capacities as men, male leaders will continue to ignore the scriptural, historical, sociological, organizational, psychological and other evidence that does not support the *status quo*.

A monolithic view of women, and of our Mother, is not only damaging to real, live women and men, but also limits the church's ability to avail itself of the full potential of all of its members. The problem is not with the idea that the most noble and glorious calling for women is motherhood; the problem seems largely rooted in how men with ecclesiastical power, growing up in a particular culture, have chosen (consciously or unconsciously) to define motherhood and womanhood. As envisioned by male church authorities, our Mother is a stereotypical, middle-class, stay-at-home Victorianesque icon, an image which neither reflects the diverse realities of women's lives, nor comes close to defining or encompassing the worthy aspirations of numberless women.

Several ironies have not escaped entirely unnoticed: first of all, Church authorities define the ideal Mormon family as a father and a mother and their children. Yet our 'approved' relationship with God is that of a Father alone with his children – a single-parent household.

Second, the argument that God the Father is completely sufficient to respond to the emotional and spiritual needs of all his children renders maternal nurturance irrelevant, further undercutting the ideal two-parent model.

Third, while there is no question that the Father does nurture us, it is obvious in both our rhetoric and practice that this particular lesson has not been divined, namely, that males can nurture, too, and that to do so is a principal role of a god. Instead, the Mormon hierarchy has persistently followed traditional Christendom's insistence on interpreting God's words to the fallen Adam and Eve as some kind of mandate to divide sex roles arbitrarily into public and private, dominant and submissive, male and female, rather than interpreting these same words as God's description of what life in a fallen world would be like, in other words, as something to be overcome, not perpetuated.

Some have asserted that the priesthood has been given only to men to help them to learn to serve others unselfishly, thereby becoming more like Christ; this assertion is frequently accompanied by a corollary argument that women do not need priesthood because they are 'naturally endowed' with Christian virtues and are 'naturally' more spiritual than men.

The problem with categorical assignations based on sex, that men by virtue or necessity of being male hold priesthood and that women by virtue or necessity of being female do not, is that there are countless individual women and men who simply do not fit the categorical definitions. Many women are not naturally possessed of those Christlike attributes which holding priesthood ostensibly teaches men. Why would not such women benefit from the 'gentle compulsion' of priesthood service? Indeed, how else can women come to fully emulate Jesus Christ if we are not given the opportunity and responsibility to learn to exercise his power?

While not generally a problem in places with a large Mormon population, the categorical restricting of certain necessary church assignments or 'callings' only to priesthood-holders has had a disastrous effect on the quality of life for many LDS families. Mormon men are burdened with multiple callings, taking them away from their families night after night, weekend after weekend; a recent survey indicated that Mormon men spend less time with their children than non-Mormon men (Duke, 1995). If the church really values fatherhood, should it not do everything in its power to keep fathers at home as much as possible? It makes utterly no sense not to use women in areas where they outnumber men eight to one or more, especially women who do not have children or whose children are grown.

Although women comprise the majority of adult members, we have no official voice in the governance of the Church. Instead, men on the general level make decisions for and about women with very little and often no input from women, not even from the women whom church authorities have called to serve as nominal leaders of female auxiliary programs. This lack of input at the general level is repeated at every level; women all over the church tell of having their views and input overlooked, ignored, or even denigrated. In practical terms, the transformation of the church's women's organization, the Relief Society, from an independent, self-financed, female-led partner with the priesthood to simply another correlated auxiliary, with a *de facto* leadership of men, has meant that countless opportunities to serve have died waiting for men to decide matters best decided by the women who would have done the work.[1]

Recently, the Church of England was torn asunder over the issue of women's ordination. One of the most specific considerations was whether a woman priest could adequately represent Christ, a question hinging on whether or not the salvific Christ transcends or is rather defined by his maleness. The conservative position holds that as Christ was a man, those who execute the priestly offices in Christ's stead must be men. In 1994, in the Catholic Church, Pope John Paul II reiterated the assertion that the fact that Jesus chose only male apostles is meant to serve as a procedural blueprint for all time. The Pope's argument that Jesus was 'perfectly free' to choose women, despite the enormous cultural and social prejudice against women in first-century Judea, is docetism of the worst sort (*Boston Globe*, May 1994).

Although Mormons have long touted the 'glorious hallmark of the restoration,' i.e., explicit doctrinal revelation from God, perhaps President Howard W. Hunter chose instead to rely on docetistic arguments when asked recently by the *Los Angeles Times* (October 22, 1994) about the possibility of ordaining women to priesthood. President Hunter replied:

> At the present time there isn't an avenue of ever changing. It's too well defined by revelation, by Scripture. And we follow strictly the scriptural passageway in matters of that kind. I see nothing that will lead to a change of direction at the present time – or in the future.

Is this God speaking, or simply Howard W. Hunter voicing an opinion? For many Mormons, this is a moot question; yet in fact there is no explicit revelation about or interdiction of women's ordination in either Mormon or biblical scripture (L. M. Anderson, 1994: 185–203). Despite a context of overwhelming patriarchal bias, the Bible refers to Deborah, Huldah, Phoebe the deacon, and so on, clearly linking women to priesthood-like offices, prerogatives, and duties. As more information becomes available about women's place and roles in ancient Israel and in the first-century Christian Church, perhaps Mormons will reconsider in light of our Sixth Article of Faith just how closely our church approximates 'the same organization that existed in the Primitive Church.'

Finally, sex-linked priesthood fosters a basic inequality that is contrary to the egalitarian model found in the Book of Mormon, one in which the leader is no better than the follower (cf. Alma 1:26). While our rhetoric proclaims that all tasks are essential to the church's proper function, and that a nursery worker is as important in her/his work as a bishop or stake president, we accord far greater honor to priesthood offices than we do to non-priesthood offices. We claim the various 'courtesies' are simply tokens of our respect for the office of the priesthood, but there is no meaningful way to divorce an office from the person called to that office. Children in particular do not see an 'office' as the recipient of respect; rather, they see human men and boys being honored, deferred to, and given privileges. When this occurs in the name of 'respecting the priesthood,' we do exactly the opposite of our stated intentions: we dishonor the priesthood, we show disrespect to that God who is no respecter of persons by upholding a hierarchical system that makes us all unequal.

While women and their Church work are vital to the proper function of the organization, their assignments are less visible, considered 'auxiliary,' and are not accorded outward tokens of respect and honor. This leaves little doubt in girls' and boys' minds that men are more important than women in and to the church. For girls in particular, this raises uncertainty about their identities and their relative value as members of the church.

Girls' feelings of being less important than boys are exacerbated at the age of twelve, when boys become part of the formal structure of the Church by being ordained as deacons. There is no equivalent experience for a twelve-year-old girl, no concrete tasks for her to perform in her congregation, no expectations for her to progress through a visible course of greater responsibility. Girls constantly read in the church's youth magazine and hear church leaders speak in glowing terms about what an enormous blessing and privilege it is for young men to hold the priesthood. What thoughtful eleven-year-old girl is not going to feel in some way cheated when she turns twelve? Or at the very least wonder what is 'wrong' with her that she cannot be ordained. And, of course, the church sends no message that she is seriously expected to prepare for the great Mormon Rite of Passage, full-time missionary service.

Not surprisingly, more young women than young men are 'inactive' in nine out of ten stakes in English-speaking North America, as reported by C. E. Asay in an address at Pittsburgh Regional Conference (October 24, 1992). Many older girls feel that the church does not see them as important in any way other than as potential wives for young men, does not value them for the same kinds of gifts and talents they, as well as young men, might bring to the Church.

Perhaps most serious of all is that a girl's questions about these differences in roles for boys and girls go unanswered. When I was twelve I marched into my bishop's office and demanded that he make me a deacon. My bishop could not answer my questions about why I could not be ordained, nor did God's Church have any authoritative explanation for excluding women. Abundant anecdotal evidence indicates that this experience is not unique, as archived messages on electronic mail demonstrate.[2] I am grateful that after my bishop's initial guffaw, he took me seriously. More than a quarter-century later, however, I still have the same unanswered questions, but now that I'm older, these questions are no longer 'cute' or 'funny' in the eyes of those in authority.

In summary, the question of ordaining women to priesthood is much more than whether girls should be permitted to distribute the sacrament as do boys, though this in and of itself is not a trivial concern. What is at stake is the knowledge of women's potential, both here and now and in the eternities, what women are, what we are to become hereafter, and what our relation is to men, to our children, and to the universe at large.

Despite the long way we Mormons have to go to overcome gender bias and prejudice, a shift is occurring in the official rhetoric: whereas once Church leaders unanimously upheld the 'patriarchal order' model of husband as the ultimate decision-maker, marriage is increasingly being portrayed as a partnership of equals, with inspiration and pragmatic considerations taking precedence over sex as to who has the ultimate say-so in any given decision. This equal partnership model, antithetical to the traditionally-defined patriarchal order, gives me hope that a larger reality may yet be realized – that we worship a God who is both our Father and our Mother together, with neither subordinated to the other. Yet until our Mother is revealed as God-with-the-Father to those governing the church, and until women's full humanity is comprehended and acknowledged, our church and our world will continue to suffer the deleterious consequences of millennia of inequity.

Some are quick to point out that it is only a relative handful of women, and men, who are questioning the *status quo*. However, the efforts of only a relative handful of women meeting at Seneca Falls, New York, in 1848, eventually led to suffrage for American women. The Church's own studies have shown that not simply a handful, but a majority of women in the Church desire to be more involved in the decision-making councils of the church at all levels (Ballard, 1994: 24–6).

Numbers 27 tells of another handful of women, the daughters of Zelophehad, who spoke with Moses about a serious inequity. Moses listened, took their concerns to God, and as a result the laws of inheritance were rewritten to include women. If the daughters had remained silent, or if Moses had refused to listen, they and countless generations of women would have been dispossessed in Israel. So we Mormon feminists try to make our experiences, our concerns and our questions known to the leaders of Christ's church, not with the idea of demanding the imposition of any specific agenda, but rather in the hope that those we look to as 'prophets, seers, and revelators' will turn to God and receive authoritative, divinely-revealed answers to take the place of flawed and limited human opinion, however well-intentioned. Who will be moved upon to ask for answers to our questions? As ever, I hope and pray it will be the current prophet.

Notes

1. Archived messages from sister-share, an LDS women's electronic mailing list. Available from lynnma@netcom.com. See Meg Wheatley, 'An expanded definition of priesthood? Some present and future consequences' (Hanks, 1992: 151ff.); Linda King Newell, 'Gifts of the Spirit: woman's share' (Beecher and Anderson, 1987); and Jill Mulvey Derr, Janath Russell Cannon, and Maureen Ursenbach Beecher (1992).
2. Abundant anecdotal evidence indicates that my experience is not unique. See archived messages from elwc-plus, an LDS electronic mailing list available from lynnma@netcom.com.

19 'Choose ye this day whom ye will serve'
LDS mothers' reaction to Church leader's instruction to remain in the home

Bruce A. Chadwick and H. Dean Garrett

Religious groups generally require their adherents to behave somewhat differently from the non-religious population, often regulating religious doctrine and sexual behavior, defining acceptable foods, influencing military service, prohibiting certain medical practices, and so on. Most who affiliate with a specific religion consider the demands of membership before they accept fellowship into the group. In an effort to mainstream membership, religious groups occasionally change their doctrine to fit shifting social norms in order to reduce the costs of affiliation for members. Conversely, doctrinal directives are maintained that have become at odds with societal norms. In the latter case, the social costs for members are increased. Many followers obey the socially unpopular instructions, commandments, or directives from their religious leaders and are socially ostracized, and in extreme cases legally prosecuted. On the other hand, some members refuse to endure the social pressures and withdraw from the religious group.

This paper explores the acceptance by a sample of women belonging to the LDS Church of a rather socially unpopular instruction from their Church leader who they regard as a prophet. In 1987, Ezra Taft Benson, then prophet and President of the Church, unequivocally stated that mothers should not enter the labor force, but rather should remain in the home (Benson, 1987). He said:

> The Lord clearly defined the roles of mothers and fathers in providing for and rearing a righteous posterity. In the beginning, Adam – not Eve – was instructed to earn the bread by the sweat of his brow. Contrary to conventional wisdom, a mother's calling is in the home, not in the market place ... With the claim on their husbands for their financial support, the counsel of the Church has always been for mothers to spend their full time in the home rearing and caring for their children.
>
> We realize also that some of our choice sisters are widowed and divorced and that others find themselves in unusual circumstances where, out of necessity, they are required to work for a period of time. But these are the exceptions, not the rule ...

Obedience to this counsel usually entails considerable costs for LDS women and their families. A majority of the mothers in the Church were employed in 1987 and the loss of income is obvious. Much has been written about the need for two incomes to cope with the economic pressures faced by American families today, especially young families. A wife remaining at home substantially lowers family income, and consequently the standard of living for her family. Another cost involves the prejudice and discrimination experienced by housewives in contemporary American society. As a large number of women have entered the labor force during the past 50 years supportive cultural values have emerged. Society began to emphasize the virtues of employment outside the home, while the role of housewife/mother became denigrated. Thus women who remain in the home are subject to subtle, and sometimes not so subtle, ridicule for choosing their lifestyle. Finally, many in society voiced concern that staying at home detracted from a woman's fulfillment and feelings of self-worth. During the 1960s and 1970s, society began to emphasize individual and self-actualization. Many feel working outside the home is essential to a woman's sense of worth and intellectual and social growth. These changing social values and norms make obedience to President Benson's instruction for mothers to remain out of the labor force rather costly and at times painful for LDS women and their families.

Because of societal pressures to the contrary, we anticipate that highly religious women accept and comply more often with this prophetic instruction than those with weaker religiosity. We tested three dimensions of religiosity – beliefs, public behavior, and private behavior – as predictors of acceptance and obedience. Religious beliefs involve the acceptance of traditional Christian and LDS doctrines concerning God, Jesus, the Holy Spirit, and man's relationship with them. Public religious behavior includes attendance at meetings and participation in Church activities. Private religious behavior includes personal worship activities such as prayer, meditation, and scripture study. We included the three dimensions because they tap rather different religious motivations. For example, it is possible that some women engage in public activities for social reasons with little religious conviction. On the other hand, private religious behavior may be engaged in because of internal convictions rather than external pressure. It is anticipated that private behavior with its strong internal motivation will be more strongly related to acceptance and compliance than public religious behavior.

At first glance it appears that all employed women have rejected President Benson's counsel. However, it is suspected that some women define both the instruction and their employment in ways which render them mutually consistent. Many working mothers may justify their employment so that in good conscience they can claim obedience to President Benson's instruction. Although employment and feelings of disobedience are strongly related, we suspect the relationship is far from perfect. We, therefore, explored how working women resolved the inconsistency between Church counsel not to work and their employment.

Consistency theory argues that individuals seek consistency between their attitude, beliefs, values, and behavior (Heider, 1958). According to this theory, inconsistency or dissonance is psychologically painful and individuals are motivated to resolve the inconsistency and reduce the pain (Festinger, 1957). Several techniques are suggested as means of so doing. Consistency may be achieved by rejecting the source of a disliked message. Women who employ this means would reject President Benson as a prophet, an inspired leader. For example, some may define him as 'an old man who has lost touch with contemporary reality,' thus ignoring his counsel. Adding cognitive elements may achieve consistency between formerly inconsistent beliefs and behaviors. Women using this strategy would reply, 'Yes President Benson is a prophet, yes his counsel is the will of God, and yes I work, but my husband is ill and can't support our family and thus my employment is acceptable.' The need to support the family excuses these women from adherence to the counsel.

This paper first ascertained the number of LDS women who complied with the prophetic instruction and then examined the ways working mothers reduced inconsistency between religious instruction and their behavior. It is expected that while a few will reject President Benson as a prophet, most women will add cognitive elements that justify their employment. Finally, we identified some of the factors related to obedience.

Methods and data collection

A mail questionnaire survey was conducted by the Center for Studies of the Family at Brigham Young University in the spring of 1991 with a sample of 3000 women between the ages of 20 and 60 who were living along the Wasatch Front in Utah. Standard procedures of multiple mailings produced a 50 per cent response rate. Comparison of the responses of women in the sample to other surveys and the 1990 census revealed the women in our sample are somewhat better educated and less likely to be divorced than the general population of women in Utah. Details about the data collection and possible bias are available in Chadwick and Garrett (1995). For this paper we analyzed the data from the 1022 married LDS women with at least one child living at home.

Measurement of variables

The demographic characteristics of age, education, marital status, and numbers of children were measured with single questions. Acceptance of President Benson's instruction to mothers was ascertained first by stating that: 'In 1987 Ezra Taft Benson, President of the Church, made the following statement.' The statement cited earlier in this chapter was then presented and each woman was asked: 'How do you feel about this statement?' Compliance to the instruction was tapped by asking: 'How does this statement apply to you and your family?'

The open-ended replies to these two questions were content-analyzed. The replies to how the women felt about the statement were coded into the categories of acceptance or rejection shown in Table 19.1 by two independent coders. The emphasis was not on whether the mother worked, but rather on whether she accepted President Benson's counsel. The women's responses about compliance to the statement were coded into the categories presented in the lower panel of Table 19.1. Over 95 per cent reliability was obtained between the two coders for responses to both acceptance and compliance.

Religious beliefs were measured with three questions on traditional Christian beliefs, such as 'There is a God,' and seven additional items about acceptance of LDS beliefs such as, 'Joseph Smith was a true prophet of God.' The five response categories ranged from 'Strongly Agree' to 'Strongly Disagree.'

Private religious behavior was measured by the frequency of personal prayer and scriptural reading. The responses ranged from 'Daily' to 'Never.' Confidential financial contributions were also included in this measure in the question, 'How much money did you give your church last year?' Respondents reported the percentage of their income they contributed.

Public religious behavior was evaluated by asking the frequency of attendance at four different LDS Sunday services. The response categories were: weekly, two or three times a month, monthly, seldom, and never. In addition, the frequency of family prayer and family scripture reading was obtained. Finally, we asked the women, 'Do you hold a Church calling(s) at the present time?'

The ten belief items, seven public items and three private behavior items, were submitted to principal components factor analysis. A scale score for each woman was computed based on the factor weights. The factor weights, eigenvalues and alpha coefficients, indicate the items combined to produce reliable unidimensional scales and are available in Chadwick and Garrett (1995). Employment status was gauged by asking, 'Are you currently employed?' The response categories included: No, Yes: part-time, and Yes: full-time.

Findings

Acceptance

About half of the LDS mothers, 47 per cent, unequivocally accepted the prophetic instruction that mothers should not work (see Table 19.1). Following are examples of accepting responses:

Because I know that Ezra Taft Benson is a Prophet called of God and acting under God's direction, I firmly believe in all that he says. I also believe that this is what a celestial family should be.

I believe it is true and inspired. Just look around in your neighborhoods. Latchkey kids have more problems, emotional and behavioral.

Our family discussed it when President Benson made the statement, and we all agreed with his counsel. We were glad that we were already living and organizing our family that way. We feel that home life and family are very important. We feel that following President Benson's advice makes a happier home with better adjusted children. We still have normal problems, of course, but we feel this is the best way.

Table 19.1 The reaction of married LDS women with children at home to President Benson's counsel and the impact on their behavior

Reaction	Per cent (N=1022)
Acceptance	
Complete acceptance	47
Accept, but have resentment	6
Accept with exceptions:	
Unless have to work	21
If children are in school	6
Subtotal	*80*
Ambivalence	
Women may choose to work (agency)	16
Mixed messages from leaders	2
Subtotal	*18*
Rejection	
Complete rejection	3
Subtotal	*3*
Total	101

Impact	Per cent (N=930)
Compliance	48
Subtotal	*48*
Partial compliance	
Work when children in school	9
Work part-time	8
Exception:	
Have to work	20
Subtotal	*37*

Noncompliance	
Reject statement and work	7
Work for self-fulfillment	6
Compensate children	1
Choose to work (agency)	1
Subtotal	15
Total	100

Some 6 per cent of the mothers accepted the statement, but resented the difficult situation it placed them in. They mentioned anger, guilt, and depression most often as negative feelings associated with their acceptance. As one mother replied:

> It makes me angry. It increases my guilt and enhances discrimination.

Another 37 per cent accepted the counsel, but with some qualifications or exceptions. The most frequently identified exception was financial difficulty: 21 per cent agreed that mothers should remain at home, unless they faced financial pressures of being a single parent, having an unemployed husband, or being in the throes of a financial crisis. Examples are:

> I believe the mother's place is in the home, but I also know of circumstances where the husband is a deadbeat and the only way to support the family is the wife working. We need stronger scripture to kick the husbands in the pants and get them to take responsibility for their children and homes.

> I would change the words to 'usual circumstances.' I see so many women in our ward [congregation] who have no choice but to work.

Some 6 per cent felt it acceptable for mothers to work while their children are in school:

> I think it is okay to work while children are in school as long as the mother is home when they are. However, if she had no energy or time to devote to them after school, then she shouldn't work.

> Small children need to be with their mother. When they are in school mothers can work away from the home.

It is remarkable that 80 per cent of the LDS married women with children living at home accepted the President's counsel as binding on the Church. This acceptance is given even though it obligates the mother to behave in ways that are likely to create economic stress on the family.

Ambivalent feelings about the statement were reported by 18 per cent of the mothers. The majority of these (16 per cent) felt that employment outside the home is a personal decision beyond the absolute influence of

Church doctrine. These women appealed to prayer and individual inspiration as an avenue for divine intervention to excuse them from their leader's instruction. They do not totally reject the counsel, but rather argue that mothers must be allowed the agency to make their own inspired decision about whether to work or remain in the home with their children as this quotation shows:

> Each sister (with husband) must determine through prayer what is appropriate for their family, with full intent to do as the Lord wishes.

The other 2 per cent argued that other Church leaders have sent a contrary message through their teachings and organizational behavior. The most frequently mentioned counter-message was the appointment of women with professional careers to leadership positions in the Church. For example:

> Also, it would be wonderful if the Women on the General Board were women who stayed home to raise their children (homemakers) whether they had college or not. Some women who stay at home are just as intelligent and capable.

> It always bothers me to read about women who are chosen for the General Board. They are mostly college graduates who have been or are working mothers. They have worked while raising children and had a career also. Is the church sending mixed messages to its women members? I think so!!

Finally, as can be seen in Table 19.1, only 3 per cent of the women rejected outright the prophet's instruction, and these often argued that his counsel is unrealistic and out-of-sorts with contemporary society as these examples show.

> I think he's full of crap!

> Dream on!!! It's always nice to live in a fantasy world.

> If I had been born 100 years earlier, I would be helping my husband plow fields, feed farm animals, milk cows, gather eggs, or in other ways work to provide sustenance for my family. I don't feel I am doing any different. I probably have more time to spend with my family than someone who had to heat water to wash clothes by hand, grow and prepare all the food for a family, and hand sew all clothing.

LDS mothers to a very large degree accept the instruction from President Benson to remain in the home with their children rather than working outside the home. Only 3 per cent flatly rejected the counsel.

Compliance

Nearly half of the mothers (49 per cent) complied with the President's instruction, which is almost identical to the 47 per cent who completely accepted it. The amount of married women with children who work in American society is over 70 per cent (*Statistical Abstracts*, 1995) and thus the influence of the prophetic instruction in keeping LDS mothers out of the labor force is substantial. For many of these women, compliance meant quitting a job and returning to the home. In some cases the loss in income was a major sacrifice. For example:

> Within a few months of this statement I quit my full-time job to stay home. Maybe in heaven I'll get blessings for obeying but since then we have struggled financially so much that it nearly broke up our marriage. Things are better now. Maybe we don't have enough faith, or something, but we need my income to buy food and pay bills.

> We have always tried to abide by this concept, and while it hasn't been easy, some months we've barely got by, but we feel we've been blessed with a stronger family unit.

An additional 17 per cent of the women claimed they partially comply by working only when their children are in school or else by working only part-time.

> That's why I work part time and where I can see my kids every day. I would not want to work full time. I thoroughly enjoy being a homemaker. Because my husband started his own business, this job helps for family expenses.

> By working part-time (school hours) I don't feel the family pays too high a price. I feel fine about it.

It is remarkable, given the costs incurred, that about two-thirds of the LDS mothers feel they are to a large degree obeying the prophet's instruction. As can be seen by the comments presented, the majority of the LDS women tried as best they could, given their family circumstances, to comply with this difficult counsel.

An additional 20 per cent of the mothers reported they work because of economic necessity. They are divorced or widowed, have husbands unable to work or who are temporarily unemployed, or whose families face a serious economic crisis such as a failed small business or crushing medical expenses. Examples are:

> If I don't work, we don't eat. We're in debt and can't get out if I don't, and the church won't help!!

> I believe it with all my heart! I'm writing this with tears in my eyes because I look forward to the time when our 'unusual circumstances' end and I can stay home.

If I had enough faith I could quit and all would be taken care of. However, I really don't know how we'd pay medical bills, support missionary, etc. I could be resentful of the fact that neither my ex-husband nor current husband can adequately support me and my kids, but it only adds stress to an already stressful situation, so I try to maintain a positive attitude.

Frustrated! I would like to be home, or more likely work just part-time, but my husband doesn't earn anywhere near enough to support us, so I work. I am the main financial support (with insurance, etc. too) for our family.

Only 7 per cent of the women made it clear they completely reject the counsel and work. These women reported that President Benson is out of touch with reality and thus they are not obeying his counsel. One illustrative comment is:

I get angry at this statement. Yes, I would love to stay home and live in the rose-covered cottage with the white picket fence. But life is hard and no one cares.

Many words and phrases in the Bible are difficult to comprehend in today's world; their meanings are no longer known or used. To be realistic, this statement no longer seems feasible or desirable to women today. Some like to work, some have no choice. It's possible to still be a good mother. Pioneers worked.

Some 6 per cent disobey the President's counsel because working provides them with feelings of self-fulfillment, self-worth, personal growth, and accomplishment.

And for myself, working is mandatory for my emotional, spiritual, and physical well-being! I have no qualms whatsoever pursuing part-time employment to enhance my life and the lives of my children.

I stayed home for awhile, became the neighborhood baby sitter – bored, depressed. My children are in school. I go to work after they do, get home just after they do. I feel good about myself and stay informed about the world and what's going on. For me to work is great!

A group of 1 per cent work, but attempt to compensate for doing so by giving their children special experiences and opportunities. Extravagant vacations, music lessons, attendance in sports camps and similar opportunities were most often mentioned.

I do feel guilty about working, but do like giving my children extra things they wouldn't have if I didn't work. Working isn't my life though. So when I'm not at work I donate a lot of time and energy to my children's well-being and happiness.

Finally, 1 per cent of the mothers work outside the home because they feel personal inspiration is supportive of them doing so.

My husband and I give President Benson's statement a great deal of prayer and feel that given our circumstances, the Lord accepts my working. This is best for our family.

After much prayer and fasting, we sold a successful business that my husband and I ran so we could spend more time at home. Especially me.

Compliance to President Benson's statement is high, as nearly two-thirds report they are doing as instructed. Only 7 per cent simply rejected the counsel and worked. Most of the working mothers regretted it and reported they work only because of economic necessity. A sizeable number of the women are struggling to reduce the negative consequences for their children by working only part-time, especially when their children are in school. Many indicate strong yearnings to eventually help their family resolve its debt and then to retire to the home.

Religiosity, acceptance, and compliance

The powerful influence of religiosity on the acceptance of and compliance with President Benson's instruction is evident in Table 19.2. For example only 22 per cent of the mothers with weak religious beliefs accept the counsel compared to 55 per cent of those women with strong beliefs. Of the mothers with weaker religious beliefs 11 per cent completely rejected the statement, while none of the women with stronger beliefs did so.

Table 19.2 The reaction of married LDS women with children at home to President Benson's counsel to remain at home by religiosity

| | Belief Per cent | | Public behavior Per cent | | | Private belief Per cent | | |
| | Low | High | Low | Medium | High | Low | Medium | High |
Reaction	(N=205)	(N=788)	(N=330)	(N=328)	(N=331)	(N=347)	(N=206)	(N=436)
Acceptance								
Complete acceptance	22	55	29	50	62	34	51	56
Accept, but resent	11	4	6	4	5	7	5	5
Accept with exceptions								
Unless *have* to work	25	20	29	23	14	26	21	18
If children at school	4	6	7	5	5	7	2	6
Subtotal	62	85	71	82	86	74	79	85
Ambivalence								
Women free to choose								
to work (agency)	25	13	22	14	12	21	15	12
Mixed messages from								
leaders	2	2	2	3	1	1	4	2
Subtotal	27	15	24	17	13	22	19	14

Rejection of statement								
Complete rejection	11	0	6	1	1	5	2	1
Subtotal	*11*	*0*	*6*	*1*	*1*	*5*	*2*	*1*
Total	100	100	101	100	100	101	100	100

Differences between high and low belief and high, medium, and low public and private behavior are statistically significant at the 0.001 level.

Of the mothers with weaker beliefs, 28 per cent comply with the counsel while 54 per cent of those with strong beliefs are housewives as shown in Table 19.3. Some 20 per cent of mothers with low religious beliefs rejected the statement and worked, while only 2 per cent of the believers did so.

Table 19.3 The impact of President Benson's family counsel on married LDS women with children at home by religiosity

Impact	Belief Per cent		Public behavior Per cent			Private belief Per cent		
	Low (N=193)	High (N=709)	Low (N=297)	Medium (N=295)	High (N=298)	Low (N=309)	Medium (N=192)	High (N=405)
Compliance	28	54	34	44	64	39	43	58
Subtotal	*28*	*54*	*34*	*44*	*64*	*39*	*43*	*58*
Partial compliance								
Work when children in school	6	10	7	11	8	9	11	8
Work part-time	10	8	8	10	6	6	13	6
Exception:								
Have to work	26	21	28	24	16	26	22	19
Subtotal	*42*	*39*	*43*	*45*	*30*	*41*	*46*	*33*
Noncompliance								
Reject statement and work	20	2	16	3	3	10	5	6
Compensate children time, opportunities, etc.	1	1	0	2	0	1	1	0
I choose to work (agency)	4	1	3	0	2	2	0	2
I work for self-fulfillment	5	3	4	6	1	7	5	1
Subtotal	*30*	*7*	*23*	*11*	*6*	*20*	*11*	*9*
Total	100	100	100	100	100	100	100	101

Differences between high and low belief and high, medium, and low public and private behavior are statistically significant at the 0.001 level.

The same large differences in acceptance and obedience occurred for public and private religious behavior. Only 3 per cent of women with high public religious behavior and 6 per cent of those with high private religious behavior rejected and disobeyed the President's instruction as compared to 16 per cent and 10 per cent of those with lower levels of religious behavior. Interestingly, public religious behavior seems to have a little stronger relationship to acceptance and compliance than either belief or private behavior. The strong relationship between religiosity and obedience to prophetic counsel is not surprising, but it should be noted that a small number of highly religious women do reject the message and/or disobey it.

Employment, acceptance, and compliance

As mentioned earlier, we anticipated a very strong, but less than perfect, relationship between current employment and acceptance of and compliance with the President's counsel. The results supported this hypothesis with 75 per cent of the housewives completely accepting the statement as compared with 21 per cent of the mothers who work part-time and with only 6 per cent of those who work full-time as in Table 19.4. Most of the working mothers have not rejected the statement, rather they have defined exceptions which make employment acceptable. Some 48 per cent of mothers employed full-time indicated that employment is justified because of financial pressures. Another 9 per cent felt that working while children are in school is not a violation of the counsel.

Surprisingly, the number of employed women who simply reject the President's counsel is rather small and not much larger than the percentage of housewives. Only 4 per cent of those employed full-time and 2 per cent of those working part-time rejected the statement as unrealistic or out-of-date. Fourteen per cent of the mothers in both groups felt that women have the right to exercise their own personal inspiration which may allow them to work. Altogether, 18 per cent of the mothers employed part-time rejected the counsel in some way as did 21 per cent of those employed full-time.

Interestingly, 6 per cent of those mothers working full-time claim they are complying with the prophetic counsel, while 15 per cent claim partial compliance. Obviously, they have justified their employment to the point that they have defined it as being consistent with the Prophet's counsel. These women have included themselves in the 'unusual circumstances' category mentioned in the instruction as justifying their employment. Of those mothers working part-time 30 per cent defined their behavior as compliance. Another 20 per cent reported they partially complied by working part-time, while an additional 19 per cent complied because they only work while their children are in school.

Table 19.4 The reaction of married LDS women with children at home to President Benson's counsel and input on their behavior, by current employment status.

| | Employment status Per cent | | |
Reaction	Not employed (N=373)	Part-time (N=314)	Full-time (N=296)
Acceptance			
Complete acceptance	75	21	6
Accept, but resent	3	5	10
Acceptance with exceptions:			
Unless have to work	8	44	48
Work if children in school	2	6	9
Subtotal	*88*	*76*	*73*
Ambivalence			
Women may choose to work	10	21	20
Mixed messages from leaders	1	2	3
Subtotal	*11*	*23*	*23*
Rejection			
Complete rejection	1	2	4
Subtotal	*1*	*2*	*4*
Total	100	101	100

Impact	Not employed (N=269)	Part-time (N=210)	Full-time (N=128)
Compliance	94	30	6
Subtotal	*94*	*30*	*6*
Partial compliance			
Work when children in school	1	19	10
Work part-time	1	20	5
Exception:			
Have to work	2	21	60
Subtotal	*4*	*60*	*75*
Noncompliance			
Reject statement and work	1	2	3
Work for self-fulfillment	0	5	12
Compensate children	0	1	2
Choose to work (agency)	1	2	2
Subtotal	*2*	*10*	*19*
Total	100	100	100

Differences between not employed, part-time and full-time employment are statistically significant at the 0.001 level.

Only 3 per cent of the full-time employed mothers reported that they rejected the prophet's statement and worked. The other 97 per cent have provided justification for their employment. As noted above, 21 per cent argue that they complied or at least partially complied. The majority of the women have reduced the inconsistency between their religious beliefs and their behavior by justifying their employment on the grounds of family financial urgency. Most of the mothers working part-time who defined their employment as disobeying the President's instruction also justified their behavior because of financial difficulties.

Leaders of the LDS Church have always stressed developing strong families and the rearing of a righteous generation. General statements encouraging mothers to stay at home with their children have occasionally appeared in the past 50 years. Explicit instructions forbidding LDS mothers from entering the labor force, except in unusual circumstances, were voiced by President Ezra Taft Benson in 1987. At this time, over half of all LDS mothers were already working outside the home and to give up employment entailed considerable sacrifice by the women and their families.

A large majority of the women accepted the counsel as divine. Most continue to try to organize their lives so that they are in the home, and if they work, they try to minimize the impacts of their employment on their children. Two-thirds at least partially obey the instruction and most of the remaining women feel that circumstances force them to remain in the labor force. Only a very small number of LDS mothers work in defiance of their leader's counsel. It is remarkable how seriously LDS women take such statements from Church leaders and how valiantly they struggle to comply. Iannaccone and Miles (1990) analyzed the LDS Church's response to women's issues and concluded that the Church has sought accommodation. They interpret this shift in LDS doctrine and practice as an effort to retain members. This study has found contradictory evidence that LDS women have readily accepted non-accommodation concerning maternal employment. These findings clearly demonstrate the religiosity of these women is a very powerful influence as most strive to live according to the Church's doctrines and practices.

Part VI
Mormon Scripture and Theology

20 Does the Book of Mormon support 'My country right or wrong,' just war or pacifism?

Andrew Bolton

My father was a British soldier in World War II for seven long years. As a Catholic he was told by priests that he was fighting a just war. He could accept that, but what he could not accept was why, in a proudly international church, German Catholics were not told by their priests that they were fighting an unjust war. Perhaps the biggest scandal this century for Christians in Europe is Catholic killing Catholic, Protestant killing Protestant and Christian killing Christian.

I am afraid this scandal extends to Latter-day Saints. Leaders of both the Church of Jesus Christ of Latter-day Saints (LDS) and the Reorganized Church of Jesus Christ of Latter Day Saints (RLDS) have encouraged their young men to fight for their country, even if they were on opposite sides with the possibility of killing each other. Conscientious objection in both movements is a repressed tradition.[1]

As both churches become more fully international we need to question our accommodation to nationalism. Thus to look at what the Book of Mormon says about the ethics of war is important for it is foundational to the whole movement. It is, after all, described twice in the Doctrine and Covenants as containing the fullness of the gospel.[2]

The early Latter-day Saint movement expressed quite unequivocally the importance of peace.[3] Yet the early Saints became increasingly militant, particularly in Far West and Nauvoo (Romig and Siebert, 1993). However, it could be argued that the militaristic response in the early days was simply one of reacting to persecution and was defensive rather than offensive. The RLDS church was the first to react against the militancy of the early church. For instance, in 1874 it chose as its seal or logo the depiction of universal peace described in Isaiah 11 with a child standing between a lion and a lamb just above the word 'peace' and surrounded by the name of the Church.

Subsequently, leaders in both movements have spoken frequently for peace, not least in the 1980s. LDS leaders spoke courageously against the MX nuclear missile system in 1981 (Cahill, 1981; Hildeth, 1984). RLDS prophet-president Wallace B. Smith in 1984 brought inspired direction to the church in terms of the building of a temple in Independence, Missouri, dedicated to the pursuit of peace (RLDS D&C 156:5a).

If the RLDS Temple is dedicated to peace then this implies that this is the central mission of all RLDS members. The question then arises: how should we incarnate peace? By simply obeying whatever our nations legally command us? That maintains a civil peace of some kind, but does it bring international peace and does it compromise the witness to peace of a self-consciously international church? Or do we incarnate peace by a discerning just-war theory which involves selective conscientious objection? Or, again, by adopting non-violent pacifism and thus an absolute conscientious objector position and joining the ranks of the historic peace churches like the Amish, the Mennonites, the Hutterites, or the Quakers?

This debate has scarcely started in the RLDS faith community. But at some point we will have to deal with the Book of Mormon and its expression of the fullness of the gospel – does it have a clear message about war or is it simply ambiguous or even contradictory?

The origins of the Book of Mormon

I want to state at the outset that I am not going to get into the debate about whether the Book of Mormon is real history or inspired parable. I acknowledge the debate exists, but whichever position is true, the Book of Mormon and its message is still clearly part of the Latter-day Saint canon of scripture. Whether Mormon is the real editor of a real historic people's record or whether Joseph Smith Jr is the real editor reworking the collective subconscious of his culture I do not know. For me it is enough that I am inspired by the teachings of this scripture to want to take it seriously whatever its origins. For ease of expression, though, I am going to speak of the Book of Mormon as it is written and not qualify at every turn whether the real editor is Mormon or Joseph.

The editor according to the Book of Mormon

Modern biblical scholarship has worked hard at uncovering the work of often hidden editors. Matthew's gospel, for instance is considered to have been put together by an editor drawing on Mark's gospel, the source and the editor's own material. In the Book of Mormon, however, the editor is up front right at the beginning. His name is Mormon and he acknowledges what he has done in the preface: an account written by the hand of Mormon upon plates taken from the plates of Nephi. He continues by saying it is an abridgement and elsewhere, at strategic places in the Book of Mormon, he tells about his task of selecting and that he can only use a hundredth part of the things of his people.[4]

What do we know about Mormon?

Mormon lived between AD 310 and 385.[5] He was a scholar and a general, living after the golden age of his people at a time of wilful rebellion against God. He is custodian of the records of his people and his life's project is to furnish an abridgement of this record which, after completion by his son Moroni, comes to us as the Book of Mormon. He is also a soldier and it can be suggested that his career as a soldier deeply colors his task of selecting and editing materials to form the Book of Mormon. His example suggests that you can serve with good conscience the Church as a missionary and scholar and the State as a soldier. Or can you?

Mormon's position is complex. He is ethical about war and holds some form of what we would call just-war theory. Just-war theory can be described as an ethical theory about war that attempts to set clear rules about what is and is not permissible. Mormon not only holds such a theory; he acts on it. There comes a point when Mormon's army becomes so vengeful that he refuses to lead it (RLDS BM 1:76; LDS BM 3:11).

In Mormon's refusal to fight we have an attempt to be ethical about war; he is a selective conscientious objector. In other words you cannot always serve your people in war with a good conscience. However, he does return as his people's leader when their situation is desperate and is killed (RLDS BM 2:25–26, 4:2; LDS BM 4:23 – 5:1, 8:3). I wonder if there are so many wars in the Book of Mormon because Mormon, a believer in Christ, was struggling as a soldier to be ethical about war? The fullest expression of just-war theory is in the latter part of Alma, right in the middle of the Book of Mormon, where it is placed in tension with pacifism. The time is 90–77 BC.

Just war and pacifism in Alma

The Nephite Ammon is successful in his somewhat violent and zealous witness to the Lamanite King Lamoni and his people (RLDS Alma 12:29–180; LDS Alma 17:19 – 19:36). The people are converted, bury their weapons of war and then, totally vulnerable, are attacked by other Lamanites, 1005 of them being slaughtered. The non-resistance of these new converts so moved some of the attackers that they also repented and joined them (RLDS Alma 14:11–54; LDS Alma 23:6 – 24:26). It is an extraordinary scene, reminiscent of events in the life of Gandhi or Martin Luther King. Even more significant, it exemplifies the admonition of Jesus in the Sermon on the Mount:

> Do not resist one who is evil. . . .
> Love your enemies and pray for those who persecute you. (Matthew 5:39, 44 RSV)

These converted Lamanites fulfil this teaching completely at this time. To return to the narrative in Alma, Ammon gives this commentary:

> For behold, they had rather sacrifice their lives than even to take the life of their enemy; and they have buried their weapons of war deep in the earth, because of their love towards their brethren. And now behold I say unto you, Has there been such great love in all the land? Behold, I say unto you, Nay, there has not, even among the Nephites. For behold, they would take up arms against their brethren; they would not suffer themselves to be slain. (RLDS Alma 14:118–121; LDS Alma 26:32–34)

The story continues, however, with these converted Lamanites, now called the people of Ammon, fleeing the murderous unconverted Lamanites to the safety of the Nephites, who grant the refugees land and military protection provided they help feed the Nephite armies (RLDS Alma 15:15–26; LDS Alma 27:15–24). Later their sons, numbering 2060, do fight alongside the Nephites as Helaman's striplings (RLDS Alma 24:63–79; 26; LDS Alma 53:10–23 and chs 56–58). The Nephite general at this time is called Moroni. He is described as an ethical soldier, a man who did not delight in bloodshed . . . firm in the faith of Christ (RLDS Alma 21:132, 134; LDS Alma 48:11, 13). There is, here, a clear rationale for just war which makes it just for Nephites to fight provided they are not guilty of the first two offences and that they are defending themselves and their families, their lands, their country, their rights, and their religion (RLDS Alma 20:50–52; LDS Alma 43:45–47).

So the pacifist witness of the converted Lamanites, later known as the people of Ammon, is set in a clear context of a just-war norm, sanctioned by the Lord. However, there remains in this whole story a suggestion that a pacifist witness is born of a deeper, more repentant love, than the love supporting a just-war ethic. Nevertheless, in the tension between the just-war ethic and pacifism, the just-war ethic is clearly dominant in Alma, as it is in Mormon's thinking and for most of the Book of Mormon. However, there is one very significant exception: the record of Jesus' personal ministry and the response of those who believe in him during the subsequent 200 or more years.

After a cacophony of storms and earthquakes, witnessing of Christ's crucifixion, the melody of the Book of Mormon symphony changes quite dramatically with the appearance of Jesus (RLDS III Nephi 4:6–45; LDS 3 Nephi 8:5 – 9:15). The melody of just war utterly disappears and the melody of the people of Ammon, the melody of suffering love, now returns and triumphs completely. The interwoven themes that make up this melody include the Lordship of Christ, the fundamental importance of repentance and baptism, the gift of the Holy Ghost, the Sermon on the Mount, the Blessing of the children – one of the most moving passages for me in all of the world's scriptures – the healing of the sick and the reiteration of the significance of the scriptures of Isaiah. Isaiah is significant because he is the Old Testament prophet who witnesses the transformation of swords into plough-shares, the prince of peace, the lion lying down with the lamb, and the suffering servant. All these passages from Isaiah are very significantly quoted in the Book of Mormon.

The inclusion of the Sermon on the Mount is particularly significant. It is *the* scripture for non-violence. The Beatitudes do not in any way support the just-war theory, concluding as they do with the blessedness of the persecuted which follows directly after the Beatitude stating the blessedness of the peacemakers (RLDS III Nephi 5:69–70; LDS 3 Nephi 12:21–22). The Sermon continues with five passages using the formula:

Ye have heard that it hath been said . . ./ it is written . . . But I say unto you . . .

This formula emphasizes the distinctive difference between the teaching of Jesus and that of previous prophets and teachers. Let us look at three of them directly relevant to our topic:

Ye have heard that it hath been said by them of old time, and it is also written before you, that thou shalt not kill . . .
But I say unto you, whosoever is angry with his brother shall be in danger of his judgement . . . and whosoever shall say, Thou fool, shall be in danger of hell fire. (RLDS III Nephi 5:69–70; LDS 3 Nephi 12:21–22)

And behold, it is written, An eye for an eye, and a tooth for a tooth.
But I say unto you, that ye shall not resist evil, but whosoever shall smite thee on thy right cheek, turn to him the other also . . . (RLDS III Nephi 5:84–85; LDS 3 Nephi 12:38–39)

And behold, it is written also, that thou shalt love thy neighbour and hate thine enemy;
But I say unto you, Love your enemies, bless them that curse you, do good to them that hate you, and pray for them who despitefully use you and persecute you. (RLDS III Nephi 5:89–90; LDS 3 Nephi 12:43–44)

Note that these teachings were prefaced by these words:

For verily I say unto you, that except ye shall keep my commandments, which I have commanded you at this time, ye shall in no case enter into the kingdom of heaven. (RLDS III Nephi 5:68; LDS 3 Nephi 12:20)

Then observe that these teachings conclude with these words:

Old things are done away, and all things have become new; therefore I would that ye should be perfect even as I, or your Father who is in heaven is perfect. (RLDS III Nephi 5:92; LDS 3 Nephi 12:47–48)

Is the just-war theory, as portrayed in the Book of Mormon, part of the old and imperfect to be done away with? Is non-violent resistance the new commandment? Would we be further helped to see how new and different this all is if we had a page called 'The New Testament of the Book of Mormon' separating the chapters containing the personal ministry of Jesus from the earlier part of the Book of Mormon?

188 Andrew Bolton

There is much more we could say from the repeated Sermon on the Mount and the rest of Jesus' teaching and personal ministry. However, in having the Sermon on the Mount twice, Latter-day Saints, above all people, should have taken it seriously.

The response of the people to the ministry of Jesus is described very beautifully in the Fourth Book of Nephi. This is the golden age of the repentant and responsive Nephites who, in keeping the commandments of Jesus, enjoy peace, faithful marriages, and all things common for nigh on 200 years. The fundamental reason is given in this passage:

> And it came to pass that there was no contention in the land, because of the love of God which dwelt in the hearts of the people. (RLDS IV Nephi 1:17; LDS 4 Nephi 1:15)

Here we have an echo of the deep love in the hearts of Ammon's newly converted Lamanites. Later as the golden age began to decline we read this:

> Nevertheless, the people did harden their hearts, for they were led by many priests and false prophets to build up many churches, and to do all manner of iniquity. And they did smite the people of Jesus . . .

What, though, was the response of those still faithful to Jesus? It was that, 'the people of Jesus did not smite again' (RLDS IV Nephi 1:36–37; LDS 4 Nephi 1:34).

This passage is very significant for my thesis that the Book of Mormon is an anti-war scripture which, whilst allowing the just-war theory because of the weakness and lack of love of some disciples, teaches the more faithful way of suffering love. This more faithful way is the suffering cross rather than the sword, where 'mercy . . . overpowerth justice,' to echo an earlier Book of Mormon discussion on the atonement (RLDS Alma 16:216; LDS Alma 34:15).

From this point on in Fourth Nephi we almost need another heading page to say: 'End of the New Testament of The Book of Mormon, The Beginning of Apostasy.'

I would also argue that Mormon, even though entrusted with editing the plates of Nephi and producing the Book of Mormon, is not only living in an apostate age but is also tragically fallen. However, he cannot help but faithfully record the teaching of Jesus and the response of those disciples which resulted in a golden age of almost 200 years of peace and all things in common.

Moroni, Mormon's son and the final editor who completes the Book of Mormon, includes the plates of Ether which conclude with an account of the mutual destruction of the opposing armies of the Jaredites. This tragedy, after Moroni bears witness of the destruction of his own people and the death of his own father, is hauntingly prophetic of the possible holocaust in our own day. Nuclear weapons, if ever used, promise the total destruction of not only one or two peoples and their cultures but all people and all cultures. This seals for me the Book of Mormon as an anti-war scripture. The earlier, almost romantic, view of war in Alma is now replaced by grim, frightening realism.

Conclusion

Does the Book of Mormon support 'My Country right or wrong,' just war or pacifism? The Book of Mormon nowhere speaks of blind obedience to government. At the very least it speaks of *selective* conscientious objection. Mormon's own refusal to fight when his own just-war ethic was violated means that every Latter-day Saint in or considering the military must still use his or her conscience. The Book of Mormon does *not* support 'My Country right or wrong.' However, as has been mentioned, both LDS and RLDS church leaders have encouraged Church members to accept conscription unreservedly. To teach, in effect, complete subjection to kings, presidents, rulers and magistrates, in obeying, honoring and sustaining the law in terms of conscription is dangerous.[6] After all, the Church in 1835 approved a resolution speaking of the importance of conscience (RLDS D&C 112; LDS D&C 134). To be blindly subject to the law puts the flag above the cross, the constitution above the scriptures and Parliament or Congress above Christ. Joseph Smith Jr was told in the first vision that 'all their creeds were an abomination in [God's] sight; that all those professors were all corrupt:' we have forgotten the condemnation due to the creeds of nationalism and those who advocate them.[7]

The Book of Mormon does speak positively about a just-war ethic, but I have argued forcefully that this ethic is superseded by the reiteration of the Sermon on the Mount by Jesus and the example of those who lived during the golden age of the Nephites and who refused, when hit, to strike back. However, if Latter-day Saints are to persist in teaching a just-war theory from their scriptures then they must be much more rigorous about its implementation and be aware how easily the just-war theory is subverted by nationalism. J. H. Yoder, for example, attempts to push just-war thinkers to take their theory rigorously (1984).

Latter-day Saints argue that their churches are restorations of the pure teachings of Christ, and of the early church. Apostasy has traditionally been dated from about AD 312 when the Roman Emperor Constantine began the process of change that led to the enforcing of Christianity as the official religion of the empire. It is significant for me that the early church was arguably pacifist *before* Constantine and that the just-war theory was not developed until *after* Constantine.[8] Thus it could be argued from the early church histories, in both Old and New Worlds, that pacifism is normative Christianity and that just-war is apostasy.

Why have Latter-day Saints not thought this way? I suspect it is because both Puritanism and secular American culture were soaked in just-war theology.[9] After all, what could be more just than the war against the British in 1776? The culture of Latter-day Saints has helped make them blind to reading the Book of Mormon in the way I have suggested as more faithful to the text.

Finally, Conrad has perceptively argued that: 'To be a Reorganized Church member is to live with the tension, to choose *both* Mormon origins *and* Protestant openness' (1991: 228). Whilst agreeing with him I want to say that we should be more choosy over those Protestant partners with whom we are open and those with whom we are in fruitful tension. I have argued elsewhere that they ought to include Anabaptists, that is Hutterites and Mennonites in particular, because of significant parallels between our two movements (Bolton, 1993: 13–24). Their way of interpreting scripture is important and sees Christ as the key to understanding. Not all scripture is equal. The Old Testament is not equal to the New Testament, Christ is the hinge, the watershed, in him is the real fullness of the gospel (Klaassen, 1984: 5–10). Anabaptists can remind us of the utter importance of what Joseph was told on seeing Christ in his first vision: 'Hear him.' Furthermore, the Anabaptist tradition of seeing and following the suffering Christ can help us highlight the significance of Joseph declaring he saw and heard the crucified Christ in his first description of the first vision (Howard, 1980: 97). Finally, Anabaptists also have the great virtue, one we presently lack, of being really committed to peace through non-violence.

William Juhnke, a Mennonite professor at the RLDS Graceland College in Iowa, wrote:

> As a latter-day Anabaptist, I frequently ask myself: Will it ever be possible for humankind to respond from strength with non-violent love? Just imagine for a moment: What if the Mormons – with all their visionary leadership, their positive Zion-building energy, their organizational and administrative genius, and their opportunity of a frontier haven – had responded from strength with non-violent love? Would they have failed miserably, losing their lives and their vision? Or would they have transformed the world? (1982: 44)

Do the modern Latter-day Saint movements, now self-consciously international, need to reconsider their accommodation to nationalism, their present doctrines on war and peace, and their shameful neglect of the Sermon on the Mount? I think so.

Notes

1. The LDS church is the group which, after Joseph Smith Jr's death in 1844, followed Brigham Young from Nauvoo, Illinois, to the Great Salt Basin in Utah and became what is sometimes called the Mormon church. The LDS church identifies with the Nauvoo era (1839–44) and is a continuation of developments there. Today this church numbers internationally over nine million members. The RLDS church arose in 1852 in the mid-West and consisted of dissenting and more democratic Latter-day Saints who were anti-polygamous, non-militant and identified with the Kirtland era (1831–37), rather than the later Nauvoo era (1839–45). They sought to be faithful to early Latter-day Saintism and yet be

open to Protestantism. They looked forward to the leadership of Joseph Smith Jr's son, Joseph Smith III, who eventually in 1860 assumed the position of prophet and served until his death in 1914. Today, under the leadership of Wallace B. Smith, the great-grandson of Joseph Smith Jr, the RLDS number about a quarter of a million members world-wide.

For the RLDS position on conscientious objection see, for example, President F. M. Smith's position (he was against 'slackers and cowardly pacifists') as described in Hunt (1982). For the LDS position see H. J. Grant, Clark, and Mckay (1942): 93–5. C. D. Tate Jr (1992: 311) states that 'Church leaders have discouraged conscientious objection in every conflict of the twentieth century.'

2. The RLDS and LDS have their own editions of the Doctrine and Covenants with some differences in revelations and section numbering and versification. Therefore both are quoted. See RLDS D&C 26:2a, 42:5a; LDS D&C 27:5, 42:12.

3. E.g. The Book of Mormon: 'And whoso shall publish peace, yea, tidings of great joy, how beautiful upon the mountains shall they be.' Both the RLDS and LDS churches have their own editions of the BM with different chapter numbers and versification. The RLDS old authorized edition, based on the 1908 edition, is used in this paper since the words are almost identical to the LDS edition. The RLDS new authorized edition has modernized English. See RLDS BM I Nephi 3:189; LDS BM 1 Nephi 13:37.

   Revelation at Kirtland, August 6, 1833: 'therefore, renounce war and proclaim peace' in RLDS D&C 95:3a; LDS D&C 98:16.

4. RLDS BM, see Words of Mormon 1:8, III Nephi 2:92, III Nephi 12:1; LDS BM, see Words of Mormon 1:5, 3 Nephi 5: 8, 3 Nephi 26:6.

5. Information for this paragraph is obtained from RLDS BM Mormon 1:1–33 and Words of Mormon 1:1–13; LDS BM Mormon 1:1 – 2:9 and Words of Mormon 1:1–9.

6. PGP (1967):59, Article of Faith no. 13.

7. *The History of the Reorganized Church of Jesus Christ of Latter Day Saints* 1: *1805–1835* (1951): 9. Independence, MO: Herald House; PGP 2:19.

8. I am aware that the pacifist nature of the early church is debatable. For instance, those supporting the argument include Yoder (1983), Bainton (1960), and Driver (1988). Scholars sounding a note of caution include Helgeland, Daly, and Burns (1987). Though these admit that:

   1. 'Modern exegetes generally agree with the ancient fathers that, however differently one may try to apply it in practice, the basic thrust of the Lord's teaching is clearly towards nonviolence' (1987: 12).

   2. The just-war theory is not 'equally well grounded in the NT as is nonviolence' (ibid.: 15).

   3. 'Observing the list of military metaphors from the NT, one is immediately aware that none are from the gospels, Jesus apparently did not speak this way. His preaching is an example of vivid teaching employing seemingly endless metaphors and parables, yet none are drawn from military life' (ibid.: 16). Cf. Young (1989).

9. See statements on just war in the Lutheran, Anglican, and Presbyterian creeds in J. H. Yoder, *Christian Attitudes to War, Peace, and Revolution – A Companion to Bainton*: 111. Goshen, IN: Goshen Biblical Seminary. See also Graham Stott's discussion about Real Whig formulations of just war during the revolutionary period in Stott (1988).

21 The death/rebirth mytheme in the Book of Mormon

Seth D. Kunin

In recent years the Book of Mormon has begun to be analyzed from a variety of new approaches. Some of these are discussed in Metcalfe's *New Approaches to the Book of Mormon* (Metcalfe, 1993). One approach which has yet to be applied to this body of material is anthropological or Lévi-Straussian structuralism. This methodology, which focuses on underlying patterns of cultural communities, has the potential to illuminate many aspects of the Book of Mormon specifically and the Mormon community in general. Structuralism offers a bridge between text (myth) and other elements of culture, e.g. social and political structure.

Structural theory suggests that culture, or any of its aspects, can be analyzed on a number of related levels. These levels are progressively deeper within the mind and more abstract. In order to facilitate our understanding we may think of this structure as divided into four levels, each represented by a letter and a number. S^1 is the deepest level of structure. It represents the biological level of structure which is part of all human beings' genetic inheritance. This level is both universal and contentless. It consists of empty unrelated categories which are minimally dyadic. For example, categories A and B, the two are empty and as yet unrelated.

The second level of structure, S^2, is the level at which the biological categories are defined in relation to each other. This definition might include a positive negative or neutral relation, e.g. A+B, A–B, or A=B. S^2, however, like S^1, is an abstract equation or relation and therefore is contentless. The relation between categories is culturally determined and maximally functions in a group of related cultures.

The third level, S^3, is that at which content is added to the equation, e.g. A(Pure[cow])–B(Impure[pig]). The equation organizes and structures this information. S^3 is culture or subculture specific. Each culture or community will add information which is significant to their cultural situation or context.

It is at this level that mythemes are found. Mythemes are mythological units which are irreducible and are the components out of which a myth (or ritual) is composed. N, the final level, is the narrative or story level of the text or the progression of actions in a ritual. By analyzing the relationship and development of these different levels in a specific community, many apparently unrelated aspects of the culture can be shown to work, at the level of structure, in similar ways.

The Book of Mormon presents fascinating possibilities for the application and testing of this structuralist theory and methodology.[1] It is written over and against the Hebrew Bible and New Testament, both consciously and unconsciously, yet its cultural context is very different. This suggests that while it may include mythemes which are found in the Hebrew Bible and New Testament, these mythemes should be characterized by significant transformation reflecting the cultural differences. Structure is not an artifact, theoretically it should be sensitive to different cultural contexts. Thus when a mythological element is used in a new cultural context, it should be structurally transformed to reflect the needs of its new context.[2]

Transformation is found on two levels, S^3 and S^2. S^3 may be transformed in two respects. First, as a result of cultural transformation mythological elements and crises which were once significant may not be significant and thus S^3 will deal with different issues. Second, the elements out of which the myth is constructed may also be transformed. As Lévi-Strauss indicates, myth-making is a process of *bricolage*, of using the materials and symbols available to create a structurally meaningful construct (1966: 16–33). Thus myths created in nineteenth-century United States should contain elements and fragments from that context as well as elements taken and adapted from the biblical texts.

Transformation is also found at S^2. The S^2 or structural matrix is culture or culture area specific. Thus structuralist theory predicts that when a myth is created or recreated in a different cultural system S^2 will be transformed. The Book of Mormon emerged from a very different cultural, temporal, and geographic context from the Hebrew Bible and New Testament and therefore is based on a fundamentally different structural equation.

This paper examines this process of transformation by focusing on a single mytheme: death/rebirth. The death/rebirth mytheme is central to all three texts. Its transformation in each reveals significant areas of cultural and structural transformation. It should be noted, however, from the outset that there is a long historical gap between the writing of the New Testament and that of the Book of Mormon. Future research is necessary to determine the process of structural transformation during that period.

The death/rebirth mytheme is found in two primary forms in the Hebrew Bible: sacrifice and murder. The sacrifice variant of the mytheme is exemplified by the 'Sacrifice of Isaac, i.e. Genesis 22.' The murder variant is exemplified by the 'Murder of Joseph, i.e. Genesis 37.'[3] These two variations are structural inversions of each other. Figure 21.1 illustrates both aspects of the death/rebirth mytheme as it is developed in the Hebrew Bible. A and A^1 represent father, B and B^1 chosen son, C and C^1 non-chosen sons, and b and b^1 the animal killed in place of B and B^1 respectively.

194   *Seth D. Kunin*

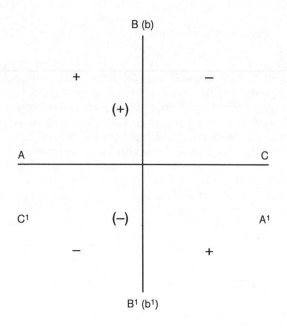

Figure 21.1 Death/rebirth mytheme in the Hebrew Bible

The diagram indicates that there is a positive (+) qualitative relationship between A and B while there is a negative (–) relationship between A, B and C. The positive quality is emphasized by the sacrifice and upward movement while the negative quality is emphasized by murder and downward movement. All variations of the mytheme occur in liminal space. The sacrifice variant occurs in positive liminal space, between heaven and earth. The murder variant occurs in negative liminal space, between earth and Sheol.[4] The negative relations are found in the bottom left and top right quadrants and the positive in the top left and bottom right. A and B share several attributes: both were the divinely chosen son (albeit at different diachronic positions), both are genealogical ancestors of Israel, and both are divinely (symbolically) reborn. C, however, shares none of these characteristics.

In a more generalized analysis of the terms, A and B represent Israel while C represents the nations.[5] Thus 'A,B not C' indicates a strong ideological boundary between Israel and the nations. Israel is genealogically and qualitatively (through divine rebirth) distinct from the nations. The key aspect of biblical structure is indicated by the location of the symbolic variant. Death and/or rebirth is symbolic while genealogy is real. Thus the structure uses symbolic rebirth to emphasize and strengthen genealogical distinctiveness. Israel is defined by genealogical rather than ideological factors.

The brothers appear to be mediators.[6] They share some characteristics of Israel, i.e. apparent genealogical kinship (they often share one or both parents). But like the nations which are not closely related, they are not divinely reborn. They bridge the gap between Israel and the nations. Such a mediator, however, is not structurally acceptable. The equation 'A not B' relies on there being no mediators which lessen the distance between the two categories. Thus by creating ideological distance through murder and rejection and qualitative distance through rebirth the brothers are moved from a mediatory position to a clearly negative position.

The development of the death/rebirth mytheme in the New Testament is superficially identical to that of the Hebrew Bible. In Figure 21.2 A represents the father, i.e. God. B represents Jesus the son. C represents the Jews and (C^1 Judas the brother). Judas is structurally identified as Jesus' brother by several texts, e.g. Matthew 13:55.[7] Although the Judas mentioned in that text may be a different Judas, on the level of structure the similarity of names suggests structural identity (at least in terms of role). The upper two quadrants represent the sacrifice aspect of the myth and the lower two, the murder elements.

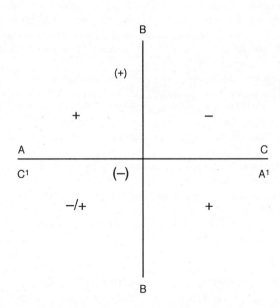

Figure 21.2 Death/rebirth mytheme in the New Testament

If the diagrammatic presentations of the two are compared there is only one apparent change, the mediating b (ram or lamb) is removed and B is actually sacrificed. Thus in the New Testament sacrifice/murder is actual rather than symbolic. There are, however, several subtle changes. The identity of A reflects the move to actual rather than symbolic sacrifice.

Whereas in the Hebrew Bible A is a biological father reflecting the genealogical pattern of descent and divine rebirth (and origin) is symbolic, in the New Testament A is God, suggesting actual divine birth and thereby denying genealogy.

The denial of genealogy is also developed on two other levels. In the sacrifice aspect of the myth C represents the Israelites who remain at the bottom of the cross (or not even there) and who are not transformed. Thus, the text creates structural opposition between Jesus and the Jews. This opposition weakens or denies Jesus' genealogical connection to Israel. The denial of genealogy is found in several other texts, e.g. Luke 8:19–21. This text suggests that actual genealogy is replaced by symbolic genealogy. Jesus' family are those who hear the word of God rather than those who are biologically related to him. This transformation is also reflected in the murder aspect. C^1, Judas, is identified with both Jesus' biological family and Israel. Thus, the rejection of Judas is equally the rejection of genealogy and Israel.

The second level in which the denial of genealogy is developed is that of passing the divine seed. In the Hebrew Bible, the chosen son gains fertility after his transformation and passes the divine seed to his son. In the New Testament, however, Jesus has no biological children, thus ending the biological chain of descent. Jesus' 'children' are not biological, they are spiritual. In the Hebrew Bible, death and rebirth are symbolic while genealogy is real. In the New Testament, however, death and rebirth are real and genealogy is symbolic.

Thus, although the mytheme contains the same structural relations as that of the Hebrew Bible, through an inversion of key elements the myth develops a different underlying structural equation. On the surface the equation appears to remain the same A (God, Jesus and his spiritual descendants) not B (Israel). This, however, is actually not the case. B, through spiritual transformation, can become A. Therefore there is not found the absolute opposition suggested by 'A not B.' The equation is rather 'A neutral B' in which a positive mediator, Jesus, allows movement from B to A. The mediatory aspect of Jesus is emphasized by his containing both human and divine elements.

The transformation in mythological structure reflects a transformation in social structure. Unlike the culture which created the Hebrew Bible, whose definition of self was based on a purely genealogical model and a pattern of endogamy, the community which created the New Testament defined itself through faith which created a symbolic genealogical relation (e.g. the term 'father' used in respect to the priesthood and communities of 'brothers' and 'sisters').

In line with this transformation in social organization and structural equation it is likely that the diagram presented opposite needs to be adjusted. Figure 21.3 presents the new model for the death/rebirth mytheme in the New Testament. The two changes are in the qualitative relations between B and C, and B and C^1. The relation is now categorized as neutral to reflect the positive mediator. This qualitative transformation is supported on the mythological level. In respect to the relation of B and C

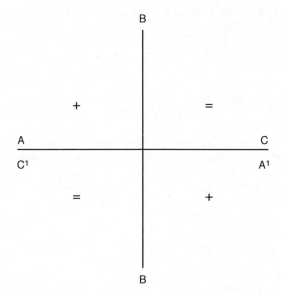

Figure 21.3 Death/rebirth mytheme in the New Testament (adjusted)

on the sacrifice level, C includes the apostles and Israel, i.e. symbolic brothers as well as real brothers, both of which can be transformed through the sacrifice. In respect to B and C^1, i.e. Judas's role in the death of Jesus, mediators, the Romans, are added to reduce Judas's (and the Jews') culpability.

The Book of Mormon includes several variations of the death/rebirth mytheme. Not surprisingly, as the mytheme relates to origins and transformation, most of these are found in the first several sections. In its development in the Book of Mormon the mytheme betrays characteristics of both the Hebrew Bible and the New Testament variants.

One textually early variant of the mytheme is 1 Nephi 7:16–22. This text includes several mythological associations with biblical versions. Nephi is bound by his brothers with the intent of killing him.[8] Thus, one main focus of this text is the murder variant of the mytheme. The text includes narrative elements which associate it with Genesis 37, e.g. Nephi, the chosen son, is sent out with his brothers into the wilderness, the mention of wild beasts as the cause of death. Murder creates ideological distance, thereby creating an opposition between Nephi, the chosen son, and his brothers who are the ancestors of other peoples. This opposition is weakened in two respects: Nephi is not actually killed and his brothers repent and are forgiven.

The murder element, however, is not the only aspect of this version. The text also includes several elements connecting it to the sacrificial model, e.g. binding with cords. The presence of Ishmael and the sacrifice (rather than slaughter) of the replacement animal also supports this association. The geographic location of the narrative also supports the development of both variants simultaneously: it is on the flat in the wilderness, i.e. neutral rather than positive or negative liminal space. The interesting transformation of the sacrifice variant is that the brothers perform the sacrifice. This weakens the opposition between Nephi and his brothers.

Thus, although this text transforms Nephi through symbolic death and rebirth, this transformation does not create absolute opposition between transformed and untransformed. Although the aspect of rebirth, as in the Hebrew Bible, is symbolic, the divine element of the transformation is strengthened through the divine action in removing the bonds.

Chapter 18 of 1 Nephi also includes a variant of this mytheme. In a sense, the chapter as a whole is a rebirth narrative. The ship is structurally and narratively related to the story of Noah in Genesis which functions as a rebirth/recreation text.[9] It is significant that all Nephi's family are included in the rebirth, and the other peoples are not wiped out (as in the flood). The journey across the sea, and the rebirth that it suggests, create opposition between the new Israel and the old, but not an insurmountable barrier (as indicated by subsequent movements across the sea).

Chapter 18 also includes a more specific example of the death/rebirth mytheme. As in the chapter 7 version, being bound is the symbol of death. The non-chosen brothers Laman and Lemuel seek to kill Nephi, thus creating horizontal opposition. This opposition is strengthened by the association of the brothers with the children of Ishmael.

The text also creates vertical association between Nephi and his father Lehi. Lehi argues for Nephi's freedom and his own life is threatened. This is further emphasized by the possibility that Lehi and his wife might die on account of these events (verse 18). The symbolic death of Nephi's parents also strengthens the symbolic rebirth. In many biblical rebirth texts, biological parents are removed to emphasize the divine nature of the rebirth.

This text creates less ambiguity in the structural oppositions developed. On the vertical level, as in the sacrifice variation, a positive valence is found (between Son and Father). On the horizontal level, the murder variant, strong negative valence is found (between Brother and Brother). As in the version in chapter 7, however, the death and rebirth remain symbolic and the brothers are ultimately forgiven. In this respect both are similar to the final version of the death/rebirth mytheme in Genesis. Because of narrative constraints all of Jacob's sons must be within Israel, thus they are ultimately forgiven. Equally, although Nephi's brothers will be rejected and excluded, ultimately there is the possibility of their return. This is emphasized by the fact that they go through a process of rebirth by crossing the sea.

The structural relations developed in the Book of Mormon are diagrammed in Figure 21.4. A represents Lehi (and God in the initial version), B Nephi, and C Laman and Lemuel (and the Ishmaelites). The two significant quadrants are the bottom left and top right, both of which are neutral. Although the structural relations are similar to those of the New Testament there is a fundamental difference in emphasis. As found in the Hebrew Bible rebirth is symbolic. This suggests that genealogy should be significant. This is further suggested by the genealogical element essential to the narrative (Nephi is the biological son of Lehi, suggesting the passage of the

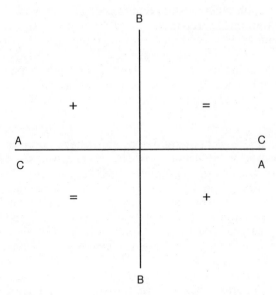

Figure 21.4. Death/rebirth mytheme in the Book of Mormon

divine seed). It is significant, however, that it is Jacob rather than Nephi's children who inherits the divine seed. This is due to the triadic rather than dyadic aspect of Mormon structure. This element is discussed below.

The genealogical element, however, is not sufficient to explain the neutral valences within the structural model. These elements suggest that like the New Testament there should be an overlap between categories, i.e. elements should be able to move from one category to the other. Laman and Lemuel and their descendants are rejected initially on the genealogical level, but through faith can be reintegrated. The faith aspect of self-definition is highlighted in several texts, see for example 2 Nephi 26 and 30. Both texts emphasize the possibility of transformation through faith rather than descent.

The two elements, genealogical opposition and transformation through faith within a dyadic system, are paradoxical. They suggest two incompatible methods of self-definition. One half suggests that mediation is possible, and therefore movement between categories is possible. The other suggests that mediation is impossible. One resolution could be the adoption within a genealogical model of those transformed, as indeed happens within the Mormon Church. This solution is adopted in Jewish tradition. A proselyte is transformed and adopted into the Jewish genealogical model as a child of Abraham and Sarah. If such a resolution was completely adopted, however, we would expect a similar structural pattern to the Hebrew Bible rather than the structural pattern found in the Book of Mormon. The neutral element within the structural pattern weakens the opposition of 'A not B.' This suggests that a different structural pattern is at work.

In order to resolve the paradox, two related elements must be analyzed: the role of mediation; and the model of categorization. If a dyadic model is correct, then the middle element in sets of three should mediate between the other two. Several sets of three are developed in the text. One such set is the six sons of Lehi. The sons can be divided into three pairs: Laman and Lemuel (A); Nephi and Sam (B); and Joseph and Jacob (C). Nephi and Sam should structurally overlap with the other two pairs. There are elements which support this model, e.g. both A and B are born in Jerusalem, while both B and C are divinely chosen. A and C also have elements which distinguish them from B, A being non-chosen (bearer of non-divine seed) and C being the bearer of the divine seed (in essence A is the opposite of C). There are, however, several elements which suggest that B is an independent category rather than a mediator. It is B, or more specifically Nephi, who is divinely reborn. The initial chosen land is also named after Nephi. Similarly on a structural level the relationship between B and the other two elements support this characterization. B is differentially related to the other two and thus does not bridge the gap. B is negatively or neutrally related to A, while it is positively related to B (A=/−B+C). It is likely that B is a distinct category rather than a mediator.

Thus, there is a pattern of structural transformation regarding mediation among the three texts examined here. In the Hebrew Bible mediators were negative: 'A not B' allows no mediation. In the New Testament they are positive: 'A neutral B' allows (perhaps demands) movement between the two. In the Book of Mormon, however, mediators are transformed into categories. Thus Nephi and Sam are not mediators between the other two sets of brothers but a category in and of themselves. Nephi is reborn (as Jesus is reborn), perhaps defining the middle category as outside made inside (perhaps within the faith model of transformation suggested below). It is Jacob, however, who is born inside (representing the genealogical model of descent), who takes up the reins of leadership and thus genealogically passes on the divine seed. This pattern is also developed in regard to the trinity, each element of which is given independent existence in Mormon theology.[10]

This is further supported when the models of categorization are examined. If the early chapters of the Book of Mormon are analyzed, the structure seems to be based on three categories, i.e. triadic, rather than two, dyadic. Triadic structure is indicated on several levels. Lehi's sons are only one of many examples. Within the three pairs of sons there is progressive transformation from non-chosen to chosen to chosen with divine seed, yet each category is distinct. The world is initially divided into three geographic units: Jerusalem, Laman, and Nephi, each one transforming into the next. A similar pattern is evident in respect to nations. Humanity is divided into three groups: Gentiles, the Jews, and Israel. The transformative aspect in respect to humanity is developed both in texts like 2 Nephi 26:33 and metaphorically in the parable of the vineyard (Jacob 5) and that of the olive tree (1 Nephi 15). The significant element of both parables is the mixing of grafted and natural branches, grafted branches representing joining

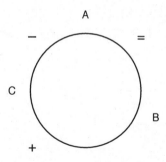

Figure 21.5 The structural equation of Mormon thought

through faith and natural through genealogy. The parables also reveal a circular aspect to the triadic structure.

Rather than a linear equation, we find in the Book of Mormon a circular equation illustrated in Figure 21.5. In principle A can transform into B which can transform into C and possibly back into A. The full circular pattern is found in the history of nations. Nations move the full circle of development from negative or neutral to positive and back to negative. This pattern is highlighted above in respect to the parables of the olive tree and the vineyard. Similarly humans move through a transformational cycle which ultimately ends in divinity.

Genealogy provides a definition of self and category but it is not suffi-cient. Faith (or baptism) is a transformational factor. It allows elements to move (and remain) between categories. Thus the structural pattern found in the Book of Mormon supports a pattern of double identification. Faith allows movement from outside to inside and genealogy both past and present supports a structure of internal cohesion.

The pattern of transformation in emphasis is illustrated in Table 21.1. In the Hebrew Bible the emphasis is on genealogical relation and definition; thus the symbolic death mythologically supports the opposition between those within the genealogical community and those outside of it. In the New Testament, in which faith is emphasized, actual death and rebirth denies the genealogical chain. It removes the qualitative distinction between peoples and thereby opens membership. In the Book of Mormon both elements are emphasized allowing a strong internal cohesion and model of self-definition while still being able to transform those who are not yet within the community.

Table 21.1

	Symbolic death	Actual death	Symbolic genealogy	Actual genealogy	Self-defining genealogy	Self-defining faith
Hebrew Bible	+	–	–	+	+	–
New Testament	–	+	+	–	+	+
Book of Mormon	+	–/=	=/+	+	+	+

This preliminary analysis of a single mytheme from the Book of Mormon indicates areas of transformation from the structures of the Hebrew Bible and the New Testament. The most significant of these is the transformation of the mediator (negative and positive in the Hebrew Bible and New Testament respectively) into a distinct category giving Mormon thought a triadic rather than dyadic structure. In a sense the structure found is a synthesis of the two foci of other traditions, e.g. genealogy and faith. With emphasis placed on both rather than one or the other. The transformations found raise several questions requiring further analysis. First, is the pattern of transformation found in other mythemes? Second, what is the origin of the transformation? Is it historically linked to Joseph Smith or can a pattern of continuous transformation be found in earlier and contemporary texts? Finally, to what degree are individuals able to effect significant transformations in underlying structure – can private idiosyncratic structure become public?

Notes

1. The structuralist theory used in this paper is anthropological rather than literary. It is partially based on the work of Claude Lévi-Strauss (see especially 1963, 1969, 1981, 1988), of E. R. Leach (e.g. 1969 and Leach and Aycock, 1983), and of Turner (1977). See also Kunin (1995): 18–48.
2. This pattern of transformation is illustrated by the transformation in the structure of the flood story when it is used in the biblical text. See, for example, Kunin (1995): 170–3.
3. Both of these texts are examined in detail in Kunin (1994): 57–81 and (1995): 91–103.
4. There is a third version of the mytheme which includes elements of the other two. This mytheme typically occurs on flat liminal space, e.g. the wilderness. Two examples of this type are Exodus 4:18–26 and Genesis 32:4–33. These texts usually include elements of both sacrifice and murder.

5. Genesis 37 is structurally a perfect inversion of Genesis 22. Thus at the level of structure, Joseph's brothers represent the nations. This equivalence is found in every other version of the mytheme, e.g. in the 'Murder of Abel.' On the narrative level, because of the placement of the myth, i.e. at the end of the process of genesis, Joseph's brothers are not excluded from Israel and thus are not absolutely equivalent to the nations. On the level of structure, however, diachronic or narrative placement is irrelevant. Thus in respect to their structural role they represent the nations in opposition to Joseph who represents Israel.
6. Mediation on the level of underlying structure refers to the area of overlap between categories and its qualitative valance.
7. Structuralism assumes that similarity of names in mythological texts is not coincidental. If similar names are used, especially in cases where one of the uses is not significant, structuralist theory suggests that a relation or identification between the two figures is developed. Thus Judas, by similarity of name, is identified with Jesus' brother Judas.
8. It is interesting that Ishmael is mentioned in the first section of the chapter. This suggests a structural association with Genesis 22. This association is also strengthened by the binding.
9. See for example, Kunin (1995): 170–2.
10. The transformation in respect to theology is significant. In Jewish structure God and man are absolutely divided, mirroring the structural equation (S^2) A–B. In classical Christian structure Jesus mediates between humanity and God – he is both human and divine, reflecting the equation A=B (with positive mediation). In Mormon structure, which is circular, there is a progressive transformation towards the divine, with Jesus as an independent intermediate category.

22 Must God be incorporeal?

David L. Paulsen

Though the earliest Christians believed God to be embodied, thinkers within the classical Christian tradition have reasoned that God must, logically, be incorporeal, without body or parts. Yet Christians commonly affirm that Christ was once mortal and now exists everlastingly with a resurrected body. But if God must be incorporeal, then the embodied Christ cannot be God. How is this apparent paradox to be resolved? In this paper, I attempt to show that the arguments used by classical Christian thinkers are not sufficient to prove that God cannot have a body.

The pattern of reasoning that arguments for God's incorporeality typically follow is set out in the eleventh century by Anselm (Deane, 1966: ch. 2). By defining God as 'that than which none greater can be conceived,' Anselm felt that he was able to prove not only that God existed, but also what he is like. In particular, Anselm argues that this definition of God entails that God must be incorporeal.

In order to see why, it is helpful to examine what Anselm meant by *greatest*. Anselm explains that the 'greatest conceivable being' would lack nothing that is good and would be 'whatever it is better to be than not to be.' Most commentators have interpreted the value terms *good* and *better* in these sentences as signifying religious values. Thus, when Anselm calls God the 'greatest conceivable being,' he means 'the most worthy object of religious worship.' Using this formula as a basis, I will now examine some of the arguments which Anselm and others believed could prove God's incorporeality.[1]

Argument from divine infinity

From the statement 'God is the greatest conceivable being,' Anselm first derives that 'God cannot be limited in any way.' Following Anselm, J. N. Findlay has recently suggested that it is 'wholly anomalous to worship anything limited in any thinkable manner. For all limited superiorities are tainted with an obvious relativity, and can be dwarfed in thought by still mightier superiorities' (1965: 116). Then, from the conclusion that God is wholly unlimited, Anselm infers that God cannot have or be a body. He argues:

> For altogether circumscribed is that which, when it is wholly in one place, cannot at the same time be in another. And this is seen to be true of corporeal things alone. But uncircumscribed is that which, as whole, at the same time everywhere. And this is understood to be true of thee alone. (Deane 1966: 20)

Anselm's argument can be summarized as follows:
1. God = the most worthy object of religious worship.
2. The most worthy object of worship cannot be limited in any way.
3. If God were corporeal, he would be limited to being in only one place at one time – not 'as whole, at the same time everywhere.'
4. Hence, God cannot be corporeal. (1) (2) (3)

As a first objection to premise 2, if it is understood literally, even Anselm himself cannot consistently affirm it. If God were absolutely unlimited in any way, he would have to be the whole of reality and not the Creator-God of theism who is ontologically distinct from his creations. It is presumably the existence of this Creator-God that Anselm attempts to prove. Furthermore, if God has no limits, then he can have no determinate attributes, negative or positive. For example, if God were immutable, he would be limited in that he would not be able to change. Thus, Findlay describes a wholly unlimited God as 'a deific absence of any definite.' But Anselm employs his deity-formula to generate 18 divine attributes. Findlay's assertion that it is 'wholly anomalous to worship anything limited in any thinkable manner' fails to recognize that some limitations, as limitations, are not defects. Being limited in qualities such as ignorance, selfishness, or cruelty is obviously a good thing. Anselm makes it clear that God would be unlimited only in admirable qualities. However, it is also possible to have too much of a good thing. It is possible to be too trusting, too generous, or too helpful. In addition, Charles Hartshorne explains that not all values, especially in their superlative form, are logically compassable; unlimited compassion and unlimited bliss, for example, preclude each other (1964: 1–56).

No doubt what Anselm meant, or should have meant, is 2': the most worthy object of religious worship must be unlimited in every aspect in which to be so is (1) possible, (2) admirable, and when conjoined with other excellences, (3) worshipworthy maximizing (hereafter WWM). But if I replace premise 2 in Anselm's argument with 2', the argument is no longer valid.

The argument from divine power

In order to make Anselm's argument work now, I shall have to supply an additional premise to show some aspect in which God must be absolutely unlimited that is both possible and WWM and simultaneously incompatible with incorporeality. Unlimited power would seemingly satisfy these conditions. If so, I can use unlimited power to form the following argument:

1. God = the most worthy object of religious worship.
2'. The most worthy object of religious worship must be absolutely unlimited in every respect possible and WWM.
5. It is possible and WWM for God to be absolutely unlimited in power.
6. N (If God is corporeal, then God is not absolutely unlimited in power).
7. Hence, God cannot be corporeal.

I must now consider whether premise 5 is true. Is it possible for God to be unlimited in power? The possibility of unlimited power seems to lead to inconsistencies, such as the well-known paradox that God could create a stone so large that he could not lift it. To salvage a rationally coherent view of God, many have proposed definitions of omnipotence considerably more restricted than its etymology suggests. For example, Anthony Kenny has recently proposed that omnipotence be understood as 'the possession of all ... powers that is possible for a being with the attributes of God to possess,' where 'attributes' are 'properties of God which are not themselves powers' (1979: 98). But if these attributes are to be determined by Christian revelation, which affirms that God the Son has a resurrected body, then omnipotence must mean all power that an embodied God could have. Thus, there would be no conflict between omnipotence and corporeality.

If instead the divine attributes are derived from Anselm's formula, I must ask how much power does God need to be a WWM? For this assurance, it seems that God must be supreme and have power over all things so that no one or no thing can thwart the fulfillment of his will. Let us use the term *almighty* to refer to this degree of power. To insist that God must possess power beyond this degree is to affirm that power has something worshipworthy about it, *per se*, apart from any good ends it makes possible. Such a belief is not religiously or morally necessary.

If my reasoning is correct, it is neither possible nor WWM for God to be absolutely unlimited in power. Thus premise 5 is false, and must be changed to:

5'. The most worthy object of religious worship must be almighty. To make Anselm's argument work, I must then show:

8. N (if *x* is corporeal, then *x* is not almighty).

If 8 is true, it is by no means self-evident. Anselm's argument suggests that it could be linked with a further premise about omnipresence to form a further argument.

The argument from divine omnipresence

This argument can be stated as follows:

1. God = the most worthy object of religious worship.
5'. The most worthy object of religious worship must be almighty.
9. N (if God is almighty, then God is omnipresent).

10. N (if God is omnipresent, then God is not corporeal).

11. Hence, God cannot be corporeal.

Religiously, the affirmation of God's omnipresence is the assurance of God's loving awareness of all that is transpiring, his constant watchful care, and his ability to intervene in our lives to fulfil his purposes and promises. Thus it seems that divine omnipresence is related to God's power and that if God is almighty, he must be omnipresent.

This understanding brings me to consider premise 10. Is it true that an embodied being could not be omnipresent? Grace Dyck (1977: 85–91) has recently examined this question.[2] She points out that, in the most relevant sense of the word *present*, (a) It is not the case that I am present only in the volume of space occupied by my body; and (b) to be present at x means, most essentially, to be aware of what is going on at x, and, perhaps, be able to influence it to some extent. For instance, surely a speaker addressing the Senate would be said to be present in the entire Senate Chamber, not just in the spatial coordinates of his or her own body. Similarly, if a Senator slept through the reading and discussion of a bill, he or she could not be said to be present.[3] Dyck concludes that if God has a spatially extended body somewhere in the universe, and from the position he knows and is able to influence everything, he could properly be called omnipresent. If Dyck's analysis is correct, the argument from omnipresence is obviously invalid.

The argument from divine indestructibility

Anselm suggested a further argument for incorporeality when he wrote: 'For whatever is composed of parts is not altogether one, but is in some part plural, and diverse from itself; and either in fact or in concept is capable of dissolution' (Deane, 1966: 24). The following seems to capture this reasoning:

1. God = the most worthy object of religious worship.

12. The most worthy object of religious worship cannot be destructible in fact or in concept.

13. N (if God is corporeal, then God is composite).

14. N (if God is composite, then God is destructible, in fact or in concept).

15. Hence, God cannot be corporeal.

Considering premise 12, it seems evident that the most worthy object of worship cannot be destructible in fact. And let us grant, *arguendo*, that a corporeal being would be composite. But is it necessarily true that whatever is composite is thereby destructible in fact? According to Plato's *Phaedo*, all natural or physical bodies, being composite, can be destroyed through the process of decomposition. From this it is concluded that all composite bodies are destructible. This, of course, does not deductively follow. Even if we grant that all natural bodies do decompose, it does not follow that a *pneumikos* body does. Finally, even if a *pneumikos* body were not inherently indestructible, it would not follow that God could not forever sustain that body in being.

What about Anselm's concern that God should not be destructible in concept? Even if God's body could somehow conceptually be destroyed, our faith in God and his promises is ultimately grounded in the integrity of the divine character and will and not in conceptual necessity. Thus, it seems that divine indestructibility does not require divine incorporeality.

The argument from divine self-existence

In his book, *Concepts of Deity*, H. P. Owen (1971) provides two additional arguments for divine incorporeality. He first claims that corporeality is logically incompatible with self-existence:

> God's incorporeality can also be proved from his self-existence . . . No material entity can be self-existent; for each is a determination, or mode, of being. Consequently we can always ask of any such entity: 'What are its causes and conditions?' (ibid.: 18)

The following seems to capture his reasoning:
1. God = the most worthy object of religious worship.
16. The most worthy object of religious worship must be self-existent.
17. N (if x is self-existent, then s is not a determination or mode of being).
18. If God had a material body, he would be a determination or mode of being.
19. Hence, God cannot have a material body.

Premises 17 and 18 seem in need of clarification. Owen has not explained what he means by a 'determination or mode of being,' but apparently he means something like a species or category of being: as contrasted with what? Totally undifferentiated being? If so, it seems that 17 proves too much. For personality as well as corporeality appears to be a mode or determination of being. By parity of reasoning it would follow that personality could not be self-existent. I see no basis for such a claim. Owen apparently provides the following argument for premise 17: (a) Of any determination or mode of being, one can always intelligibly ask, What are its causes and conditions?; (b) Of a self-existent being, one can never intelligibly ask, What are its causes and conditions?; (c) Hence, a self-existent being cannot be a mode or determination of being.

Premise (b) appears to be analytically true and (c) does follow from (a) and (b). But premise (a) does not appear to be analytically true. If I understand 'determination or mode of being' correctly, it does not grammatically imply the need for a cause or condition. Whether some particular determination or mode of being is caused or uncaused depends on reality, not on the meaning or structure of our language. Thus, this support for premise 17 fails, and the premise remains inconclusive. The argument from self-existence thus fails to prove that God must be incorporeal.[4]

The argument from moral perfection

Owen's second argument is based on the claim that pure spirit is the most perfect form of being. He says:

> Moreover, if a dualistic view of mind and matter is correct we can see, not only that God's pure spirituality is possible, but also that it is the most perfect form of being. All human behavior approaches perfection to the extent that it expresses wisdom, goodness and love. Yet although the body aids these spiritual properties in so far as it offers a medium for their expression, it also inhibits them in many – and some tragically frustrating – ways. Hence only pure Spirit can constitute an absolutely perfect form of personal existence. (1971: 19)

His argument can be summarized as follows:
1. God = the most worthy object of religious worship.
20. The most worthy object of religious worship must constitute an absolutely perfect form of personal existence.
21. Only pure Spirit can constitute an absolutely perfect form of personal existence.
22. N (If x is pure Spirit, then x is incorporeal).
23. Hence, God cannot be corporeal.

Owen acknowledges that the cogency of this argument depends on the Cartesian view that mind and body are ontologically distinct, a questionable view that he does not attempt to justify. But assuming *arguendo* that there could be totally unembodied mind, why should this be considered the most perfect form of personal existence? Though Owen refers to the body inhibiting spiritual properties, he does not explain how the body constitutes such an inhibiting agent. Personally, I find the idea hard to grasp. It seems entirely gratuitous to assign all of the good properties, such as wisdom and goodness, to the mind, and assign all negative qualities to the body.

However, even granting that the body is the source of certain desires for food or sexual gratification, these desires are not inherently evil, and would not necessarily inhibit one from always choosing rightly. The New Testament describes Christ as one who was tempted in all points, but without sin. It might even be wondered if one who was so tempted but overcomes is more worthy of worship than one who has never experienced such a conflict. Thus, it seems that premise 21 is false, and this argument also fails to prove God's incorporeality.

In sum, it appears that none of the arguments for divine incorporeality considered here are sufficient to prove it; and thus none ought to be a stumbling block to rational acceptance of the Father or the Son as embodied beings.

Notes

1. Whether this is a correct interpretation of St Anselm's premise is irrelevant for present purposes; while highly plausible, the interpretation is also interesting in its own right, providing the fundamental premise for much of contemporary rational theologizing.
2. My thinking on the issues discussed in this chapter has been significantly aided by Dyck (now Jantzen)'s articles and her later book (1984).
3. My illustrations are similar to and suggested by Dyck's.
4. Certainly ordinary believers do not believe Christ's resurrected body to be self-existent, but that Christ is self-existent and antedated both his resurrected and mortal bodies. It is perfectly consistent to think of God as a self-existent person with some acquired properties.

Part VII
The Future of Mormon Studies

23 Mormon Studies: progress and prospects

David J. Whittaker

Latter-day Saints have been commanded to study, to seek knowledge out of the best sources of information they can find. Such knowledge is viewed as a central part both of their missionary enterprise and of their efforts to build the latter-day Zion. Their early establishment of schools, libraries, and even temples was a part of this zest for learning.

Many of their early efforts were focused outward on the outside world, not inward on themselves. When they did publish books and pamphlets, or books of information about themselves, they were generally defensive. This was particularly so in an era of anti-Mormon polemics and activity. It was not that early members failed to keep records of their inner lives. Joseph Smith's leadership in record-keeping activities led others to gather and compile large quantities of official and unofficial records. He also encouraged a journal-keeping tradition that is still strong in the Church he founded.[1]

Early histories

The first important histories of the Mormon Church which attempted a look inward to the group and backward through time were by British converts seeking to understand both their adopted faith and a new country.[2] Unfortunately T. B. H. Stenhouse's *Rocky Mountain Saints* (1876) was flawed by his critical stance toward Brigham Young and his use of history to defend the Godbeite cause. But the history did provide several interpretive models used by later writers. Especially important were his perspectives on early Mormon conflict which he presented in a context of federal–state and church–state relationships.[3]

The most important and influential of the British converts was B. H. Roberts, whose historical and biographical works culminated in his six-volume centennial history *A Comprehensive History of the Church* in 1930. Rich in detail and defensive in tone, the work remains a standard history of the Mormon Church by one of its finest minds.[4]

Students of nineteenth-century Mormonism are also benefited by the perceptive observation of a number of travelers who met Latter-day Saints on their journey. For example, Richard Burton's *The City of the Saints* (1861) remains an important volume in this genre. There are literally hundreds of travel and curiosa accounts, not all of which were written to attack. And given the large number of these works, it is clear that the reading public was interested in Mormons and publishers were eager to meet the public demand.[5]

Hubert Howe Bancroft's *History of Utah, 1546–1886* (1889) was a serious attempt by an indefatigable collector of Western Americana to research his topic and to try to tell the story fairly. This he attempted by placing the pro-Mormon version in the text with critical and anti-Mormon views in the footnotes.[6]

It is difficult to assess the use by Latter-day Saints of these histories. During the first century (1830–1930), many potential readers had lived the history or knew people who had, hence this group memory of shared trials and experiences made 'professional' history unnecessary. For example, when Mormon artist C. C. A. Christensen traveled around giving lectures and showing his panoramas of church history, in his audiences were people who had lived through the very events he had painted; they added details to his compositions and thus made the artistic renderings more true to their own memories.[7]

There are other explanations as well. As a lay church, Mormon members have kept records, but they have generally stressed living memory over archival research. Thus personal testimonies and group stories have been far more powerful in creating the Mormon sense of the past. Then too, much of the Mormon foundational experience was recorded in an age when there was no real difference between those who wrote history and those who compiled or edited it. Thus during the first century, there was a much stronger tradition of *documentary* history as opposed to *interpretive* history. Much of the work of Andrew Jenson clearly fits into the former category.[8] Finally, as a missionary church, Mormons have had little time to reflect seriously on the past. The challenges, especially of today's fast growth, thrust enough problems needing solving upon the membership to allow much time for looking back.

By the 1880s Mormon students were seeking education beyond the confines of their Great Basin refuge. The first generation, concentrating in the area of law, medicine, and the agricultural sciences, were generally untouched by the critical approaches of the seminar system emerging in the social sciences.[9]

The emergence of graduate programs in history and the organization of professional associations such as the American Historical Association (1884) and the American Society of Church History (1888) testify to the growing specialization and sophistication of historical study. Such organizations would shape the historical professional in the twentieth century with their emphasis on high standards of research, a broad collegiality, and the establishment of professional publications which provided outlets for the new research and thinking.

It was just a matter of time before Mormon students entered these graduate programs and applied the advanced training they received to their own history.[10] These individuals included Levi Edgar Young, Milton R. Hunter, Daryl Chase, Heber Snell, T. Edgar Lyon, Leland Creer, LeRoy R. Hafen, Russel B. Swensen, Andrew Love Neff, William J. Snow, Joel Ricks, Ephraim E. Erickson, Joseph A. Geddes, Lowry Nelson, Thomas C. Romney, Andrew Karl Larson, Juanita Brooks, and Feramorz Y. Fox. Other individuals, such as J. Cecil Alter, long-time editor of the *Utah Historical Quarterly*, and Dale Morgan must be included in this list of the first generation of historians upon whom the contemporary flowering of Mormon Studies depends.[11]

Thus, when Bernard DeVoto complained in 1936 that 'a complete bibliography of articles by qualified scholars' on Mormon Studies would not fill one page,[12] he was not aware of the emerging work of those students mentioned above. Of course, DeVoto was not speaking of Mormon Studies broadly defined, but the majority of the people noted above were working in Utah and Western history, and they nevertheless were asking hard questions and writing books and articles that would push Mormon Studies to a new level.

Professionalization of Mormon Studies

By the end of World War II a new generation of LDS students was emerging from various graduate schools. Building on the earlier work of their mentors with better access to archival collections, newer volumes of Mormon history began to appear.[13] A good example of this second generation of professional scholars is Leonard J. Arrington. In many ways his revised (1952) PhD dissertation, published in 1958 as *Great Basin Kingdom, An Economic History of the Latter-day Saints, 1830–1900*, was a culmination of these earlier studies. Its extensive bibliography provides a valuable index to Mormon Studies at the time of the volume's publication.

Arrington has continued to write Mormon and Western history.[14] His colleagues and students have produced large numbers of scholarly monographs on all aspects of Mormon Studies. In 1965 they organized the Mormon History Association and it was merely a logical development in Mormon studies. Other professional publications, such as *Brigham Young University Studies, Dialogue: A Journal of Mormon Thought,* and *Sunstone,* have provided important outlets for scholarly work in Mormon history and culture.

Arrington's position as the official historian of the Mormon Church from 1972 to 1982 furthered the growth and development of Mormon Studies. His own staff of trained scholars generated an enormous amount of published material which, when combined with the more open access to the Church's own extensive archives, helped encourage a new generation of students to investigate all dimensions of the LDS past.[15]

Mormon Studies: an overview

While no one essay can do justice to the recent renaissance of Mormon Studies during the past 30 years, a brief summary will exhibit the breadth of Mormon scholarship today. We will only highlight the significant works in the following categories, hoping that such a sampling will suggest the rich amount of material that is now available on Mormon history and culture. Much of our emphasis will be on bibliographical works which will assist students into the larger corpus of Mormon Studies.

Archival sources

One of the keys to the flowering of Mormon Studies has been the growing descriptions and availability of manuscript sources. The large amount of material that Bancroft gathered for his history of Utah is now housed in the library named after him on the campus of the University of California at Berkeley. Because of the key role Mormons have played in the religious history of the United States and also because of their central role in the American westward movement and the subsequent settlement of the Great Basin, libraries have been interested in collecting Mormon material for most of the twentieth century. Detailed histories of these gathering efforts with descriptions of their respective holdings have been assembled in David J. Whittaker (ed.) *Mormon Americana: A Guide to Sources and Collections in the United States* (Provo, UT: Brigham Young University Studies Monograph Series, 1995). Archival repositories with essays in this 700-page volume include libraries from Yale to the Bancroft, and all the major collections in Utah. A concluding essay calls attention to additional collections scattered throughout the United States. Davis Bitton, *Guide to Mormon Diaries and Autobiographies* (Provo, UT: Brigham Young University Press, 1977) is the best single guide to specific items, but it is in need of revision and updating.

Encyclopedias and reference works

The best overall reference work from Mormon culture broadly defined is the multi-volume *Encyclopedia of Mormonism*, ed. Daniel H. Ludlow (New York: Macmillan, 1992). Written by a variety of scholars, its articles range broadly over the history, scriptures, institutional, and doctrinal aspects of the Church. Its graphics and photographs are valuable assets to the whole project. Useful atlases are Wayne L. Wahlquist *et al.*, *Atlas of Utah* (Ogden, UT: Weber State College, 1981); and S. Kent Brown, Donald Q. Cannon, and Richard H. Jackson (eds) *Historical Atlas of Mormonism* (New York: Simon and Schuster, 1994).

The *Deseret News Church Almanac,* generally published annually from

1974 to the present, is a very useful compilation of facts and statistics about the Church.

Bibliographical guides and indices

Scholarly periodicals dealing with Mormon history have included a number of bibliographical essays and notes on various topics. *BYU Studies* has issued annually a 'Mormon Bibliography' since 1960. *Dialogue* issued the bibliographical 'Among the Mormons' from 1977 to 1986. The Mormon History Association *Newsletter* has included a number of bibliographic essays on both period and topical subjects. Particularly useful are Susan L. Fales and Lanell M. Reeder, 'Mormonism: bibliography of bibliographies,' Mormon History Association *Newsletter* 72 (April 1989): 5–8 and 74 (October 1989): 4–7.

The important bibliographies, histories, and biographies are noted in David J. Whittaker, 'The study of Mormon history: a guide to the published sources,' in Whittaker (ed.) *Mormon Americana*: 45–90. Here attention is called only to a few of the more recent and representative: David L. Laughlin, 'A selective, evaluative, and annotated bibliography on Mormonism,' *Bulletin of Bibliography* 48 (June 1991): 75–101; Armand L. Mauss and Jeffrey R. Franks, 'Comprehensive bibliography of social science literature on the Mormons,' *Review of Religious Research* 26 (September 1984): 73–115; Thomas G. Alexander and James B. Allen, 'The Mormons in the Mountain West: a selected bibliography,' *Arizona and the West* 9 (Winter 1967): 365–84; Thomas G. Alexander, 'Toward the new Mormon history: an examination of the literature on the Latter-day Saints in the Far West,' in *Historians and the American West*, ed. Michael P. Malone (Lincoln, NE: University of Nebraska Press, 1983): 344–68; and James B. Allen, 'Since 1950: creators and creations of Mormon history,' in *New Views of Mormon History*, ed. Bitton and Beecher: 407–38.

Up-to-date bibliographical essays on key topics in Mormon studies are available in Whittaker (ed.) *Mormon Americana*: Carol A. Edison, 'Material culture: an introduction and guide to Mormon vernacular' (306–35); Brad Westwood, 'Mormon architectural records' (336–405); Stanley B. Kimball, 'Mormon emigration trails' (406–36); William A. Wilson, 'Mormon folklore' (437–454); Eugene England, 'Mormon literature: progress and prospects' (455–506); Richard Neitzel Holzapfel and T. Jeffery Cottle, 'Mormon-related material in photoarchives' (506–21); Steven L. Olsen, 'Museums and historic sites of Mormonism' (522–37); Michael Hicks, 'The performing arts and Mormonism: an introductory guide' (538–58); Richard F. Haglund Jr and Erich Robert Paul, 'Resources for the study of science, technology, and Mormon culture' (559–606); and Richard G. Oman, 'Sources for Mormon visual arts' (607–66).

More specialized guides include Susan L. Fales and Chad J. Flake (comps) *Mormons and Mormonism in U.S. Government Documents: A Bibliography* (Salt Lake City, UT: University of Utah Press, 1989); Kip

Sperry, *A Guide to Indexes to Mormon Works, Mormon Collections, and Utah Collections* (Salt Lake City, UT: Historical Department of The Church of Jesus Christ of Latter-day Saints, 1974); Russell T. Clement (comp.) *Mormons in the Pacific: A Bibliography* (Laie, HI: The Institute for Polynesian Studies, BYU, Hawaii Campus, 1981); David J. Whittaker, 'Mormonism in Victorian Britain: a bibliographic essay,' in *Mormonism in Early Victorian Britain*, ed. Richard L. Jensen and Malcolm R. Thorp (Salt Lake City: University of Utah Press, 1989): 258–71.

History and biography

Two excellent one-volume histories of the Church are available: James B. Allen and Glen M. Leonard, *The Story of the Latter-day Saints*, 2nd edn, rev. and enl. (Salt Lake City: Deseret Books, 1992) takes a chronological approach and supplies an extensive bibliography; Leonard J. Arrington and Davis Bitton, *The Mormon Experience: A History of the Latter-day Saints* (New York: Alfred A. Knopf, 1979) takes an interpretive, topical approach. Of the histories of Mormon-dominated Utah, the most comprehensive and bibliographically useful is the multi-authored *Utah's History*, ed. Richard D. Poll, Thomas G. Alexander, Eugene E. Campbell, and David E. Miller (Provo, UT: BYU Press, 1978).

The most comprehensive aid to students seeking biographical information on Mormons is Marvin Wiggins, *Mormons and Their Neighbors: An Index to over 75,000 Biographical Sketches from 1820 to the Present*, 2 volumes (Provo, UT: Harold B. Lee Library, Brigham Young University, 1984). Interpretative essays on the state of Mormon biographical writing provide useful overviews of the current status of biographical works: Davis Bitton, 'Mormon biography,' *Biography: An Interdisciplinary Quarterly* 4 (Winter 1981): 1–16; Ronald W. Walker, 'The challenge and craft of Mormon biography,' *BYU Studies* 22 (Spring 1982): 179–92; and David J. Whittaker, 'The heritage and tasks of Mormon biography,' in *Supporting Saints: Life Stories of Nineteenth Century Mormons*, ed. Donald Q. Cannon and David J. Whittaker (Provo, UT: Religious Studies Center, Brigham Young University, 1985): 1–16. The large body of personal history writing in the Church is studied in one geographical area in Susan Hendricks Swetnam, *Lives of the Saints in Southeast Idaho: An Introduction to Mormon Pioneer Life Story Writing* (Moscow, ID: University of Idaho Press, 1991).

Women and the family

Several bibliographical guides are available for students of Mormon women's experiences: Carol Cornwall Madsen and David J. Whittaker, 'History's sequel: A source essay on women in Mormon history,' *Journal of Mormon History* 6 (1979): 123–45; Patricia Lyn Scott and Maureen Ursenbach Beecher, 'Mormon women: a bibliography in process,

1977–1985,' ibid. 12 (1985): 113–27; and Karen Purser Frazier (comp.) *Bibliography of Social Scientific, Historical, and Popular Writings about Mormon Women* (Provo, UT: Women's Research Institute, Brigham Young University, 1990), which lists about 1150 items organized into 30 topical categories. An important collection of essays is Maureen Ursenbach Beecher and Lavina Fielding Anderson (eds) *Sisters in Spirit: Mormon Women in Historical and Cultural Perspective* (Urbana, IL: University of Illinois Press, 1987). On the church-wide women's organization see Jill Mulvay Derr, Janath R. Cannon, and Maureen Ursenbach Beecher, *Women of Covenant: The Story of the Relief Society* (Salt Lake City: Deseret Books, 1992).

Students of Mormon plural marriage are well served by two bibliographical guides: Davis Bitton, 'Mormon polygamy: a review article,' *Journal of Mormon History* 4 (1977): 101–18; and Patricia Lyn Scott, 'Mormon polygamy: a bibliography, 1877–92,' ibid. 19 (Spring 1993): 133–55. Selected book-length studies include Kimball Young, *Isn't One Wife Enough?* (New York: Holt, 1954); Lawrence Foster, *Religion and Sexuality: Three American Communal Experiments of the Nineteenth Century* (New York: Oxford University Press, 1981); Richard S. Van Wagoner, *Mormon Polygamy: A History*, 3rd edn (Salt Lake City: Signature Books, 1992); and B. Carmon Hardy, *Solemn Covenant: The Mormon Polygamous Passage* (Urbana, IL: University of Illinois Press, 1992).

There is a great need for more scholarly studies of the Mormon family. Beginning points are Bruce L. Campbell and Eugene E. Campbell, 'The Mormon family,' in *Ethnic Families in America*, ed. Charles H. Mindell and Robert W. Habenstein (New York: Elsevier, 1981): 369–416; and Darwin L. Thomas, 'Family in Mormon experience,' in *Families and Religions: Conflict and Change in Modern Society*, ed. W. D'Antonio and J. Aldous (Beverly Hills, CA: Sage Publications, 1983): 267–88. See also Howard M. Blair and Renata Tonks Forste, 'Toward a social science of contemporary Mormondom,' *BYU Studies* 26 (Winter 1986): 73–121.

Additional studies

Significant studies of various aspects of the Mormon experience, as interpreted by scholars outside the Mormon experience (to mention only a few) include Eduard Meyer, *The Origin and History of the Mormons with Reflections on the Beginnings of Islam and Christianity*, translated by Heinz F. Rahde and Eugene Seaich (1912; reprint, Salt Lake City: University of Utah, 1961); Wallace Stegner, *Mormon Country* (New York: Duell, Sloan and Pearce, 1942); Thomas F. O'Dea, *The Mormons* (Chicago: University of Chicago Press, 1957); and Jan Shipps, *Mormonism: The Story of a New Religious Tradition* (Urbana, IL: University of Illinois Press, 1985).

Additional studies, if only a sampling, to suggest the rich breadth of current research and writing on Mormonism, include Lester E. Bush Jr and Armund L. Mauss (eds) *Neither White nor Black: Mormon Scholars Confront the Race Issue in a Universal Church* (Midvale, UT: Signature Books, 1984);

Armund L. Mauss, *The Angel and the Beehive: The Mormon Struggle with Assimilation* (Urbana, IL: University of Illinois Press, 1994); Lester E. Bush Jr, *Health and Medicine Among the Latter-day Saints: Science, Sense, and Scripture* (New York: Crossroad Publishing, 1993); Marie Cornwall, Tim B. Heaton, and Lawrence A. Young (eds) *Contemporary Mormonism: Social Science Perspectives* (Urbana, IL: University of Illinois Press, 1994); Philip L. Barlow, *Mormons and the Bible: The Place of the Latter-day Saints in American Religion* (New York: Oxford University Press, 1991); Michael Hicks, *Mormonism and Music: A History* (Urbana, IL: University of Illinois Press, 1989); Erich Robert Paul, *Science, Religion and Mormon Cosmology* (Urbana, IL: University of Illinois Press, 1992); Grant Underwood, *The Millenarian World of Early Mormonism* (Urbana, IL: University of Illinois Press, 1993); and D. Michael Quinn, *The Mormon Hierarchy: The Origins of Power* (Salt Lake City: Signature Books, 1994).

The growing scholarship on the groups that have broken from mainstream Mormonism is surveyed in Steven L. Shields, *The Latter Day Saints Churches: An Annotated Bibliography* (New York: Garland Publishing, 1987). Shields provides a brief history of these groups in *Divergent Paths of the Restoration: A History of the Latter-day Saint Movement*, 3rd edn (Bountiful, UT: Restoration Research, 1982). Such research can give valuable insight into the conflict and tensions that have been a part of the Mormon movement from its earliest years. A useful volume of essays is *Differing Visions: Dissenters in Mormon History*, ed. Roger D. Launius and Linda Thatcher (Urbana, IL: University of Illinois Press, 1994).

Prospects

In order to know where you are going or where you should go, you must have a sense of where you have been. This is especially true of historical studies, for we all stand on the shoulders of those scholars who preceded us. A large bibliographical project scheduled for release in 1996 is an attempt to provide a comprehensive mapping of Mormon Studies. To be published by the University of Illinois Press, it will provide a comprehensive bibliography of the books, graduate theses and dissertations, and articles that address the Mormon history in a significant way. Compiled and edited by James B. Allen, Ronald W. Walker, and David J. Whittaker, with contributions from Armand L. Mauss, and currently containing about 11,000 separate items, *Studies in Mormon History* will give students of the Mormon experience a broad mapping of where we have been in Mormon Studies. It will also contain a number of scholarly essays on select topics which will provide historiographical analyses of key subjects.

Such a project has suggested several areas that need more work in the future. These include: international studies, works that place Mormonism more fully and factually into the larger world in which it now finds converts; textual studies of Mormon scriptures from the earliest manuscripts to the current editions; more accurate and complete biographical works of major and minor figures with sensitivity to the full context of an individuals life; studies of Mormon women and the larger story of the LDS family, stressing both its successes and its challenges; studies of Mormon thought that are sensitive to both official and unofficial sources; the religious context of the Mormon movement; and better edited editions of notable Mormon manuscripts, including professionally prepared editions of the papers of the Presidents of the Church, and possibly a new edition of the *History of the Church*. Important projects have begun to appear, including the papers of Joseph Smith, but more needs to be done.[16]

No one studying Mormonism can ignore the life and thought of its founding prophet Joseph Smith Jr. An essential place to begin is with Dean C. Jessee, 'Sources for the Study of Joseph Smith,' and with the items gathered in David J. Whittaker, 'Joseph Smith in recent research: a selected bibliography.'[17] His successors in the Presidency are gradually receiving scholarly attention, but much more needs to be done.[18]

So much of the research mentioned in this essay has remained in academically oriented publications, with only bits and pieces finding their way to the general public, in or out of the Church. But there are signs that a people who have kept such good records of their lives are beginning to look closer at their inner lives and seek a fuller understanding of the religion that has defined so completely their corporate and private worlds.[19] All of this suggests a great future for both scholars and Church members as we approach the twenty-first century.

Notes

1. See Dean C. Jessee, 'Joseph Smith and the beginnings of Mormon record keeping,' in Porter and Black (1988): 138–60.
2. For an overview of the Mormon historical writing see Bitton and Arrington (1988). See also Arrington (1968): 56–66.
3. See especially Walker (1974). On another early British convert who wrote Mormon history see Lye (1960) and Walker (1976).
4. See Bitton (1968).
5. Most of these works can be found in Flake (1978), and the ten-year supplement, Flake and Draper (1989). A title index to both volumes was issued in 1992. On Burton see Brodie (1970). A useful overview of the British travel literature is E. J. Snow (1991).
6. See Ellsworth (1954). Bancroft's *History of Utah* included an extensive bibliography of sources he had gathered and used for this volume. His history also devoted over 200 pages to the pre-Utah history of the Mormons.
7. For an overview of Christensen's life and work with reproductions of his Mormon history paintings see the exhibition catalogue prepared by Jensen and Oman (1984).
8. See Perkins (1971), and Reinwand (1973).
9. These changes in American education are beyond the scope of this essay. For more detail, with sources, see Whittaker (1980): 293–327.
10. See Dunford (1965). For one experience see Swensen (1972).
11. See Bitton and Arrington (1988): 87–125; and Ellsworth (1972).

12. DeVoto (1936): 82–3.
13. Many of these studies first appeared as dissertations. See the overview in Arrington (1966), which includes a listing of dissertations.
14. For a chronological listing of his published work see David J. Whittaker (comp.) 'Leonard J. Arrington: a bibliography,' in Bitton and Beecher (1987): 439–69.
15. On the history of the Historical Division of the LDS Church under Arrington's direction, see Arrington (1992); Bitton (1983).
16. Two volumes of the Joseph Smith Papers have appeared under the editorship of Dean C. Jessee. It is anticipated that when finished the project will comprise eight volumes.
17. Both are in Whittaker (1995): 7–28, 29–44.
18. For example, see Arrington (1985), and Alexander (1991). For additional references see Whittaker, 'The study of Mormon history: a guide to the published sources,' in Whittaker (1995): 70–4. Especially needed are biographical studies of the wives of Mormon leaders.
19. One index to this is to survey the large number of organizations and periodicals devoted to Mormon life and culture. See Waterman (1994).

24 Views of an international religion

Douglas J. Davies

Each chapter in this book displays the energy which non-Mormon and Mormon scholar alike give to the subject. As a focus of academic studies Mormonism increasingly becomes a fertile area for research as data and theory yield a cumulative insight into the Latter-day Saint way of life.

In many respects Rodney Stark's 1984 article on Mormonism, entitled 'The rise of a new world faith,' offered an inevitably provocative yet comforting view of the LDS future. For some fellow sociologists its prediction of a massive rise in LDS membership into the twenty-first century was deemed an unwise move on the part of a social scientist; some LDS sociologists also expressed caution (L. A. Young, 1994: 43ff.). But, equally, for some Mormons, its vision of greatly enhanced membership figures, coming as it did from an extremely well known yet non-Mormon sociologist, serves as a kind of secular testimony to the potency and potential of the faith.

Given Mormonism's traditional preoccupation with the detail of history, this extrapolation of membership figures into the future functions as a kind of reversed history, depicting a future of a profoundly positive profile. The Mormon interest in Stark's analysis is, obviously, grounded in faith and in the hope that this religion of the Restored Gospel will establish itself in large numbers across the world. This reflects an ideal whose roots go far into the early and mid-nineteenth century with the birth of the Mormon Church and the eager expectation that Zion was being established upon the earth.

For social scientist and historian alike this hope furnishes an interesting phenomenon open to study. Against it is set the realistic constraints of changes of Mormon identity as the church organization moves far beyond Utah, as explored in the section on the 'Expansion of Mormonism' as well as in the first section on 'Dimensions of identity.' Certainly Mormonism will continue to serve as a fertile laboratory for analyzing the transformation of a new religious tradition as also for exploring the complex relationships between the dominant cultural ethos of North America in interaction with several South American and other cultural complexes.

The topic of identity, in both its sociological and psychological domains, also stands open to illustrate the power of religion to construct corporate and private lives. And all this within the broad theoretical framework of secularization, fundamentalism, and postmodernity. Just why some religious movements go on to become world religions and others fade into the historical shadows is difficult to say, though some, like Mauss, Midgley, and Duke in this volume, have astute insights into the question. Ultimately only time will tell whether we have in Mormonism a new world religion as such.

Meanwhile, as this book shows in its different sections, there remains the necessity for an interdisciplinary perspective in gaining continuing insight into this Latter-day Saint way of life which in some parts of the world currently amounts to a sub-culture while elsewhere it stands firm as a sectarian commitment. Certainly scholars of other religions can benefit from the study of a religious tradition whose birth is not too historically lost and whose contemporary transformations may yet arouse theoretical curiosity. As such, the future of Mormon Studies is assured.

Bibliography

Abbott, M. (1993) *Family Ties: English Families 1540–1920*. London and New York: Routledge.

Acevedo, R. (1990) *Los Mormones en Chile*. Santiago: Impresos y Publicaciones Cumorah.

Alder, D. D. and P. M. Edwards (1978) Common beginnings, divergent beliefs. *Dialogue* 11: 18–28.

Alexander, T. G. (1986a) Historiography and the new Mormon history: a historian's perspective. *Dialogue* 19: 25–49.

Alexander, T. G. (1986b) *Mormonism in Transition: A History of the Latter-day Saints, 1890–1930*. Urbana, IL: University of Illinois Press.

Alexander, T. G. (1991) *Things in Heaven and Earth: The Life and Times of Wilford Woodruff*. Salt Lake City: Signature Books.

Allen, J. H. (1930; original 1902) *Judah's Sceptre and Joseph's Birthright*. Boston, MA: A. A. Beauchamp.

Allen, J. H. and G. M. Leonard (1976) *The Story of the Latter-day Saints*. Salt Lake City: Deseret Books.

Allport, G. W. and J. M. Ross (1967) Personal religious orientation and prejudice. *Journal of Personality and Social Psychology* 5: 432–43.

Anderson, D. (ed.) (1992) *Drinking to Your Health: The Allegations and the Evidence*. London, Social Affairs Unit.

Anderson, L. F. (1993a) The LDS intellectual community and church leadership: a contemporary chronology. *Dialogue* 26(1): 7–66.

Anderson, L. F. (1993b) Apprenticeship in fear. Paper presented May 1993.

Anderson, L .F. (1993c) Letter to the First Presidency. Dated October 23.

Anderson, L. F. (1994) The year of the axe. Paper at November meeting of the B. H. Roberts Society.

Anderson, Lynn Matthews (1994) Towards a feminist interpretation of LDS Scripture. *Dialogue* (Summer).

Anderson, M. (1971) *Family Structure in Nineteenth Century Lancashire*. Cambridge, UK: Cambridge University Press.

Anderson, N. (1942) *Desert Saints*. Chicago: University of Chicago Press.

Mormon identities in transition

Arens, W. (1979) *The Man-eating Myth*. New York: Oxford University Press.

Ariès, P. (1962) *Centuries of Childhood*. New York: Vintage Books.

Arrington, L. J. (1966) Scholarly studies of Mormonism in the twentieth century, *Dialogue* 1: 15–32.

Arrington, L.J. (1968) The search for truth and meaning in Mormon history. *Dialogue: A Journal of Mormon Thought* 3: 56–66.

Arrington, L. J. (1985) *Brigham Young, American Moses*. New York: Alfred A. Knopf

Arrington, L. J. (1992) The founding of the LDS historical department, 1972. *Journal of Mormon History* 18: 41–56.

Arrington, L. J. and Davis Bitton (1979) *The Mormon Experience: A History of the Latter-day Saints*. New York: Alfred A. Knopf.

Asay, Carlos E. (1991) Address, Pittsburgh Regional Conference. October.

Ashment, E. H. (1990) Making the scriptures indeed one in our hands. In Vogel (1990).

Ashment, E. H. (1992) Historiography of the Canon. In Smith (1992).

Bachman, D. and R. K. Esplin (1992). In Ludlow (1992).

Bainton, R. (1960) *Christian Attitudes to War and Peace*. Nashville, TN: Abingdon.

Ball, B. W. (1975) *A Great Expectation: Eschatological Thought in English Protestantism to 1660*. Leiden: Brill.

Ballard, M. (1994) *Fireside* 11: 94. Provo, UT: Brigham Young University.

Barber, I. and D. Gilgen (1996) Between covenant and treaty: emerging cultural diversity in the New Zealand Latter-day Saint tradition. *Dialogue* 29: 1.

Barker, E., Beckford, J. A. and K. Dobbelaere (eds) (1993) *Secularization, Rationalization, and Sectarianism: Essays in Honour of Bryan R. Wilson*. New York: Oxford University Press.

Barlow, P. L. (1991) *Mormons and the Bible: The Place of the Latter-day Saints in American Religion*. New York: Oxford University Press.

Barth, F. (1969) *Ethnic Groups and Boundaries*. Boston: Little Brown.

Beck, A. T. (1976) *Cognitive Therapy and Emotional Disorders*. New York: International Universities Press.

Beck, S. H., Cole, B. S. and J. A. Hammond (1991) Religious heritage and premarital sex: evidence from a national sample of young adults. *Journal for the Scientific Study of Religion* 30(2): 173–80.

Beckwith, F. J. (1992) Philosophical problems with the Mormon concept of God. *Christian Research Journal* 14:4: 24–9.

Beckwith, F. J. and S. E. Parrish (1991) *The Mormon Concept of God: A Philosophical Analysis*. Lewiston, NY: The Edwin Mellen Press.

Beecher, Maureen Ursenbach and L. F. Anderson (1987) *Sisters in Spirit: Mormon Women in Historical and Cultural Perspective*. Urbana, IL: University of Illinois Press.

Bellah, R. N. *et al.* (1985) *Habits of the Heart*. Berkeley, CA: University of California Press.

Bennion, L. C. and L. A. Young (1996) The uncertain dynamics of LDS Church growth, 1950–2020. *Dialogue* 29(1).

Benson, E. T. (1987) *To the Mothers in Zion*. World-wide satellite broadcast and pamphlet PXMP0594.

Berger, P. L. (1969) *A Rumor of Angels*. Garden City, NY: Doubleday.

Bergin, A. E. (1983) Religiosity and mental health: a critical reevaluation and meta-analysis. *Professional Psychology: Research and Practice* 14(2): 170–83.

Bergin, A. E., Masters, K. S. and P. S. Richards (1987) Religious and mental health. A study of an intrinsically religious sample. *Journal of Counselling Psychology* 34:2: 197–204.

Berquist, J. A. and P. Kamber Manickam (1976) *The Crisis of Dependency in Third World Ministries: A Critique of Inherited Missionary Forms in India*. Madras: Christian Literature Society.

Berzano, L. and M. Introvigne (1994) *La sfida infinita. La nuova religiosità nella Sicilia centrale*. Caltanissetta, Sicily and Rome: Salvatore Sciascia Editore.

Bitton, D. (1968) B. H. Roberts as historian. *Dialogue* 3: 25–44.

Bitton, D. (1983) Ten years in Camelot: a personal memoir. *Dialogue* 16: 9–33.

Bitton, D. and L. J. Arrington (1988) *Mormons and Their Historians*. Salt Lake City: University of Utah Press.

Bitton, D. and Maureen Ursenbach Beecher (eds) (1987) *New Views of Mormon History: A Collection of Essays in Honor of Leonard J. Arrington*. Salt Lake City: University of Utah Press.

Blair, A. R. (1973) The Reorganized Church of Jesus Christ of Latter Day Saints: moderate Mormonism. In F. M. Mckiernan, A. R. Blair, and P. M. Edwards (eds) *The Restoration Movement: Essays in Mormon History*. Lawrence, KS: Coronado Press.

Blair, A. R. (1985) RLDS views of polygamy: some historiographical notes. *John Whitmer Historical Association Journal* 5: 16–28.

Bloch, M. (1992) What goes without saying. In A. Kuper (ed.) *Conceptualizing Society*. London: Routledge.

Bohn, D. (1994) The larger issue. *Sunstone* 16(8): 45–63.

Bolton, A. (1993) Learning fron Anabaptism: a major peace tradition. In D. Caswell (ed.) *Restoration Studies V: A Collection of Essays About the History, Beliefs and Practices of the Reorganized Church of Jesus Christ of Latter-day Saints*. Independence, MO: Herald House.

Brinkerhoff, M. B. and M. M. Mackie (1986) The applicability of social distance for religious research: an exploration. *Review of Religious Research* 28(2): 151–67.

Brodie, F. W. (1970) Richard F. Burton: exceptional observer of the Mormon scene. *Utah Historical Quarterly* 38: 295–311.

Brooke, J. L. (1994) *The Refiner's Fire: The Making of a Mormon Cosmology 1644–1844*. Cambridge, UK: Cambridge University Press.

Brown, R. A. (ed.) (1994) *Theology: Authority, Membership, and Baptism*. Independence, MO: Graceland-Park Press.

Brown, S. Kent (1992) Israel overview. In Ludlow (1992).

Bruce, S. (1993) Religion and rational choice: a critique of economic explanations of religious behaviour. *Sociology of Religion* 54: 193–205.

228 *Mormon identities in transition*

Buerger, D. J. (1987) The development of the Mormon temple endowment ceremony. *Dialogue* 20(4): 33–76.
Bull, M. (1990) Secularization and medicalization. *British Journal of Sociology* 41(2): 245–61.
Bull, M. and K. Lockhart (1990) *Seeking a Sanctuary: Seventh-day Adventism and the American Dream.* San Francisco: Harper and Row.
Burgon, G. L. (1992) God the Father, Name of God. In Ludlow (1992).
Burgoyne, R. H. and R. W. Burgoyne (1977) Belief systems and unhappiness: the Mormon woman example. *Journal of Operational Psychiatry* 8: 48–53.
Bushman, R. L. (1984) *Joseph Smith and the Beginnings of Mormonism.* Urbana, IL: University of Illinois Press.
Cahill, J. P. (1981) First Presidency statement on the basing of the MX missile. Press statement, May 5, 1981. Salt Lake City: The Church of Jesus Christ of Latter-day Saints.
Cameron, K. N. (ed.) (1969) *Percy Bysshe Shelley: Selected Poetry and Prose.* New York: Holt, Rinehart and Winston.
Cate, R. M. and S. A. Loyd (1992) *Courtship.* Newbury Park, CA: Sage Publications.
Chadwick, B. A. and H. D. Garrett (1995) Women's religiosity and employment: the LDS experience. *Review of Religious Research* 36(3): 277–94.
Chadwick, B. A. and B. L. Top (1993) Religiosity and delinquency among LDS adolescents. *Journal for the Scientific Study of Religion* 32(1): 51–67.
Clark, B. B. and R. K. Thomas (eds) (1964) *Out of the Best Books* (5 volumes). Salt Lake City: Deseret Books.
Clouse, R. G. (ed.) (1977) *The Meaning of the Millennium: Four Views.* Downers Grove, IL: InterVarsity Press.
Conrad, L. W. (1991) Dissent among the dissenters: theological dimensions of dissent in the reorganization. In R. D. Launius and W. B. Spillman (eds) *Let Contention Cease: The Dynamics of Dissent in the Reorganized Church of Jesus Christ of Latter-day Saints.* Independence, MO: Graceland-Park Press.
Conrad, L. W. and P. Shupe (1985) An RLDS reformation? Construing the task of RLDS theology. *Dialogue* 18: 92–103
Cornwall, M., Heaton and L. A. Young (eds) (1994) *Contemporary Mormonism: Social Science Perspectives.* Urbana, IL: University of Illinois Press.
Cowan, R. O. (1985) *The Church in the Twentieth Century.* Salt Lake City: Bookcraft.
Cowan, R. O. (1993) From footholds to strongholds: spreading the gospel worldwide. *Ensign* 23(6): 56–61.
Crowther, G. and H. Finlay *et al.* (1990) *India: A Travel Survival Kit.* Berkeley, CA: Lonely Planet Publications.
Cunningham, P. H. (1992) Activity in the church. In Ludlow (1992).
Davies, C. (1982) Sexual taboos and social boundaries. *American Journal of Sociology* 7(5): 1032–63.
Davies, C. (1983) Religious boundaries and sexual morality. *Annual Review*

of the Social Sciences of Religion 6: 454–77.

Davies, C. (1993) Aspects of illegitimacy. *Social Biology and Human Affairs* 58(1): 34–44, 58(2) 26–37.

Davies, D. J. (1973) Aspects of Latter-day Saint eschatology. In Michael Hill (ed.) *A Sociological Yearbook of Religion in Britain*. London: SCM Press.

Davies, D. J. (1983) Pastoral theology and folk-religion as a category of self-absolution. *Research Bulletin*, Birmingham Institute of Worship and Religious Architecture. Birmingham, UK: Birmingham University.

Davies, D. J. (1984) *Meaning and Salvation in Religious Studies*. Leiden: Brill.

Davies, D. J. (1987) *Mormon Spirituality: Latter-day Saints in Wales and Zion*. Nottingham University.

Davies, D. J. (1995) Jural and mystical authority in Mormonism. Paper delivered to British Association for the Study of Religion. *Diskus* 3(2).

Davies, J. A. and T. W. Smith (1994) *General Social Surveys, 1972–1994: Cumulative Codebook*. Chicago: National Opinion Research Center.

Davis, R. J. (1992) Antipolygamy legislation. In Ludlow (1992).

Deane, S. N. (1966) *Saint Anselm: Basic Writings, Proslogium*. LaSalle, IL: Open Court Publishing Company.

Derr, J. M. with J. R. Cannon and M. U. Beecher (1992) *Women of Covenant: The Story of the Relief Society*. Salt Lake City, UT: Deseret Books.

DeVoto, D. (1936) The Centennial of Mormonism: a study in utopia and dictatorship. In *Forays and Rebuttals*. Boston: Little, Brown & Co.

Dillenberger, J. and R. B. Keller (1992) Restoration Protestantism. In Ludlow (1992).

Dobbelaere, K. (1987) Some trends in European sociology of religion: the secularisation debate. *Sociological Analysis* 48: 107–37.

Dobbelaere, K. and Voye, L. (1990) From pillar to post-modernity: the changing situation of religion in Belgium. *Sociological Analysis* 51 (special issue): 1–13.

Douglas, M. (1966) *Purity and Danger*. London: Routledge and Kegan Paul.

Douglas, M. (ed.) (1970) *Witchcraft Confessions and Accusations*. London: Tavistock.

Douglas, M. (1975) *Implicit Meanings*. London: Routledge and Kegan Paul.

Draper, M. L. (1968) Theocratic democracy – restoration church government. *Saints' Herald* 115: 800–1, 842–4.

Draper, M. L. (1982) *Isles and Continents*. Independence, MO: Herald House.

Driver, J. (1988) *How Christians Made Peace with War: Early Christian Understandings of War*. Scottdale, PA: Pennsylvania Herald Press.

Duke, J. T. (1995) Cultural continuity and tension between the Church of Jesus Christ of Latter-day Saints and American society. Mormon Studies Conference, University of Nottingham, UK, April 6.

Duke. J. T. (ed.) (1996) *Latter-day Saint Social Life*. Provo, UT: Religious Studies Center, Brigham Young University.

Duke, J. T. and B. L. Johnson (1981a) The dimensions of religiosity among Mormons and their consequences in family relationships. Paper at Southwestern Sociological Association, Dallas, TX, March.

Duke, J. T. and B. L. Johnson (1981b) Happiness in Mormon families: a multivariate analysis. Paper at Association for the Sociology of Religion, Toronto, Canada, August.

Dunford, J. P. (1965) Students leave Zion: an impetus in twentieth century Utah. MA thesis, Utah State University.

Durkheim, E. (1970) *Suicide: A Study in Sociology.* London: Routledge and Kegan Paul.

Dwyer, J. C. (1985) *Church History: Twenty Centuries of Catholic Christianity.* New York: Paulist Press.

Dyck, G. M. (1977) Omnipresence and incorporeality. *Religious Studies* 13: 85–91.

Eco, U. (1990) *I limiti dell' interpretazione.* Milan: Bompiani.

Ehat, A. F. (1982) Joseph Smith's introduction of temple ordinances and the 1844 Mormon succession question. MA thesis, Brigham Young University.

Eliade, M. (1954) *The Myth of the Eternal Return.* New York: Harper and Row.

Eliade, M. (1957) *The Sacred and the Profane,* New York: Harper and Row.

Eliade, M. (1963) *Myth and Reality.* New York: Harper and Row.

Eliade, M. (1977) *No Souvenirs.* New York: Harper and Row.

Ellis, A. E. (1980) *Journal of Consulting and Clinical Psychology* 5(48): 635–9.

Ellison, C. G. (1991) Religious involvement and subjective well-being. *Journal of Health and Social Behaviour* 32: 80–99.

Ellsworth, S. G. (1954) Hubert Howe Bancroft and the history of Utah. *Utah Historical Quarterly* 22: 99–124

Ellsworth, S. G. (1972) Utah's history: retrospect and prospect. *Utah Historical Quarterly* 40: 342–67.

Embry, J. L. (1992) Ethnic groups in the LDS church. *Dialogue* 25.

Embry, J. L. (1994) *Black Saints in a White Church: Contemporary African American Mormons.* Salt Lake City: Signature Books.

Emery, S. (1992) A four dimensional analysis of sex role attitudes in a Mormon population: personal control, self esteem, dogmatism and religious affiliation. Abstract from ProQuest File: Dissert. Abstracts 9131175.

Enstrom, J. T. (1989) Health practices and cancer mortality among active California Mormons. *Journal of the National Cancer Institute* 81(23): 1807–14.

Evans-Pritchard, E. E. (1937) *Witchcraft, Oracles and Magic Among the Azande.* Oxford, UK: Clarendon Press.

Festinger, L. (1957) *A Theory of Cognitive Dissonance.* Evanston, IL: Row Peterson.

Findlay, J. N. (1965) Can God's existence be disproved? In Plantinga (1965).

Finke, R. and R. Stark (1992) *The Churching of America. 1776–1990: Winners and Losers in Our Religious Economy.* New Brunswick, NJ: Rutgers University Press.

First Presidency of the Church of Jesus Christ of Latter-day Saints (1991) Standards of morality. November 14.

First Presidency of the Church of Jesus Christ of Latter-day Saints (1993) Statement regarding disciplinary councils. November 2.

Flake, C. J. (1978) *A Mormon Bibliography, 1830–1930: Books, Pamphlets, Periodicals, and Broadsides Relating to the First Century of Mormonism*. Salt Lake City: University of Utah Press.

Flake, C. J. and L. W. Draper (1989) *A Mormon Bibliography, 1830–1930: Ten Year Supplement*. Salt Lake City: University of Utah Press.

Florence, G. H. (1992) City of Angels. *Ensign* 22.

Foster, L. (1979) From frontier activism to neo-Victorian domesticity: Mormon women in the nineteenth and twentieth centuries. *Journal of Mormon History* 6: 3–21.

Fox, M. B. H. (1995) The theology, history and organisation of the Reorganised Church of Jesus Christ of Latter-day Saints in the British Isles. PhD thesis, University of Nottingham.

Fulton, J. and P. Gee (eds) (1994) *Religion in Contemporary Europe*. Lampeter: Edwin Mellen Press.

Garrard-Burnett, V. and D. Stoll (eds) (1993) *Rethinking Protestantism in Latin America*. Philadelphia: Temple University Press.

Garrison, C. E. (1988) *Two Different Worlds: Christian Absolutes and the Relativism of Social Science*, Newark. NJ: University of Delaware Press.

Gartner, J. Larson, D. B., and G. D. Allen (1991) Religious commitment and mental health: a review of the empirical literature. *Journal of Psychology and Theology* 19(1): 16–25.

Geertz, C. (1966) Religion as a cultural system. In M. Banton (ed.) *Anthropological Approaches to the Study of Religion*. London: Tavistock.

General Handbook of Instruction (1989) The Church of Jesus Christ of Latter-day Saints.

Gorsuch, R. L. and D. Aleshire (1974) Christian faith and ethnic prejudice. *Journal for the Scientific Study of Religion* 13: 281–307.

Grant, H. J., Clark, J. R. Jr and D. O. Mckay (1942) *One Hundred and Twelfth Annual Conference Report*. Salt Lake City: Church of Jesus Christ of Latter-day Saints.

Hallowell, A. I. (1967) The self and its behavioral environment. *Culture and Experience*, ch. 4. New York: Schocken Books.

Hammond, P. E. (1992) *Religion and Personal Autonomy: The Third Disestablishment in America*. Columbia, SC: University of South Carolina Press.

Hanks, M. (1992) *Women and Authority: Re-emerging Feminism*. Salt Lake City: Signature Books.

Hanson, P. D. (1979) *The Dawn of Apocalyptic: The History and Sociological Roots of Jewish Apocalyptic Eschatology*. Philadelphia: Fortress Press.

Hartshorne, C. (1964) *Man's Vision of God and the Logic of Theism*. Hamden, CT: Archon Books.

Harvey, V. (1966) *The Historian and the Believer: The Morality of Historical Knowledge and Christian Belief*. Philadelphia: Westminster Press.

Hawks, R. D. and S. J. Bahr (1992) Religion and drug use. *Journal of Drug Education* 22(1): 1–8.

Heaton, T. B. (1988) Four C's of the Mormon family: chastity, conjugality, children and chauvinism. In D. Thomas (ed.) *The Religion and Family Connection*. Provo, UT.

Heaton, T. B. (1989) Religious influences on Mormon fertility: cross national comparisons. *Review of Religious Research* 30: 401–11.

Heaton, T. B. (1992) Vital statistics. In Ludlow (1992).

Heaton, T. B. and K. L. Goodman (1985) Religion and family formation. *Review of Religious Research* 26(4): 343–59.

Heaton, T. B., Goodman, K. and T. Holman (eds) (1994) In search of a peculiar people: are Mormon families really different? *Contemporary Mormonism*.

Heider, F. (1958) *The Psychology of Interpersonal Relations*. New York: John Wiley.

Helgeland, J., Daly, R. J. and J. P. Burns (1987) *Christians and the Military: The Early Experience*. London: SCM Press.

Henry, W. A. III (1990) Beyond the melting pot. *Time*, April 9: 28–9.

Hervieu-Leger, D. (1990) Religion and modernity in the French context: for a new approach to secularisation. *Sociological Analysis* 51 (special issue): 15–25.

Hildeth, S. A. (1984) Mormon concern over MX: parochialism or enduring moral theology? *Journal of Church and State* 26(2): 227–53.

Hinkley, G. B. (1988) Priesthood restoration. *The Ensign*, October: 70–1.

Hinkley, G. B. (1991) Cornerstones of responsibility. Regional Representative Seminar, Salt Lake City, April 5.

Hoge, D. R. and F. Yang (1994) Determinants of religious giving in American denominations: data from two nationwide surveys. *Review of Religious Research* 36: 12.

Howard, R. P. (1980) An analysis of six contemporary accounts touching Joseph Smith's first vision. In M. Draper (ed.) *Restoration Studies I: A Collection of Essays About the History, Beliefs, and Practices of the Reorganized Church of Jesus Christ of Latter-day Saints*. Independence, MO: Herald House.

Howard, R. P. (1983) The changing RLDS response to Mormon polygamy: a preliminary analysis. *John Whitmer Historical Association Journal* 3: 14–29.

Hunt, L. E. (1982) *F. M. Smith: Saint As Reformer*. Independence, MO: Herald House.

Hunter, H. W. (1994) Exceeding great and precious promises. *Ensign*, November 7–8.

Iannaccone, L. R. (1991) The consequences of religious market structure: Adam Smith and the economics of religion. *Rationality and Society* 3: 156–77.

Iannaccone, L. R. (1992) Religious markets and the economics of religion. *Social Compass* 39: 123–31.

Iannaccone, L. R., Ellison, C., Chaves, M. and N. J. Demerath (1995) Symposium on the rational choice approach to religion. *Journal for the Scientific Study of Religion* 34(1): 76–120.

Iannaccone, L. R. and C. A. Miles (1990) Dealing with social change: the Mormon church's response to changes in women's roles. *Social Roles* 68(4): 1231–50.

James, W. (1929) *The Varieties of Religious Experience*. New York: Longmans.

Jantzen, G. M. (1984) *God's World, God's Body*. London: Darton, Longman and Todd.

Jarvis, J. C. (1991) Mormonism in France: a study of cultural exchange and institutional adaptation. Unpublished PhD dissertation, Washington State University, Pullman, WA.

Jensen, L. C., Jensen, J. and T. Wiederhold (1993) Religiosity, denomination, and mental health among young men and women. *Psychological Reports* 72: 1157–8.

Jensen, R. L. and R. G. Oman (1984) *C. C. A. Christensen 1831–1912: Mormon Immigrant Artist*. Salt Lake City: Museum of Church History and Art, Church of Jesus Christ of Latter-day Saints.

Jessee, D. C. (1984) *The Personal Writings of Joseph Smith*. Salt Lake City.

John Paul II (1993) *Veritatis Splendor: The Splendor of the Truth Shines*. Vatican City: Libreria Editrice Vaticana.

Johnson, B. L., Eberly, S., Duke, J. T. and D. H. Sartain (1988) Wives' employment status and marital happiness of religious couples. *Review of Religious Research* 29(3): 259–70.

Johnson, R. V. (1993) South Africa: land of good hope. *Ensign* 23(2): 33–41.

Jones, B. (ed.) (1987) *Becoming Makers of Peace: The Peace Symposium at Kirtland, Ohio, June 20–21, 1986*. Independence, MO: Herald House.

Jorgensen, C. (1994) Fall from grace: LDS stake counselor's story. Salt Lake *Tribune*, September 3.

Judd, D. K. (1985) Religiosity and mental health: a literature review 1928–1985. Master's thesis, Brigham Young University.

Judd, D. K. (1986) Religious affiliation and mental health. *AMCAP* 12(2) 71–108.

Judd, D. K. (1987) Not as the world giveth . . . Mormonism and popular psychology. In R. Millet (ed.) *To Be Learned Is Good If . . .* Salt Lake City: Bookcraft.

Juhnke, W. E. (1982) Anabaptism and Mormonism: a study in comparative history. *The John Whitmer Historical Association Journal* 2: 41–4.

Kenny, A. (1979) *The God of the Philosophers*. Oxford, UK: Clarendon Press.

Kimball, E. L. (1982) *The Teachings of Spencer W. Kimball*. Salt Lake City.

Klaassen, W. (1984) Anabaptist hermeneutics, presuppositions, principles and practice. In W. M. Swartley (ed.) *Essays on Biblical Interpretation: Anabaptist-Mennonite Perspectives*. Elkart, IN: Institute of Mennonite Studies.

Knapp, W. J. (1982) Professionalizing religious education in the church: the new curriculum controversy. *John Whitmer Historical Association Journal* 2: 47–59.

Knowlton, D. (1996) Mormonism in Latin America: toward the twenty-first century. *Dialogue* 29(1).

Kromminga, D. H. (1945) *The Millennium in the Church: Studies in the History of Christian Chiliasm.* Grand Rapids, MI: Eerdmans.

Kunin, S. D. (1994) The death of Isaac: structuralist analysis of Genesis 22. *Journal of the Society of Old Testament Studies* 64: 57–81.

Kunin, S. D. (1995) *The Logic of Incest: A Structuralist Analysis of Hebrew Mythology.* Sheffield, UK: Sheffield Academic Press.

Kunz, P. R. and O. S. Yaw (1989) Social distance: a study of changing views of young Mormons towards black individuals. *Psychological Reports* 65(1): 195–200.

Larson, D. B., Sherrill, K. A. *et al.* (1992) Associations between dimensions of religious commitment and mental health. *American Journal of Psychiatry* 149(4): 557–9 and *Archives of General Psychiatry 1978–1989.*

Launius, R. D. (1987a) Methods and motives: Joseph Smith III's opposition to polygamy, 1860–90. *Dialogue* 20: 105–21.

Launius, R. D. (1987b) Politicking against polygamy: Joseph Smith III, the Reorganized Church, and the politics of the antipolygamy crusade, 1860–1890. *John Whitmer Historical Association Journal* 7: 35–44.

Launius, R. D. (1988) *Joseph Smith III: Pragmatic Prophet.* Urbana, IL: University of Illinois Press.

Launius, R. D. (1991) Many mansions: the dynamics of dissent in the nineteenth century reorganized church. *Journal of Mormon History* 17: 145–68.

Launius, R. D. (1995a) Coming of age? The Reorganized Church in the 1960s. *Dialogue* 28: 31–57.

Launius, R. D. (1995b) The RLDS church and the decade of decision. *Sunstone* (Fall).

Launius, R. D. and W. B. Spillman (eds.) (1991) *Let Contention Cease: The Dynamics of Dissent in the Reorganized Church.* Independence, MO: Graceland-Park Press.

Lea, G. (1982) Religion, mental health, and clinical issues. *Journal of Religion and Health* 21(4): 336–51.

Leach, E. (1969) *Genesis As Myth.* London: Jonathan Cape.

Leach, E. and A. Aycock (1983) *Structuralist Interpretations of Biblical Myth.* Cambridge, UK: Cambridge University Press.

Leone, M. (1979) *Roots of Modern Mormonism.* Cambridge, MA: Harvard University Press.

Levin, J. S. and H. Y. Vanderpool (1987) Is frequent religious attendance really conducive to better health? Toward an epidemiology of religion. *Social Science and Medicine* 24(7): 589–600.

Levinger, G. (1983) Development and change. In J. Wilson (ed.) *Close Relationships.* New York: W. H. Freeman and Co.

Lévi-Strauss, C. (1963) *Structural Anthropology* Vol. 1. New York: Basic Books.

Lévi-Strauss, C. (1966) *The Savage Mind.* Chicago: University of Chicago Press.

Lévi-Strauss, C. (1969) *The Raw and the Cooked.* New York: Harper and Row.

Lévi-Strauss, C. (1976) *Structural Anthropology* Vol. 2. New York: Basic Books.

Lévi-Strauss, C. (1981) *The Naked Man.* New York: Harper and Row.

Lévi-Strauss, C. (1988) *The Jealous Potter.* Chicago: University of Chicago Press.

Lévy-Bruhl, L. (1965) *The Soul of the Primitive.* Allen and Unwin: London.

Lewis, I. (1986) *Religion in Context.* Cambridge, UK: Cambridge University Press.

Lindén, I. (1978) *The Last Trump: An Historico-Genetical Study of Some Important Chapters in the Making and Development of the Seventh Day Adventist Church.* Frankfurt am Main: Peter Lang. Band 17 of the Studien zur interkulturellen Geschichte des Christentums.

Lindsell, H. (1976) *The Battle for the Bible.* Grand Rapids, MI: Zondervan.

Ludlow, D. H. (ed.) (1992) *Encyclopedia of Mormonism* (5 volumes). New York: Macmillan.

Luhrmann, T. M. (1989) *Persuasions of the Witches' Craft: Ritual Magic and Witchcraft in Present Day England.* Oxford, UK: Basil Blackwell.

Lye, W.F. (1960) Edward Wheelrock Tullidge: the Mormons' rebel historian. *Utah Historical Quarterly* 28: 56–75.

Lyon, J. L. O. (1992) Alcoholic beverages and alcoholism and Word of Wisdom. In Ludlow (1992).

Maimonides, M. (1963) *The Guide of the Perplexed.* Chicago: University of Chicago Press.

Malinowski, B. (1948) *Magic, Science and Religion* (1974 edn). New York: Doubleday Anchor Books.

Mariz, C. L. (1994) *Coping with Poverty: Pentecostals and Christian Base Communities in Brazil.* Philadelphia: Temple University Press.

Marsden, G. (1980) *Fundamentalism and American Culture: the Shaping of Twentieth-Century Evangelicalism.* Grand Rapids, MI: William B. Eerdmans.

Marsden, G. (1991) *Understanding Fundamentalism and Evangelicalism.* Grand Rapids, MI: William B. Eerdmans.

Martin, D. (1990) *Tongues of Fire: The Explosion of Protestantism in Latin America.* Oxford, UK: Basil Blackwell.

Marty, M. E. (1959) (reprinted 1967) *A Short History of Christianity.* New York: Meridian.

Marty, M. E. (1986) *Modern American Religion, 1: The Irony of It All, 1893–1919.* Chicago: University of Chicago Press.

Marty, M. E. (1987) *Religion and Republic.* Boston: Beacon.

Marty, M. E. (1989) *We Might Know What to Do and How to Do It: On the Usefulness of the Religious Past.* Salt Lake City: Westminster College.

Marty, M. E. (1992) Two integrities: an address to the crisis in Mormon historiography. In Smith (1992).

Marty, M. E. and R. S. Appleby (1991–94) *The Fundamentalism Project* (4 volumes). Chicago and London: University of Chicago Press.

Mason, J. O. (1992) Health, attitudes towards. In Ludlow (1992).

Masters, K. S., Bergin, A. E., Reynolds, E. M. and C. E. Sullivan (1991) Religious life-styles and mental health: a follow-up study. *Counseling Values* 35: 211–24.

Mauss, A. (1994) *The Angel and the Beehive: The Mormon Struggle with*

Assimilation. Urbana, IL and Chicago: University of Illinois Press.

Mauss, A. and P. Barlow (1991) Church, sect and scripture: the protestant Bible and Mormon sectarian retrenchment. *Sociological Analysis* 52(4): 397–414.

McConkie, B. R. (1966) *Mormon Doctrine.* Salt Lake City: Bookcraft Company.

McConkie, B. R. (1978a) All are alike unto God. Church Education System Symposium. Brigham Young University, August 18.

McConkie, B. R. (1978b) *Charge to Religious Educators,* 2nd edn. Salt Lake City: The Church of Jesus Christ of the Latter-day Saints.

McConkie, B. R. (1984) The Bible a sealed book. In *Supplements to a Symposium on the New Testament* 1–7. Salt Lake City: Church Educational System, Church of Jesus Christ of Latter-day Saints.

McKay, D. O. (1976) *Gospel Discourses of David O. McKay, Ninth President of The Church of Jesus Christ of the Latter-day Saints.* Salt Lake City: Deseret Books.

Metcalfe, B. L. (ed.) (1993) *New Approaches to the Book of Mormon: Explorations in Critical Methodology.* Salt Lake City: Signature Books.

Midgley, L.C. (1990) Review of Novick (1988). *John Whitmer Historical Association Journal* 10: 102–4.

Midgley, L. C. (1992) The acids of modernity and the crisis in Mormon historiography. In Smith (1992).

Midgley, L. C. (1994) The current battle over the Book of Mormon: 'is modernity somehow canonical?' *Review of Books on the Book of Mormon* 6: 200–54.

Miller, B. C., Christensen, R. B. and T. D. Olson (1987) Adolescent self-esteem in relation to sexual attitudes and behaviour. *Youth and Society* 19(1): 93–111.

Miller, B. C. and T. D. Olson (1988) Sexual attitudes and behaviour of high school students in relation to background and contextual factors. *Journal of Sex Research* 24: 194–200.

Millett, R. J. and J. F. McConkie (1993) *Our Destiny: The Call and Election of the House of Israel.* Salt Lake City: Bookcraft Company.

Moorhead, J. H. (1984) Between progress and apocalypse: a reassessment of millennialism in American thought 1800–1880. *Journal of American History* 71, December: 524–42.

Murphy, T. W. (1996) Reinventing Mormonism locally: Abraham, Popul Vuh, and ethnicity in Guatemala. *Dialogue* 29(1).

Needham, R. (1980) *Reconnaissances.* Toronto: University of Toronto Press.

Neill, S. (1984) *A History of Christianity in India: 1707–1858.* Cambridge, UK: Cambridge University Press.

Netland, H. (1991) *Dissonant Voices: Religious Pluralism and the Question of Truth.* Grand Rapids, MI: William B. Eerdmans.

Newell, Linda King (1987) Gifts of the Spirit: women's share. In Beecher and Anderson (1987).

Novick, P. (1988) *That Noble Dream: The 'Objectivity Question' and the American Historical Profession.* New York: Cambridge University Press.

Numano, J. (1996) Mormonism and modernization in Japan. *Dialogue* 29(1).
Numbers, R. L. (1992) *The Creationists: The Evolution of Scientific Creationism.* New York: Alfred A. Knopf.
Oaks, D. H. (1971) Brigham Young University. In Ludlow (1992).
O'Day, R. (1994) *The Family and Family Relationships 1500–1900.* New York: St Martin's Press.
O'Dea, T. F. (1957) *The Mormons.* Chicago: University of Chicago Press.
Oliver, W. H. (1978) *Prophets and Millenialists: The Uses of Biblical Prophecy in England from the 1790s to the 1840s.* Auckland, NZ: Auckland University Press.
Orteaga, E. R. and E. B. Tironi (1988) *Pobreza en Chile.* Santiago: Centro de estudio del desarrollo.
Owen, H. P. (1971) *Concepts of Deity.* London: Macmillan.
Oxhorn, P. (1967) The popular sector response to an authoritarian regime. *Latin American Perspectives* 67(18:1): 66–9.
Packer, B. K. (1977) The Equal Rights Amendment. *Ensign* 7.
Palmer, D. (1979) Establishing the LDS Church in Chile. Unpublished MA thesis, Brigham Young University.
Palmer, S. J. (1979) Mormons in West Africa: new terrain for the sesqui-centennial church. Annual Religion Faculty Lecture. Brigham Young University, September 27.
Paul, E. (ed.) (1993) *Coffee, Cafeine and Health.* London: Coffee News Information Service.
Perkins, K. W. (1971) A study of the contributions of Andrew Jenson to the writing and preservation of LDS Church history. MA thesis, Brigham Young University.
Perrin, R. D. (1989) American religion in the post-Aquarian age: values and demographic factors in church growth and decline. *Journal for the Scientific Study of Religion* 28: 75–89.
Peterson, D. C. (1992) Editor's introduction: questions to legal answers. *Review of Books on the Book of Mormon* 4: vii–lxxvi.
Peterson, D. C. (1994) Editor's introduction. *Review of Books on the Book of Mormon* 6: v–xii.
Peterson, P. H. (1992) Doctrine and Covenants: Section 89. In Ludlow (1992).
Plantinga, A. (ed.) (1965) *The Ontological Argument from St Anselm to Contemporary Philosophers.* Garden City, NY: Doubleday.
Pollock, L. A. (1983) *Forgotten Children: Parent–Child Relations from 1500 to 1900.* Cambridge, UK: Cambridge University Press.
Pontifical Biblical Commission (1993) *The Interpretation of the Bible in the Church.* Vatican City: Libreria Editrice Vaticana.
Porter, J. R. (1976) *Leviticus. The Cambridge Bible Commentary, The English Bible.* Cambridge, UK: Cambridge University Press.
Porter, L. C. and S. E. Black (eds) (1988) *The Prophet Joseph: Essays on the Life and Mission of Joseph Smith.* Salt Lake City: Deseret Books.
Pratt, Parley P. (1837) *A Voice of Warning and Instruction to all People, Concerning an Introduction to the Faith and Doctrine of the Church of the*

Latter-day Saints, Commonly called Mormons. New York: Sandford.

Quinn, D. M. (1983) *J. Reuben Clark: The Church Years.* Provo, UT: Brigham Young University Press.

Quinn, D. M. (1992) Mormon women have held the priesthood since 1843. In Hanks (1992).

Quinn, D. M. (1994) *The Mormon Hierarchy: Origins of Power.* Salt Lake City: Signature Books.

Ramet, S. P. (ed.) (1993) *Protestantism and Politics in Eastern Europe and Russia: The Communist and Post-Communist Eras.* Durham, NC: Duke University Press.

Ramsay, E. D. (1873) *Reminiscences of Scottish Life and Character.* Edinburgh: Gall and Inglis.

Reinwand, L. (1973) Andrew Jenson, Latter-day Saint historian. *Brigham Young University Studies* 14: 29–46.

Ricks, S. D. (1992) Book of Mormon studies. In Ludlow (1992).

Riggs, R. E. (1992) *Reynolds v United States.* In Ludlow (1992).

Robertson, R. (1992) The economization of religion? Reflections on the promise and limitations of the economic approach. *Social Compass* 39: 147–57.

Robinson, S. E. (1991) Review of Vogel (1990). *Review of Books on the Book of Mormon* 3: 312–18.

Rogers, K. (1989) How healthy are we? *This People* 10(3): 11–15.

Romig, R. E. (1993) Contours of the kingdom: an RLDS perspective on the legions of Zion. In Carswell, D. D. (ed.) *Restoration Studies V: A Collection of Essays About the History, Beliefs, and Practices of the Reorganized Church of Jesus Christ of Latter-day Saints.* Independence, MO: Herald House.

Rose, F. F. (1986) A comparison of LDS and non-LDS responses to MMPI items. Unpublished doctoral dissertation, Brigham Young University.

Sandeen, E. R. (1970) *The Roots of Fundamentalism.* Chicago: Chicago University Press.

Sauna, V. D. (1969) Religion, mental health and personality: a review of empirical studies. *American Journal of Psychiatry* 125(9): 1203–13.

Schlumberger, H. L. and A. C. Herrera (1987) *Los Evangélicos en Chile: una lectura sociológica.* Santiago: Ediciones Literatura Reunida and Programa Evangélica de estudios socio-religiosos.

Schneider, C. (1967) Mobilization at the grassroots: shantytown resistance in authoritarian Chile. *Latin American Perspectives* 67(18:1) 92–112.

Scott, L. C. (1992) Mormonism and the question of truth. *Christian Research Journal* 15(1): 25–8.

Segal, R. A. (1978) Eliade's theory of millenarianism. *Religious Studies* 14: 159.

Shelley, P. B. (1969) *Selected Poetry and Prose,* ed. K. N. Cameron. New York: Rinehart and Winston.

Shepherd, G. and G. Shepherd (1984) *A Kingdom Transformed: Themes in the Development of Mormonism.* Salt Lake City: University of Utah Press.

Shepherd, G. and G. Shepherd (1996) On the eve of a Mormon century? The dynamics of LDS membership growth, lay activity, and missionary recruitment. *Dialogue* 29.

Smith, G. D. (ed.) (1992) *Faithful History: Essays on Writing Mormon History.* Salt Lake City: Signature Books.

Smith, J. (1845) *Book of the Doctrines and Covenants of the Church of Jesus Christ of Latter-day Saints, Selected From the Revelations of God.* Liverpool: Wilfred Woodruff.

Smith, J. (1964) *History of the Church of Jesus Christ of Latter-day Saints,* 2nd edn. Intro. and notes B. H. Roberts. Salt Lake City.

Smith, J. F. (1938) *Teachings of the Prophet Joseph Smith.* Salt Lake City.

Smith, J. F., Winder, J. R. and A. H. Lund (1966) Mother in Heaven. In McConkie (1966).

Smith, W. Cantwell (1963) *The Meaning and End of Religion.* New York: Macmillan.

Smith, W. E. (1992) Peculiar people. In Ludlow (1992).

Snow, E. J. (1991) British travelers view the Mormons 1847–1877. *Brigham Young University Studies* 31: 63–81.

Snow, L. (1901 and 1993) Greetings to the world. Reprinted from *Sunstone* 6:1 (1981): 31.

Soulay, J. (1973) Sémiotique de la nourriture, dans la Bible. *Annales* 28(11:4): 943–55.

Spendlove, D. C., West, D. W. and W. M. Stannish (1984) Risk factors and the prevalence of depression in Mormon women. *Social Science and Medicine* 18(6): 491–5.

Stark, R. (1971) Psychopathology and religious commitment. *Review of Religious Research* 12: 165–76.

Stark, R. (1984) The rise of a new world faith. *Review of Religious Research* 26: 18–27.

Stark, R. (1987) How new religions succeed: a theoretical model. In D. G. Bromley and P. E. Hammond (eds) *The Future of New Religious Movements.* Macon, GA: Mercer University Press.

Stark, R. and W. S. Bainbridge (1985) *The Future of Religion: Secularization, Revival, and Cult Formation.* Berkeley, CA: University of California Press.

Stark, R. and L. R. Iannaccone (1992) Sociology of religion. In E. F. Borgatta and M. L. Borgatta (eds) *Encyclopedia of Sociology.* New York: Macmillan.

Stewart, D. A. (1992) Scattering Israel. In Ludlow (1992).

Stoll, D. (1990) *Is Latin America Turning Protestant?* Berkeley, CA: University of California Press.

Stott, G. (1988) Just war, holy war, and Joseph Smith, Jr. In M. B. Troeh (ed.) *Restoration Studies IV: A Collection of Essays about the History, Beliefs, and Practices of the Reorganized Church of Jesus Christ of Latter-day Saints.* Independence, MO: Herald House.

Stryker, S. (1992) Identity theory. In E. F. Borgatta and M. L. Borgatta (eds) *Encyclopedia of Sociology.* New York: Macmillan.

Surra, C. A. (1990) Research and theory on mate selection and premarital relationships in the 1980s. *Journal of Marriage and the Family* 52: 844–65.

Swenson, R. B. (1972) Mormons at the University of Chicago divinity school: a personal reminiscence. *Dialogue* 7: 37–47.

Tate, C. D. Jr (1992) Conscientious objection. In Ludlow (1992).

Taylor, J. (1987) *The Gospel Kingdom*. Salt Lake City: Bookcraft.

Thomas, D. L. (1983) Family in the Mormon experience. In W. D. Antonio and J. Aldous (eds) *Families and Religion*. Beverly Hills, CA.

Thomas, G. K. (1993) Finest orientalism, western sentimentalism, proto-zionism: the muses of Byron's Hebrew melodies. *Prisms* 1: 51–66.

Torres, C. A. (1992) *The Church, Society, and Hegemony: Critical Sociology of Religion in Latin America*. Westport, CT: Praeger Company.

Toumey, C. P. (1994) *God's Own Scientists: Creationists in a Secular World*. New Brunswick, NJ: Rutgers University Press.

Towns, E. (1994) Jimmy Breland's tea and coffee truck. *The Christian Reader*, May–June: 76–9.

Troeltsch, E. (1931) *The Social Teaching of the Christian Churches*. New York: Macmillan.

Turner, T. (1977) Narrative structure and mythopoesis: a critique and reformulation of structuralist concepts of myth, narrative, and poetics. *Arethusa* 10(1): 103–63.

'Two Laymen' (1910–15) *The Fundamentals: A Testimony to the Truth* (12 vols). Chicago: Testimony Publishing House.

Tyler, S. A. (1973) *India: An Anthropological Perspective*. Prospect Heights, IL: Waveland Press Inc.

Tylor, E. B. (1958) *Primitive Culture* (first publ. 1871). New York: Harper.

US Bureau of the Census (1994) *Statistical Abstracts of the United States: 1994*, 114th edn. Washington, DC.

van Beek, W. (1996) Mormonism in the twenty-first century: western Europe. *Dialogue* 29(1).

Vlahos, C. D. (1980) Images of orthodoxy: self-identity in early Reorganized apologetics. In M. L. Draper and C. D. Vlahos (eds) *Restoration Studies* I. Independence, MO: Herald House.

Vlahos, C. D. (1981) Moderation as a theological principle in the thought of Joseph Smith III. *John Whitmer Historical Association Journal* 1: 3–11.

Vogel, D. (ed.) (1990) *The Word of God: Essays on Mormon Scriptures*. Salt Lake City: Signature Books.

Walker, R. W. (1974) The Stenhouses and the making of a Mormon image. *Journal of Mormon History* 1: 51–72.

Walker, R. W. (1976) Edward Tullidge: historian of the Mormon commonwealth. *Utah Historical Quarterly* 3: 55–72.

Wallace, A. F. C. (1967) Identity processes in personality and in culture. In R. Jessor and S. Feshbach (eds) *Cognition, Personality and Clinical Psychology*. San Francisco.

Warner, R. S. (1993) Work in progress toward a new paradigm for the sociological study of religion in the United States. *American Journal of Sociology* 98: 1044–93.

Waterman, B. (1994) A guide to the Mormon universe: Mormon organizations and periodicals. *Sunstone* 17: 44–65.

Weber, T. P. (1979) *Living in the Shadow of the Second Coming: American Premillennialism, 1875–1925*. New York: Oxford University Press.

Wheatley, Meg (1992) In Hanks (1992).

White, E. G. (1864) *Spiritual Gifts, Important Facts of Faith, Laws of Health and Testimonies. Spiritual Gifts* Vol. 4. Battle Creek, MI: Seventh Day Adventist Publishing Association.

Whittaker, D. J. (1980) Historians and the Mormon experience: a sesquicentennial perspective. In *Sidney B. Sperry Symposium, January 26: A Sesquicentennial Look at Church History.* Provo, UT: Brigham Young College of Religious Instruction.

Whittaker, D. (ed.) (1995) *Mormon Americana.* Provo, UT: Brigham Young University Studies.

Whyte, M. K. (1991) *Dating, Mating and Marriage.* New York: Aldine de Gruyter.

Wilkie, J. *et al.* (1983) *Statistical Abstract of Latin America.* University of California at Los Angeles, Latin American Center Publications.

Wilkinson, M. L. and W. C. Tanner (1980) The influence of family size, interaction, and religiosity on family affection in a Mormon sample. *Journal of Marriage and the Family* 297–304.

Willems, E. (1967) *Followers of the New Faith.* Nashville, TN: Vanderbilt University Press.

Williams, P. W. (1980) *Popular Religion in America: Symbolic Change and the Modernization Process in Historical Perspective.* Urbana, IL: University of Illinois Press.

Wilson, J. F. (1988) Modernity. In M. Eliade (ed.) *Encyclopedia of Religion.* New York: Macmillan.

Witten, M. G. (1993) *All Is Forgiven: The Secular Message of American Protestantism.* Princeton, NJ: Princeton University Press.

Woodruff, W. (1983–85) *Wilford Woodruff's Journal, 1833–1898,* ed. S. C. Kenney. Salt Lake City: Signature Books.

Wordsworth, W. (1952–59) *The Poetical Works of William Wordsworth,* ed. E. Selincourt. Oxford, UK: Clarendon Press.

Wordsworth, W. and D. Wordsworth (1988) *The Letters of William and Dorothy Wordsworth: The Later Years,* ed. E. Selincourt. Oxford, UK: Clarendon Press.

Wright, D. (1992) Historical criticism: a necessary element in the search for religious truth. *Sunstone* 16(3): 28–38.

Wrigley, E. A. and R. S. Schofield (1989) *The Population History of England 1541–1871: A Reconstruction.* Cambridge, UK: Cambridge University Press.

Yarrington, R. (1990) Changes in the Church. *Saints Herald* 137, September: 10.

Yerushalmi, Y. H. (1982) *Zakhor: Jewish History and Jewish Memory,* 1st edn. Seattle, WA: University of Washington Press. 2nd edn. (1989) New York: Schocken Books.

Yoder, J. H. (1983) *The Politics of Jesus.* Grand Rapids, MI: Eerdmans.

Yoder, J. H. (1984) *When War Is Unjust: Being Honest in the Just-War Thinking.* Minneapolis, MN: Augsburg.

Young, B. (1869) *Journal of Discourses.* Liverpool: Albert Carrington.

Young, F. (1989) The early church: military service, war and peace. *Theology* XCII (750): 491–503.

Young, L. A. (1994) Confronting turbulent environments: issues in the organizational growth and globalization of Mormonism. In Cornwall, Heaton, and Young (1994).

Index

Kimball, Spencer W.   63, 64, 81ff.
Kirtland   190

Lamanites   185, 186
lamb and lion   136, 183, 186
Latin America   15, 68–79
Leone, Mark   146
Lévi-Strauss, Claude   193
Lewis, I. M.   143
liberalism, intellectual and religious
   4, 5, 25, 27, 28
Lindsell, H.   25
Lost Tribes of Israel   138

magic   32, 143–48
Man's Search for Happiness   153
marriage   41, 48, 89, 108, 125–32, 165
Marsden, G. M.   25
Martin, D.   75
Marty, Martin   20–3
Mauss, Armand   26, 103, 219
McConkie, B. R.   17, 83, 141, 160
McKay, David O.   81, 154
memory and history   24, 146, 214
Mennonites   184, 190
mental health   112–24
Metcalfe, Brent   29, 102ff., 192
Methodists   38
millennialism   135–42
miracles   22
missionaries   15, 17–18, 69, 80, 90, 214
modernism   28
modernity   57, 140
modernization   140
Mormon   185
Mormon History Association   145, 217
Mormon Tabernacle Choir   140
Mormonism
   membership   46, 47, 68, 223
   occupation of members   73ff.
   as world religion   13, 223
Mother God   159–65
mothers   166–79
murder   197
music   17, 87, 89, 94
Muslims   21, 23, 39
myth   192ff.

nationalism   189–90
Native Americans   138
Nauvoo   55, 155, 183, 190

'new Mormon history'   23
New Testament   193–4
New Zealand   15
newspapers   49
Nigeria   84ff.
Novick, P.   29
nuclear missiles   183
nudism   17

Oaks, Dallin H.   4
O'Dea, T. F.   36
oral history   63–7
orphans   98
Owen, H. P.   208
Oxford University   2

pacifism   183–90
Packer, Boyd K.   160, 161
Partridge, Edward   138
patriarchal blessings   41, 149
patriarchy   15
peace   58
'peculiar people'   9, 11
Pentecostalism   69, 74, 121
phenomenology   29
Philippines   18, 87
Plato   207
polygamy   26, 39, 42, 105, 219
Popper, K. 30ff.
post-modernity   25, 28, 31ff.
Pratt, Parley   140
prayer   167, 172
prejudice   116
Preston   96
priesthood   9, 57, 80, 82, 104, 107,
   160–3, 198
primitivism   142
prophets   26, 59, 82, 169
Protestants (Protestantism)   25, 26, 41,
   52, 57–9, 87, 120, 123, 145, 183, 190
Puritanism   189

Quakers   184
Quinn, M. D.   29, 102

Rabbis   42
rationalism   23, 28
Ratzinger, Joseph Cardinal   30, 32
Reformation   40, 41
Relief Society   66, 85, 89, 154, 162
religiosity   112ff.

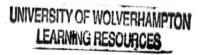
UNIVERSITY OF WOLVERHAMPTON
LEARNING RESOURCES